in bad faith

in bad
faith

in bad faith

DASSI ERLICH

with Ellen Whinnett

hachette
AUSTRALIA

Note to readers: Some names have been changed throughout this book to protect privacy.

There are harrowing details recounted in Dassi's story. If you are affected by these, have suffered abuse and trauma or are struggling, please see page 358 for important contact details and resources and don't be afraid to reach out for help and seek out an experienced trauma specialist. Be gentle with yourself as you read Dassi's story and please know there are people there to help you.

⊞ hachette
AUSTRALIA

Published in Australia and New Zealand in 2024
by Hachette Australia
(an imprint of Hachette Australia Pty Limited)
Gadigal Country, Level 17, 207 Kent Street, Sydney, NSW 2000
www.hachette.com.au

Hachette Australia acknowledges and pays our respects to the past, present and future Traditional Owners and Custodians of Country throughout Australia and recognises the continuation of cultural, spiritual and educational practices of Aboriginal and Torres Strait Islander peoples. Our head office is located on the lands of the Gadigal people of the Eora Nation.

A catalogue record for this book is available from the National Library of Australia

NATIONAL
LIBRARY
OF AUSTRALIA

ISBN: 978 0 7336 4649 2 (paperback)

Cover design by Christabella Designs
Front cover photograph courtesy of Dassi Erlich
Back cover and internal picture section photographs courtesy of the Dassi Erlich family collection
Internal picture section design by Christabella Designs
Typeset in Sabon LT Std by Kirby Jones
Printed and bound in Australia by McPherson's Printing Group

MIX
Paper | Supporting
responsible forestry
FSC
www.fsc.org
FSC® C001695

The paper this book is printed on is certified against the Forest Stewardship Council® Standards. McPherson's Printing Group holds FSC® chain of custody certification SA-COC-005379. FSC® promotes environmentally responsible, socially beneficial and economically viable management of the world's forests.

To my daughter,
the heartbeat to my resilience,
you are everything to me

Contents

Prologue

Friday, 22 June 2012 begins like any other Friday that year. Except on this particular Friday, I am on the edge of a train platform, about to choose death. *This is where it all ends,* I think. *One second of intense pain to never know pain again.*

Balaclava Station is five stops from the CBD, and at 8 a.m. on a weekday, there's a rush of Melburnians headed for the city. I have to jostle my way through a sea of black umbrellas to reach the platform edge, but despite the commotion, I feel cocooned in a circle of silence where only me and my dark deliberations exist.

I hadn't planned this. The day began as it did three days a week, every week. I crawled out of bed, packed my nursing books and drove to Balaclava Station. It was a cold morning and the biting wind and spitting grey skies mirrored my dark mood. The events of Wednesday played repeatedly in my mind; time with my one-year-old daughter would now be supervised. I would see her for two hours, five times a week while I was watched by other people. I couldn't be trusted alone with my daughter.

My mother's words ring in my ears. 'You are worthless, Dassi, rotten to the core. You don't deserve to live.' I believe her. I know she is right, and my heart struggles under the weight of this knowledge.

By the time I park outside the station, I've decided. It will be better if I am gone.

I wait for the train. Every two minutes an automated announcement reminds us to stand behind the yellow line, to ensure our safety.

The platform is wet and slippery. *It will look like a fall*, I think. One missed step will end everything.

The 8.05 arrives. I stand still as the crowd of bodies presses against me, everyone vying to board the already overcrowded train. The train leaves with me still standing on the platform. *Failure*, the voice in my head says. *Couldn't even kill yourself.*

The wind howls and I pull my jumper tighter. The moment has passed, moved on without me. I don't step away from the edge; I'm frozen in fear of myself.

It has been three months since I was last discharged from the Albert Road psychiatric clinic. I have begun the process of making a police statement against my former principal and sexual abuser, and separating myself from the exclusive, insular community I grew up and married within. It's a lot.

The sound of a baby chattering in excitement breaks me from my dissociative state. I can't do this to my daughter. Not here, not like this.

When the 8.15 train arrives I allow myself to be swept inside the carriage, and I stand pressed against the door, breathing in the sweat of the man standing beside me. I get off at Flinders Street Station, my body on autopilot while my mind plays catch-up. I trudge up Swanston Street and down Bourke Street, like I do every Monday, Wednesday and Friday, to Navitas University, where I am studying a diploma of nursing, and join my classmates outside. I am grateful for their friendship; I have only known them for a couple of months, and they are so different from the people I grew up with.

Ten minutes into the first lecture I escape the classroom in search of solitude, secluding myself in the university bathroom atop the lid of a toilet. The smell of cleaning chemicals lingers in the air. Taking out my phone, I flick through photos from a park adventure with my daughter two days before. We look happy and relaxed, wrapped up in coats, enjoying the sunny day. Two days ago, I was free to hug, bond and play with her. Now, I have just two assigned hours with her, and a pair of eyes watching our every move.

The tears fall silently, pooling on the phone screen. Two students enter the bathroom and fix their make-up in the mirror. I strangle my sobs as I wait for them to leave and analyse every choice that has led me to this moment, days shy of my twenty-fifth birthday. It is a strange place to take stock of my life, but the white walls make an appropriate backdrop to my dark thoughts.

Two years ago, I was secure in my arranged marriage, finally pregnant with our first child after three years trying to conceive. I worked as a personal assistant to the principal of a local Jewish boys' school while my husband spent his days in the synagogue, studying the Torah and praying. Our life mirrored the lives of all our friends, except they were pregnant with their second or third children.

Within eighteen months, I had given birth, separated from my husband, had three lengthy hospital admissions for postpartum depression, given a statement to the police about the sexual abuse I had suffered at the hands of my former principal, left my closed community and enrolled in a nursing degree.

I look down at myself in my short denim skirt and black leggings. Whose strange life was I living? Was this all part of secular society? Why couldn't I have stayed silent and buried my truth in the religious life destined for me?

The destructive inner voice is back, and determined to crush me. *Your new life is flimsy and unsustainable; you'll never make it.* I remember the childhood stories about those who tried to leave our community: they either ended up dead or lived on the streets as druggies and alcoholics.

I dry my eyes and leave the bathroom. I skirt towards the exit, past the half-glazed classroom windows, hoping no one will notice my red-faced escape.

It is 10.30 a.m. and the changeable Melbourne weather has turned from dreary into bright sunshine. I join the stream of slow-moving tourists shopping on Bourke Street and duck into Target. The gleaming white floors and colourful toys are soothing. I check my bank account. I have $70 to last until next week; I can make do with $40. I choose a Hoot Owl plushie for my daughter, and already, I feel lighter. I might only see her for two hours today, but I will make sure every minute counts.

I jump aboard a passing tram. Six hours until I can hold my daughter in my arms and tell her I love her. I wrap myself around a yellow pole for balance as the tram lurches the four stops to Flinders Street Station.

I enter Melbourne's oldest station under its famous clocks and catch the Sandringham line to Balaclava. Once again, I am standing on the edge of the train platform. But this time when I look down at the tracks, I realise something: I don't want to die, I want to kill something inside me.

I sit down on the now-deserted platform and speak out loud to myself.

'Dassi, you have two choices. You can feel sorry for yourself. You can give up, lean into the narrative that the system is punishing you for circumstances beyond your control. You can let it ruin you, continue the cycle of inherited trauma, prove that you are indeed a worthless mother.

Or you can get up and fight. Do the work. Take the help being offered to you and fix yourself. Prove that you are not broken. Be the mother you always wanted to be. Give your daughter the love and safety you never had.

It will be hard, but it can be done. It must be done.'

CHAPTER 1

The monster

My mother stood in the corner of my bedroom smashing my doll against the floor. I shrank back into the top bunk, trying to make myself invisible as I watched on in horror. Esther was my only doll.

Mummy was screaming, and it took me a minute to realise she was screaming at me. 'Dassi, get me a knife.' I tumbled down the ladder of the bunk and ran. Down the stairs, through the hall and into the kitchen. The sun in the backyard filtered through the windows. I stopped for a moment and stared at my bike, propped against the shed. I could hear the girl across the road laughing with her brothers as they rode up and down our dead-end street. I was envious of her life. I had spent so many afternoons watching her family from the upstairs window, while I was locked inside and forbidden to play.

'AVODAH ZARAH, AVODAH ZARAH.' My mother's yelling travelled down the stairs.

'Avodah Zarah' referred to idol worship or creating an image of God himself. This was forbidden under Jewish law. Although God had no physical form, humans are representations of God, and a human sculpture could be considered an idol. According to the strict interpretation of the Talmud's holy teachings, my doll's human-like features were an affront to God.

I needed to hurry. Panicked, I pulled open both cutlery drawers. Which knife did I bring my mother? Red or blue? Dairy or meat? I jumped up and down, gripped by indecision, then grabbed the red knife and bolted back up the stairs as fast as my five-year-old legs would carry me.

My prep teacher had taught us not to run with sharp objects, but I didn't slow. There was no time for caution.

My older sister Nicole was on her trundle bed and my younger sister Elly was on the lower bunk, clutching her own doll. The monster that had swallowed my mother stood at the back of the room, Esther trapped between her fingers.

I handed the knife to my mother and shrunk back. I retreated two steps, but her eyes told me to stop there.

The knife punctured Esther's face again and again. 'Avodah Zarah,' my mother repeated as she handed the doll back to me, her voice softer now. Elly and Nicole didn't move as my mother took their dolls and cut holes in their faces.

After she left the room, I climbed back into bed clutching my disfigured doll. *I'm sorry, Esther*, I told her, but Esther didn't look like Esther anymore. There was a hole where her face used to be.

I covered Esther's poor, damaged face and tried to retreat into the quiet world inside my mind. It didn't matter that Esther was broken or that I would get no dinner that day. I covered my head, sucked my thumb, and disappeared into the world where I felt nothing. No pain, no hunger, no fear. A world where suffering didn't exist. I had been retreating into this world since I was old enough to know it was safer than the one I was living in.

I was born during the early hours of a wintry Australian morning in June, the fourth daughter in a family that would eventually number seven children. The year was 1987 and my parents were on a religious quest. By the time I turned six my family would belong to the most exclusive Jewish ultra-Orthodox community in Melbourne. Religion, and fear of my parents, would be the defining features of my childhood.

According to strict Jewish law, a family only fulfils the commandment to 'be fruitful and multiply' if they give birth to both male and female children. My parents had my sisters Dalia, Tamar and Nicole before I came along. Despite poor health and difficult pregnancies, my mother would then go on to have my younger sister Elly and my two brothers, Isaac and Ben.

Our family was considered small in the community. According to Jewish belief, each child's soul represents a whole world, and killing that possibility with birth control is akin to murder. My mother almost died during the labour with Ben and only then received the rabbi's permission to take measures against further pregnancy.

My parents' mixed marriage was tumultuous. My father came from an English, multi-generational, upper middle-class family.

He was born in the Royal Northern Hospital in London in 1953, the same week that the Queen was crowned. The family of five – his parents and his two sisters – lived in the upmarket London suburb of Hampstead Gardens. His family, as Liberal Jews, lived a cultural expression of Judaism, engaging with the traditions of the faith while also embracing modernity, such as the use of technology and mixing with the secular community.

My mother was an exotic, dark-skinned child of Israeli immigrants, one of five daughters including a set of twins.

Her father had been a fervent follower of religious life and engaged in training to become a rabbi. My mother's early years were spent in Israel around her grandparents, who kept a strongly traditional home.

When my mother was ten, her parents moved them to England, and the family dropped many of the religious traditions as financial struggles saw her father moving away from his rabbinical training to open a restaurant in London.

Both my parents attended Habonim, a Socialist-Zionist Jewish youth movement in London. My father, at the time a nineteen-year-old university student, had walked into the club and seen a young woman sitting on the floor, and told himself he was going to marry that girl. My mother was sixteen at the time.

It was 1973. My parents began a whirlwind romance and quickly fell in love. They informed their parents that if they didn't allow them to marry, they would live together. Both sets of parents were aghast at the idea, and despite their families' wishes for them to delay the marriage until my father had finished university and my mother was older, they married later that same year. Although neither lived a religious life, their marriage was held in an Orthodox synagogue, as they intended to settle in Israel. Marrying in an Orthodox synagogue would prevent them from having to serve in the Israeli Army.

They travelled to Paris for their honeymoon and, wanting independence, chose to settle away from their families in Manchester, England. My father finished his university degree in information technology and began looking for a job. A year later, in November 1974, Dalia was born. My parents struggled to support themselves and my paternal grandmother helped them financially when she was able. Tamar was born three years later, in September 1977.

With two young kids and limited funds, my parents decided to move across the world. Warm, sunny Australia seemed ideal. My father's qualifications as a computer programmer were in high demand, and offered the growing family financial stability. So, in 1981 my parents began a new life in Melbourne.

Before their departure, my mother travelled to Israel to seek out a rabbi for a blessing. She had a secret hope of leading a more religious life, and asked the rabbi to grant her wish that my father would also embrace a religious lifestyle. The rabbi gave her a blessing, and she held that promise to heart.

After they settled in St Kilda, my father successfully developed a business in computer technology and my mother looked around for a Jewish day school where she could enrol Dalia and Tamar. She considered Yavneh College, the modern Zionist school in Elsternwick, but a chance meeting with a rabbi's wife in a Jewish bakery convinced her to instead enrol my sisters in Beth Rivka – a religious school in East St Kilda.

Beth Rivka was a staunch Lubavitch school with a philosophy promoting knowledge and religious practice. Lubavitch is a Hasidic movement within ultra-Orthodox Judaism, known for its outreach activities and its emphasis on the study of the Torah and adherence to the commandments in daily life. The movement is also sometimes referred to as Chabad, an acronym for the Hebrew words 'Chochmah, Binah, Da'at' (wisdom, understanding and knowledge).

Dalia was devoted to her religious teachings, and encouraged my mother to light Shabbat candles and keep the Shabbat – a holy day of rest that follows many strict customs. The family was warmly welcomed by Lubavitch community members, who provided them with guidance and support. To my mother's great joy, my father also began attending classes to learn how to properly observe the Shabbat.

Religious observance in our family quickly became a source of tension between my parents. My mum wanted to live a religious life while retaining the practices of her childhood, without the numerous restrictions, whereas my dad, having experienced a taste of a religious lifestyle, wanted to embrace it wholeheartedly. The religion they were taught by the community had many life-changing rules, including a married woman covering her hair, keeping a scheduled sex life, and observing dietary laws.

Once my father was exposed to religion in an authentic manner, his outlook shifted drastically. His apathy was replaced by a strong conviction. No longer was my mother leading the charge.

My parents had tried for more children, but faced fertility complications after the placenta ruptured during my mother's pregnancy with Tamar. They had conceived multiple times, but each pregnancy ended in a miscarriage. My mother was promised by a rabbi that if she took on God's law, she would be able to carry a healthy baby to term. With this promise in mind, she agreed to embrace a religious lifestyle.

At first, living a religious life seemed daunting. There were so many rules and restrictions to follow; the family would need to make many changes.

They took steps to purify their lives and banished any and all outside influences: no more television, radio, secular newspapers, catalogues or non-Jewish music. Only Jewish music was now permitted, sung solely by boys and men; women's voices in song were forbidden, deemed too immodest for a man's ears. No longer content with the secular world, the family found solace in the Torah and the many rabbis who preached its message.

My parents lived next door to a rabbi in the ultra-Orthodox community. He attended their home and showed them how to make a kosher kitchen. Dishes that had been used for non-kosher food were discarded and new ones were bought and ritualised in a holy bath. My mother, obsessed with cleanliness, took on the cleaning and 'koshering' of the kitchen with gusto. After the kitchen had been cleaned and left covered for forty-eight hours, the rabbi poured boiling water over the countertops and sinks and declared it ready for use.

From now on, meat and dairy would be cooked and eaten separately, using only ingredients found in Jewish grocery stores or approved by the governing Australian kosher authority. The Bible states not to cook a goat in its mother's milk, and the many laws from the Torah regarding eating meat and dairy together came from the translation and understanding of this quote. One was not allowed to eat meat and dairy in the same meal, and the dairy could not be consumed for six hours after eating meat. Slowly, my mother learnt to cook the foods traditional to Jewish women worldwide, and to ensure they were up to the highest kosher standards.

The rabbi's promise of a healthy baby came to fruition. My mother carried a pregnancy to term and in 1985 my sister Nicole was born.

By the time I was born two years later, in 1987, my parents aspired to an even more religious life. Although the Lubavitch community members were ultra-Orthodox, their outreach meant they were involved in the secular world. The Adass community represented the epitome of religious observance, insular and exclusive, and my mother wanted in.

CHAPTER 2

Growing up Adass

Nestled in the popular suburb of East St Kilda, Melbourne, lies the Adass Israel community – an ultra-Orthodox Jewish sect of approximately 250 families who adhere to the strictest interpretation of the commandments in the Torah. The community has its own self-sufficient services, such as kindergartens, schools, shops, synagogue, cemetery and medical service, and rarely engages with the wider community.

In 1939–40, a group of Elwood Talmud Torah members, unsatisfied with the level of observance in their congregation, decided to form their own – the Kehila Kedosha Beis Haknesses Ahawah Zion. In 1944, they affiliated with the London Adass Yisroel movement, and adopted the name Adass Israel in 1950. To be part of the movement, their constitution had to include a commitment to Orthodoxy, and had to stipulate that no one who desecrated the Sabbath or ate forbidden food could be on the governing body.

Immigration after the war laid the foundation for the Adass community, and in 1950 the work began to build a mikveh (ritual bath), which played an important role in community life for men and women. A government-recognised primary school and a kosher meat facility were also built. In 1959, a War Memorial Synagogue Building fund was established. The school building opened the night before the foundation stone for the synagogue was laid, marking the start of a new future for the congregation. My mother learnt of the Adass community through the rabbi next door, and chose to enrol her children in Adass. By 1992, we had officially become members of the Adass community.

East St Kilda was one suburb and a million miles away from its well-known neighbour St Kilda, with its famous beach, pier, Luna Park and edgy nightlife. Our suburb was inland, with standalone houses on small blocks, intersected by the tramlines carrying rattling trams between the city and Melbourne's southeastern suburbs.

Living side by side with our secular neighbours, it felt like we existed in a parallel universe. There were few reasons to leave the four-block radius we lived within – journeying to the dentist in Hawthorn, only a few suburbs over, felt like travelling to a distant world.

I remember being six years old and standing glued to the bathroom doorway with Nicole and Elly as our mother held Tamar by her hair and pushed soap into her mouth. Tamar's teeth were covered in a film of white, and I knew it would take days to rid her mouth of the taste. My mother's roar followed her down the hall as she pushed Tamar into her bedroom. 'You are not my daughter anymore, you don't deserve to be Jewish. A Jewish girl doesn't talk back to their mother like you do!' We followed her as ordered, and gathered around the bed. My father had taken down a suitcase and collected Tamar's belongings. Sixteen-year-old Tamar was being kicked out of the house. From today, we would no longer have an older sister.

I don't know what Tamar had done to anger my mother. Even at this young age I had worked out her rage had no rhyme or reason, no trigger we could predict.

When our father left to drop Tamar somewhere outside the community, Nicole, Elly and I fled upstairs and hid under our blankets. I stared at the ceiling, wondering if I would ever see my sister again. I imagined the forces of evil in the secular world convincing her to wear a shorter skirt or making her forget to say the blessings after food. I thought about how hard it would be to keep all the Shabbat rules in a strange place. Not being Jewish was the worst punishment.

Nicole told us a made-up story about Zelda the robot and sang the nightly prayers with Elly and me, as Tamar had done every night, but it wasn't the same.

When we got up the next morning, I asked my mother if Tamar would be coming home. She told us that Tamar was not a part of our family anymore, and that we would be punished if we mentioned her name. That evening, we were sent upstairs to bed without dinner as soon as we came home from school. Without Tamar to look after us we were too noisy, and our mother didn't want to see us.

The problem with going to bed at four-thirty was that both bathrooms were downstairs, and once in bed we were forbidden to come downstairs until morning. It was a long time to hold in our pee and because we were hungry, we would drink as much as we could to fill our stomachs. Sometimes, if we were very thirsty and could overcome the guilt, we would drink the negel vassar. These cups of 'nail water' standing in buckets beside our beds were for pouring over each hand three times in the morning when we woke. After we washed our hands from the impurity of the night, we would sing a short stanza to thank God for giving us a new day.

The days without Tamar are remembered by the constant taste of fear in the back of my throat. Without the shield of my big sister, I was afraid of my own shadow. I wanted to please my mother, I wanted to make her happy, I wanted her to love me, but I had no idea how. Everything I did was wrong and no matter how hard I tried, I didn't know how to make myself right.

That night Nicole, Elly and I huddled in the middle of our bedroom. Hungry, we had once again drunk water to fill our empty stomachs. We were too scared to lie down in case we peed on our sheets. The ache from holding it in was turning Elly green. I leant in close to Nicole so I wouldn't be heard and, in a series of whispers, we made our decision: we would open the corner cupboard and pee on the carpet in turns.

The cupboard door was heavy; three metres tall and made of solid wood.

Nicole stood on the bunk bed and wrapped both hands around the handle while Elly and I lay on our stomachs and pushed our fingers underneath the door. On the count of three we dragged the door towards us. There was a loud creak, big enough to fill the room and travel downstairs, and as if rehearsed, we each froze for a moment and then flew to our beds.

We listened for the sound of our mother climbing the stairs, her bare feet in hard-soled slippers. The tone of her footsteps told us everything: how red her face would be and the rage that would pour into the room. We had been reading the way she walked since we were little.

I jammed a thumb into my mouth and squeezed my legs together, holding my breath so I could hear better. I blinked back my tears and waited. Crying would only make things worse. We waited another few moments and then, without making a sound, moved together towards the cupboard again.

I didn't want to go first. I was convinced that every childhood monster lived behind that door, and the few times I had seen the cupboard open I'd been too scared to look inside. Goosebumps covered my chest. I knew our decision was wrong, but the monsters in the cupboard weren't as scary as the very real one waiting downstairs.

Nicole went first, then Elly, and I peed last. With the carpet soaked in our desperation, we closed the cupboard door and tiptoed back to our beds. It was dark and my face flushed with shame as the smell seeped into the room. I was relieved that my sisters couldn't see me. Now we had done it once, we knew we would do it again.

The following afternoon when we came home, our mother was in our bedroom, standing in front of the cupboard. The carpet hadn't dried from our sins of the previous night, and the air breathed our secret.

'Who did this?' she asked. Her voice was quiet, calm. We knew that was worse than her anger. Nicole and Elly were silent, and I bit my lip to hold back my confession. My heart was thumping in my throat and my legs were straining not to fold.

My mother spoke directly to me, as if she had read my thoughts and knew what I had done. 'Take off your clothes,' she demanded. I ripped off my uniform and tights while she glared at me, my eyes lowered with the shame of being immodest. My mother handed me a nappy. 'If you act like a baby, I will treat you like a baby,' she said. For the rest of the evening, I was ordered to crawl around on the floor with the nappy under my nightie and drink water out of a bowl under the table.

Even after that punishment, we still used that cupboard

in times of urgency. I felt dirty and wrong every time we did it. I tried to stop myself drinking after school so I wouldn't need to pee, but sometimes the hole in my stomach was greater than the shame, and I drank to mask the hunger.

On the nights we were given dinner, we then spent the time until bed sitting on the pink couch in the dining room, staring at the walls. We were robots, forbidden to move. Movement meant punishment, and punishment meant time locked in the cupboard under the stairs. It was impossible to figure out how to be the ideal child; the meaning of perfect changed as quickly as my mother's moods.

It was easy to sit still and silent. I could float into the nothing behind my eyes, to a place where my body didn't exist. I worried about Isaac and his bundle of toddler energy. One evening my mother pulled him towards the cupboard, picked up his flailing body, threw him in and locked the door. 'Twenty minutes,' she told him, but he was only two years old and didn't understand. Every time he cried to be let out, my mother started the timer again.

My heart was sore with my longing to save him. When my mother got up to use the bathroom I jumped up and ran to the cupboard door. I lay on my stomach and spoke through the crack. 'Isaac, think about the story of elephants I read to you yesterday. Think how you are an elephant, big, strong and quiet.' His words were soft and filled with fear. 'My tummy is hurting, Dassi.' I heard Nicole run into the kitchen to find something we could slip under the door.

Every moment we were away from the couch, we risked a bigger punishment, but although our young minds couldn't fathom that this was not our fault, we knew our mother was being unfair to the youngest of us.

A couple of days later we came home from school to find Tamar standing at the sink, washing dishes, like she had never left. She seemed different, quieter, and she held her head lower. She was still dressed the same – a skirt over her knees, tights, and a long-sleeved shirt that covered her neckline.

I was relieved that the non-Jewish people hadn't torn her away from the Torah. It was April, and our mother was weeks away from having our youngest brother. The pregnancy was fraught with complications. If she had no patience for us before, she had even less now. Tamar had been brought back to keep the house running.

The days without Tamar had given me a taste of life without the protection of my older sister. The following nights I tossed and turned, worrying about her leaving our home when she was older.

By now I had started prep at Adass Israel School and we were learning about Lag Ba'omer – a festival of celebration during a period of mourning in the Jewish calendar.

Each morning our teacher made the blessing for the day, before our morning prayers, and we chanted it after her, word for word.

The forty-nine days between two of the major Jewish festivals, Passover and Shavuot, are a period of mourning to commemorate the massacres that took place in Jewish history, especially the death of the great sage Rabbi Akiva. Every year during this seven-week period, we stopped listening to music, didn't get married or cut our hair.

Even as a little girl, I was fascinated by the stories of the Great Rabbis and their sacrifices under the evil Roman Empire, which forbade the learning of the Torah. 'Rabbi Akiva didn't learn how to read until he was forty years old,' our teacher taught us, 'and still he gave up his life to defend the Torah.' I wished I could find a way to sacrifice my life for such a holy cause.

One of Rabbi Akiva's famous disciples continued to defy the Romans and spent twelve years hiding in a cave, sustained by a miraculous well and carob tree, writing a key work of Kabbalah.

Lag Ba'omer, the thirty-third of the forty-nine days between the festivals, was the day the disciple died and was buried in Meron, Israel.

On that day, observant Jews around the world stopped mourning, and we celebrated his life and his teaching by building huge bonfires to symbolise the light of religious spirituality.

The weeks leading up to Lag Ba'omer were marked by the growing pile of wood in the middle of the school playground. The taunts of the boys traipsing into the yard to drop their firewood made me realise I was too old to attend. The bonfire would be surrounded by the men and boys dancing, and at almost seven years old I was too big to slip in unnoticed as I had in previous years. I was devastated.

In later years when my mother allowed us to attend, my sisters and I would stand outside the school with the rest of the women and girls, watching the men celebrate from afar. The rituals of Lag Ba'omer, like the rest of the Jewish holidays, are mainly performed and led by and for the men.

I accepted this. Our way of life was the holiest way to live.

I recall being amazed when the non-Jewish girl who lived next door told me that, although she was a girl, she was allowed to sing in church.

We had been warned never to speak to her, given her lack of Jewish faith, but one weekend I was biking up and down Avoca Grove, coasting on the applause of our Jewish neighbours for learning to ride without training wheels, when a little girl in a white dress caught my eye.

Perhaps it was the confidence boost I had received that gave me the courage to defy my parents' order and stop outside her gate, but without thinking, I yelled out hello. 'I've just come home from church,' she explained to me.

'What's church like?' I asked her.

I felt incredibly naughty for saying the word 'church' out loud. I knew it was a dirty word that described a sinful place. When walking to the synagogue with our father on Shabbat, we crossed the road when passing a church so we wouldn't walk on church grounds.

Mary was five years old, and she sang us a hymn she'd learnt that day. I was glad she was allowed to participate in the prayers. She had a beautiful voice; it would be wasted if she couldn't sing. I yearned for her life. As the guilt began to bite at my chest, I yelled goodbye and rode away. That night I chastised myself over and over. *You're an awful, terrible girl, Dassi, you deserve to die right now and go to Gehinnom.* (Gehinnom was an afterlife of torment for the wicked dead.) I promised myself to never think of her life again.

Fifteen days after Lag Ba'omer came Shavuot – the festival to celebrate the giving of the Torah to the Jewish people. We observed the holiday with festive meals of dairy foods, and the men stayed up all night to learn the Torah.

That year our mother was in hospital with complications from her pregnancy, so instead of going to the synagogue to study, our father walked to the hospital after the traditional meal. It was half an hour away, but the rules of the major Jewish holidays were the same as Shabbat, and driving was forbidden.

At home alone that night, we danced around Tamar, too excited to sleep. We knew our mother had gone to the hospital to bring home a baby. We changed out of our holiday clothes, which were only to be worn on holy days, and brought our blankets down to the living room. I tried to stay awake, waiting for my father to come home with the news of our sibling, but as dawn crept closer my eyes were too heavy to keep open.

'It's a boy!' my father announced, bursting through the door at 4 a.m. We all jumped up and down in excitement. My father pulled Tamar into the hall to speak privately, then returned to the hospital. 'Your mother is very unwell,' he told her. 'It's a life or death situation.'

My mother was fighting for her life due to complications with the birth, but I had no idea. To me, it was the best Shavuot ever. Tamar sat at the head of the table, and we each received our Shavuot chocolate pudding without anyone missing out, as often happened. Isaac zoomed through the house, and we chased him up and down the stairs, through the halls and out the back door. At the end of the day, we all fell into cuddles in the middle of the living room floor.

When our mother came home a week later, the children we had been during Shavuot ceased to exist; we snapped back into the little soldiers she expected us to be.

A month later, in June 1995, I turned seven.

I only remember two other events of that year – Dalia's wedding and Tamar leaving for a religious seminary a month later.

Dalia had left for a Jewish girls' seminary in England when I was five. Tamar would follow her a year later. The next time I saw Dalia, I was six years old, and she was engaged. The matchmaker had set her up with an Australian boy studying in Manchester Yeshiva, the men's seminary. A week later, they were engaged, and the wedding preparations began.

It was my first wedding. All my friends came from bigger families, and were related to many other families in the community. Every other week one of my classmates had the day off school to attend a wedding, and now, finally, it was my turn. My mother was on a mission to prove her worth to the Adass community she had only recently joined. To do that, she would make sure Dalia had the perfect Jewish wedding.

My mother kept a constant count of how much money we cost her, and when it seemed too much, she would yell at us, 'I wish you were dead.' Despite this, every Sunday for months before the wedding, we were taken to a seamstress to have bespoke dresses made, just like other families in the community did. 'Higher, higher,' my mother would rally the seamstress, until the neckline was so tight around my neck, I felt like I was choking. It was a sin to parade your collarbone. My mother would stop at nothing to ensure our modesty.

Dalia's wedding was held at Clarence Receptions in Elsternwick, with 250 guests in attendance. All night, I waited eagerly for the buffets of food and the dessert tables.

My mother frequently used food withdrawal as a punishment. Always hungry and frequently starved, I thought about food constantly. But when the waiters pulled out the chocolates with Dalia's name on them, I wanted to throw up with the pounding in my head. As well as my first wedding, I was also experiencing my first migraine, a condition that would haunt me all my life. On the one night I could eat what I wanted, I felt too ill to indulge.

For me, the unintentional highlight of Dalia's wedding was when a woman got too close to the celebratory candles and her wig caught on fire. She didn't feel it until half her head was ablaze. Fortunately, she was unharmed.

A month after Dalia's wedding, Tamar left for the seminary. I knelt on the couch by the window and waved until I couldn't see her anymore. I was overcome by fear, sadness and dread. We were alone now, without the protection of our big sisters. Tamar was gone, and she would never live with us again.

Our last years at the house on Avoca Grove are hazy in my memory. My childhood was characterised by constant fear and anxiety. I lived in a heightened state of vigilance, experiencing intense emotional distress. I didn't quite understand why I didn't feel safe with my father – that understanding would come much later. My brain, intent on keeping me alive, found creative ways to protect me. Each day when I woke, I felt like I was a different Dassi to the one who had existed the night before. Every morning, I was a Dassi not yet been betrayed by the people supposed to protect her.

This dissociation allowed me to lock parts of the same memories in different boxes inside my brain. That way, even if I gained access to one part, I would never remember everything and become overwhelmed. My primary school reports talk about my lack of focus, insisting that better concentration would help me fulfil my potential. I spent a lot of time wondering if I was real, and disappearing into a dreamlike world where I was an inanimate object that didn't think or feel.

Many summer days were spent locked upstairs, to keep us away from our mother. We would pass the time watching life outside the big panoramic window in Dalia and Tamar's former bedroom-turned-rumpus. There was no air-conditioning; we were sweaty, hungry and grumpy. 'I wish we had icy poles,' Nicole would say to me as we watched our neighbours on the street. 'I wish we were allowed to ride our bikes,' Elly would say. 'I wish I was dead,' I would say under my breath.

After Tamar left, my mother expected nine-year-old Nicole to run the house as Tamar had done. The vacuuming was delegated to me, and I was slapped each time the vacuum bumped into the walls. The machine was bigger than I was.

When I was eight, Tamar came home from the seminary. Following the same path all young women in the community were expected to take, the matchmaker set her up with a local boy and a month later they were engaged. The following months were dominated by the tension of my mother's stress as she organised the wedding.

Two days before the wedding, at 6.30 a.m. there was a knock at the door. Our father was at the synagogue, our mother and Tamar were sleeping, and Nicole, Elly and I ignored the door as we had been taught. But before we could stop him, Isaac ran to the door and pulled it open. 'It's Dalia,' he shouted into the house as we all ran to hug her. We had been told she had a new job in Manchester and wasn't able to come to the wedding, so this was a wonderful surprise. Dalia placed her finger over her mouth and crept up the stairs as we trailed behind her to wake Tamar. My heart felt like it would burst with happiness. My two big sisters were home again.

The Sheva Brachot (seven blessings) followed Tamar's wedding. For seven nights, friends in the community hosted Tamar, her husband and our family for an elegant meal where the wedding blessings were recited again, asking God's blessings for the new couple. I was old enough to be invited to several of these occasions, and I took advantage of the food on offer.

When the wedding festivities had ended, my mother compelled my father to take us on a short holiday to the country before Dalia returned to her husband overseas. For two glorious nights our mother played gracious hostess, and after a day picking cherries with Dalia, Tamar and her husband drove up to join us for an evening. When I scrambled up to the high bed and snuggled in next to Elly, my dreams were filled with laughter and love, like I was a princess in my own land of angels. Now that the stress of both weddings was over, I believed my mother had changed, and we would never see the rage monster again.

But when we returned home, Nicole, Elly and I cleaned the car and carried our belongings into the house under our mother's stern gaze. 'Get to your rooms and don't make a sound. Take Isaac upstairs with you,' she told us. 'One sound and you'll go without dinner.' It was 2 p.m. – for four hours we had to keep Isaac from running around. Downstairs, our mother was putting Ben down for a nap. He was a gorgeous toddler, with bright eyes and chubby cheeks; the apple of her eye. I wondered what it was like to be loved like that.

But Isaac wouldn't settle. He scampered from one end of the room to the other, never growing tired or out of breath. His energy had no end, his world was bound by nothing but his own imagination. 'Quiet!' my mother screamed when she heard his feet thumping overhead. Isaac didn't register, he didn't hear the panic in our voices as we pleaded for him to calm. He was lost in his head, playing out his favourite storybook characters and having fun.

'Bring him down,' she screamed. *Him* – the boy that doesn't deserve a name. I'm scared for Isaac, but I know disobedience isn't an option, so I lead him down the stairs towards her.

I feel as though I am standing outside the window looking at the four children gathered around the fridge.

Four children and a monster. I know my body is in that room, but I am not. I am floating outside, beyond her reach. I watch as the monster holds a chilli pepper up to the little boy's mouth and tells him to open wide. I have been forced to eat a hot pepper before, and then forbidden to rinse the burn from my throat. I know the pain. The little boy looks around, eyes wide with fear, then opens his mouth and squeezes his eyes shut.

I see his eyes watering and the tears stream down his face. He is choking on the pepper as she pushes it down his throat. 'Look at your brother,' the monster screams, and I watch as the pepper comes back up, along with his breakfast. The vomit makes the monster bigger. The oldest girl begs for her brother, but the monster pays her no attention. The boy is pushed onto his hands and knees and she forces his face into the vomit. I watch outside, waiting for the monster to give me back my mother.

As I return to my body, I hear my mother telling us we won't be having dinner tonight. We put ourselves to bed in silence. My mouth is dry, and my chest feels narrow and cramped. I pretend the noises of my stomach belong to someone else. The hope that our mother would be different has disappeared.

As I grew older, I became more creative in finding ways to appease the hole in my belly. I would wait until the middle of morning prayers, then put up my hand to use the toilet. On the way to the bathroom block I would pass through the locker room, where the students' bags were kept. Glancing around to make sure I wasn't being watched, I would stick my hand into an open bag, open the lunch box and pull out a snack. I never took more than one snack from the same child. Finding something I had never been allowed to eat, like a lolly, was the ultimate treat. I would stuff it into my pocket, race to the bathroom and quietly eat it in the privacy of a cubicle.

When the students complained of a thief, the head teacher gathered us in the hall. 'Thou shalt not steal,' she reminded us – one of the ten main commandments of the 613 in the Jewish Torah. My classmates looked around, whispering about who they thought it could be. They didn't look at me. I was a girl who never made a peep. I couldn't be the thief. Although I felt enormous guilt, that never outweighed my hunger. My hunger was bigger than anything.

When I was in Grade Three, my parents sold the house on Avoca Grove – at a loss, as Australia was still recovering from the recession. We moved from a five-bedroom, double-storey house into a three-bedroom rented property, the first of three rented properties I would live in with my parents. Anything that wasn't deemed an essential and didn't serve a Jewish purpose was thrown out. Nicole and I did most of the packing, along with the cleaner my mother hired, who stayed on despite my mother accusing her of stealing. 'You can't trust non-Jews for a second,' she warned us. 'They would steal from you, all of them.'

Somehow despite my parents' strict rules, a few ABBA tapes had escaped the earlier culling; Dalia and Tamar had occasionally pushed against the rules and played them. I remember listening to them fascinated to hear a woman's voice in song. As I packed the dishes, my mother walked into the kitchen, pulled out the tape reel and threw them away. 'From now on we will *only* be listening to Jewish music,' she told us. ABBA's lively beats were replaced by the haunting sounds of boys' choirs singing about the Torah and its holy messages.

The cassettes were a small part of my childhood, but they held memories of our older sisters. It felt like any remnants of our lives with Dalia and Tamar had been thrown away. From this point on, it would be up to Nicole, Elly and me to look out for each other. We would watch each other's backs, and together we would survive. I would keep the monster away from my brothers, I would make sure they were fed, and I would pray every day that my mother would love me.

CHAPTER 3

New York

The second hand didn't tick. I watched as it made its smooth journey around the clock above the fridge. I had never seen a second hand that didn't tick before. The clock was the most interesting thing to watch in the apartment. I thought about sitting down to follow the hand as it passed the minutes, but I was worried my mother would come in and catch me being lazy. It was 9.30 a.m. on a Tuesday, and I had been alone in my auntie's New York apartment with my two- and three-year-old cousins for an hour.

I was eleven years old, and I had arrived in New York with my mother twenty-four hours earlier, because my grandfather was having heart surgery. 'Double bypass,' my auntie told me, but no one explained what that meant. I knew by the way they whispered to each other that the whole family was worried.

Flying had lived up to every word of Nicole's description – she had experienced it two years earlier when she travelled with my mother, and I had questioned her endlessly about it. Being under twelve years old, my ticket was half the price of an adult ticket, so my mother took me along to help with the younger kids.

'Make sure your two cousins don't get into trouble, and the house better be spotless when we come home,' my mother had told me that morning with a stern face.

I had never met my maternal grandfather. After my parents married, my mother's family had chosen to lead an ultra-Orthodox Hasidic life, and moved to settle in one of America's thriving Hasidic communities in Brooklyn.

The older cousins went to school and my four aunts and my mother left for the hospital. When my mother told me I would be looking after the two youngest kids every day, I had been ecstatic, imagining all the food I could eat. Six weeks meant thirty whole days, excluding weekends, without my mother, in an apartment bursting with kosher goodies, and no one to forbid me from eating.

When the door closed behind them, I waited five minutes and then ran to the pantry and studied the rows of cereals. I had never seen so many choices. Twice a year, a shipment of dry kosher goods arrived in Australia from the US or Israel and was sold by the two kosher groceries in Balaclava and Elsternwick. The choices were limited, especially compared to what I could see here, and once items were sold out, we would have to wait for the next shipment. It was a highlight to visit the kosher groceries in Melbourne right after a shipment came in and see the crowded shelves.

I grabbed a box of Kellogg's Froot Loops and filled a bowl to the brim. I lifted the spoon to my mouth, then stopped. I had forgotten to say a blessing. I searched the box for the ingredients to help me work out which blessing I should make. Not being familiar with the ingredients, I made two to cover all bases.

I couldn't get the sugary goodness in my mouth fast enough. I finished one bowl and then poured myself a second. I was soon rubbing my stomach. This full to bursting sensation was a new feeling.

Lost in food bliss, I forgot about the two toddlers I was supposed to be babysitting until a scream reminded me of my duties. I took one last bite and rushed to see what was happening. The toddlers were fighting, so I picked up the two-year-old and cuddled him. The three-year-old demanded my attention, whimpering 'Ikh vil a flash, ikh vil a flash' as he pulled on my dress.

I didn't understand what he was saying. I got down on my knees beside him. 'What do you want?' I asked. He looked at me blankly, not understanding. My older cousins had learnt some English in school, but the little ones spoke only Yiddish – a language spoken by Jewish people in Central and Eastern Europe prior to the Holocaust. It had its roots in German, and included words from Hebrew and other modern languages.

'Ikh vil a flash, ikh vil a flash, ikh vil a flash!' He was on the floor, screaming and kicking. I sat down beside him and, in my panic, began to cry. I was alone, there was nobody to call, and I didn't speak the right language.

I spoke to myself quietly through my tears. 'Dassi, stop crying. You're eleven years old and your aunties trusted you with their kids. You don't want to disappoint them.' Somehow, after a lot more crying, screaming and hand gestures, I realised the three-year-old wanted a bottle. Years later, I came to understand that one of the reasons the community didn't teach the children to speak fluent English was to make it harder for them to leave.

My grandfather underwent his surgery, but his recovery was uncertain. The weeks passed with the toddlers making a mess while I rushed after them, frantically cleaning to ensure the house would be spotless when the adults came home from the hospital. Every day my mother would ask my auntie if the house had been cleaned as she'd instructed. One evening in the fourth week, my aunt and mother came home tired and irritated. My grandfather was gravely ill, and the stress had led to my grandmother being admitted too. It had been a long day with the toddlers. They'd kept pointing at the door, demanding to go outside and play, but I had to pull them away and tell them no. I wasn't allowed to leave the apartment.

My aunt called my mother into the bathroom, and I heard loud words being exchanged. I stood in the hall, pulling my hair and biting my knuckles. I was desperate for my auntie to like me and to be proud of me. When my mother yelled for me, I raced to her side, and she slapped me across the face.

'Why can I see stains here?' she screeched into my ear, pointing at the unclean toilet bowl.

'I'm so sorry, I'm so sorry,' I cried. I looked up at my auntie, wishing she would say something, but when I tried to catch her eyes she avoided my gaze. I could feel the red creeping over my face. I was used to the pain, but knowing she was watching hurt more.

Later that night, while I tried to get to sleep lying top-to-toe in my cousin's bed, I overheard my mother apologising to her sisters for her disobedient daughter. I shrivelled up inside, wishing I could disintegrate into dust. I had tried so hard to be good, but now everyone could see who I really was. The good girl was just an act. Deep inside, I was a terrible girl.

I spent most of my days staring out the lounge room window at a nearby railway bridge, wondering about the

New York my friends had seen. Although my family was not wealthy, we lived in an affluent community, and until this trip I'd been one of the few girls who had not yet been abroad. I thought about the stories my classmates had shared and the questions they would ask me when I got back. I was determined to see more than the trash-lined streets between my aunt's and grandmother's apartments.

I begged my auntie to let me go to school with my older cousins. In broken English, they had described their huge classes – a hundred or more kids, all Jewish, all Hasidic. They told me there were many schools like theirs. I couldn't wrap my head around the sheer enormity of the Jewish community in Brooklyn compared to my class of sixteen at home.

At Adass Israel School in Melbourne, we were learning how intermarriage and assimilation into the wider society could threaten the continuity of the Jewish community. Our teachers emphasised the importance of preserving our culture and heritage in order to prevent our people from disappearing. When I was finally allowed to go to school for a day with my cousin and saw the throngs of girls all speaking Yiddish, I stopped fretting about the future of Jewish communities. There were too many of us around the world. In New York, surrounded by so many Jewish people, I was proud of my religion.

After six long weeks with the toddlers in the apartment, finally it was time to go home. I was eager to show off the new phrases I had learnt, and to tell the story of attending a maths class taught in Yiddish.

I enjoyed flying. The cramped economy class cabin meant I was protected from my mother's anger, and I spent hours watching the other families, imagining what it would be like to live their lives. I was enthralled by the kids' packs the attendants handed out, even though they were targeted at younger children. The person sitting beside me was watching their screen, and when my mother caught me looking, she swapped me to the seat beside the window. Movies were unkosher and I was forbidden to touch the screen. Landing back home was bittersweet. I was going back to the same hell I had left, but at least I wasn't alone. In Australia, I had my siblings.

Several weeks after our return, my mother decided she was going to move into a respite home for a week. We were making her sick, she told us. All our badness was eating her up, and she needed to get away from us. On the day my father was to drive her to the country house, I woke up hot and feverish and couldn't go to school. 'Please can I stay home alone?' I begged, but my mother refused. I had been left alone with two toddlers for six weeks in a country I didn't know, but she wouldn't let me have a day to myself in our own home. My brothers and sisters were sent to school and I had to travel with my parents.

I took my blanket into the car and slept across the back seat. Midway through the three-hour journey, my mother demanded that my father turn around and go home. 'I have a chush (sense) that something is wrong,' she insisted.

At home, my sisters and brothers had been dropped off after school and walked into a ransacked house. Someone had wrapped their arm in a shirt from the washing line, smashed the dining room window, and thrown all the cupboards across the floor in search of money. Nicole ushered the younger kids into the bathroom and locked the door. They sat squashed in the bath together, shaking, certain that the thief was still there. They wouldn't unlock the bathroom door until we got home. When the police arrived to take a report, we were sent to our rooms. This was one of the very rare times my parents reached out to the secular world.

For months afterwards, we all had nightmares of a robber breaking in. In our minds, the robber represented all the dangers of the outside world, a scary monster that was coming to drag us away from our family and the Torah. My fear of evenings grew.

Each night at 10 p.m. I would fall into bed after completing my chores and homework, desperate to journey into my imagination and the world of nothing, but my ears would perk up at the slightest sound. Was it the robber at the window, or the footsteps of one of my parents? The fear kept me stuck in the present, unable to escape into my imaginary world. My mother knew about our fear of the dark, and night-time became her favourite playtime.

She would walk around the house checking our cleanliness. One night, she wiped a finger over the top of a bookshelf and came away with a speck of dust. I could hear all the books, at least three hundred of them, being swept to the floor. A moment later she was in our bedroom, telling me to get up. 'If I find one speck of dust when that bookshelf is back in order, I will throw it all down and you will start again. I will do this all night if I have to!' I was out of bed and in the dining room before she finished speaking, frantically wiping the books and returning them to the bookshelf. Dusting was my job, so this was my fault.

I stacked the books as she stood over me. When I had one shelf back up, she threw it all down again; the books were in the wrong order. 'I give you food. I give you a roof over your head. Why do you behave like this? You are an ungrateful child who takes and takes from me.' Her anger was growing. I knew my sisters would be listening – on another night, it would be them.

Knowing what I did wrong was better than having to guess. 'I have spies watching your every movement,' she would tell us, and she would prove it by describing happenings at school we hadn't disclosed to her.

Confessing to something was terrifying, but not confessing was worse. I racked my brain, trying to work out what I had done wrong, but I was a shy student who abided by the rules. It was never something I had knowingly done, so it was up to me to analyse my actions and figure out what she'd found lacking. 'I have a sense you're keeping something from me,' she said. Ever since her sense had been right about the robbery, she'd also developed the power to know our thoughts.

Eventually I confessed to playing with a friend she had forbidden me to spend time with, because they didn't come from a good enough family. After I was punished, I was ordered into my bedroom to write an apology letter.

Dear Aba and Mummy,
I am sorry I was a bad girl. I am sorry I am stupid and terrible. I know how hard you have tried all my life to teach me to be better and I have chosen not to listen. I'm sorry. I'm sorry you have a daughter like me. I will try to use everything you have taught me so lovingly to be a better daughter.

I wrote in big letters, because the apology letter had to cover at least half a page to be deemed acceptable.

My mother read the letter and sent it back. 'The letter is disgusting,' she said. 'Where is your apology for making me so angry that I was forced to punish you so you would listen?'

Dear Aba and Mummy,
I am sorry I made you angry. It was my mistake that made you
angry because I am a stupid child.
Love Dassi

Back and forth I went all night until I had written a letter
that was deemed acceptable. If I looked the wrong way,
wrote the wrong way, said sorry the wrong way, the letter
would be torn up and I would have to start again.

After all this, I was still given a punishment. No food
for the next day, or a day kept home off school to do
deep cleaning around the house. One mistake meant the
punishment started again. Once, towards the end of Grade
Five, I was kept home the entire week and missed an
excursion I had been waiting for all year. I was devastated,
but when my face betrayed my feelings, my mother simply
told me if I was a better child this wouldn't be happening.

I entered my last year of primary school with a newfound
determination to prove that I was worthy of my mother's
love. I wanted nothing more than to become the child she
had been hoping for.

CHAPTER 4

Bat mitzvah

It was an Aviara (sin) to kill yourself, I knew that. My Grade Six teacher had taught us that our bodies belonged to God, and that only He would decide if we lived or died. Which is why, on the eve of my twelfth birthday, I lay in bed begging Him to take my life. 'Please, Hashem (God), please, I want to die in my sleep,' I whispered into my hands.

I didn't want my sisters to hear me, but my voice grew loud with desperation. I covered my face with my hands. 'Please, Hashem, please, if you leave me here one more day, by night my soul will be covered in filth. I want to leave this material world before it's too late.' When the sun set the next evening, I would be twelve years old. In the eyes of my religion, I would be a woman, responsible for my own sins.

I thought about the relief I would feel to not wake in the morning. The Torah said, 'Honour thy father and mother.' It was one of the most important commandments and my mother's disapproval made clear I had already broken it. Hashem could read my mind; tonight was the last time my soul would fly to Him as the pure and white soul of a child.

Tomorrow, I would be responsible for the true darkness I harboured within.

I closed my eyes and tried to listen for God's voice telling me I would be joining Him in heaven, but all my mind provided were pictures of my soul choking, blackened by misdeeds. It wasn't working. God was leaving me here to test me, and I was already failing.

I stopped begging and crept into my nothing world inside, as I did every night. It was my favourite place to be, and I fell asleep imagining I never had to leave. I tried to disappear into this world in the daytime too, but it wasn't the same. I kept trying, though, sure that if I could just stop thinking and feeling, I wouldn't be hungry and tempted to sin.

I woke up with a stone in the middle of my stomach. It was ten hours until my birthday, and today was the last day I had to tell my classmates that the bat mitzvah party I had invited them to had been called off.

That morning, while my mother was in the bathroom, I made her bed and peeked into her cupboard. The box of party favours she had been collecting was still there. When I first saw the box, I was so sure the party would go ahead. Why else would she spend money on party favours? But over the weekend my mother had called me into her room and yelled, 'Dassi, you do not deserve anything, let alone a party, you're such an ungrateful child.' That was it – no explanation, and no party for me.

Don't feel anything, Dassi, I told myself. *A bat mitzvah party doesn't mean anything to a nothing. You are a nothing. You don't feel, you don't think.* But no matter how hard I tried, I still cried myself to sleep.

I was the oldest in my class, so I would be the first to have a bat mitzvah party. Every day this week I had tried to tell my classmates the party was off, but when I opened my mouth, the words wouldn't come. Now it was the end of the week and there was no time left – I had to tell my classmates there would be no party.

Aba dropped us off at school and I ran towards the bathroom block beside the playground. The halls were empty; Aba dropped us off just after 8 a.m., and only a few other families dropped their children off that early. I walked past all the cubicles until I reached the last one, at the back of the block: the disabled toilet. It was twice the size of the other cubicles, and it had its own sink and mirror. A room to hide all my dread and shame until I was ready to face the world again.

I lifted my feet onto the closed seat so the gap under the cubicle door wouldn't reveal my secret. For a minute I imagined myself as a girl who had the guts to run away. *I could live here*, I thought. No one would find me. I would save up my snacks for a week and stuff a blanket into my bag. When the school was quiet, I could hop off the toilet and sleep on the floor using my bag as a pillow. I smiled at the thought of a private oasis; even the smell didn't bother me. I wasn't that girl, though. I wasn't that brave. Not yet.

I glanced at the Mickey Mouse watch Dalia had sent me for my birthday; it was almost 9 a.m. If anyone arrived any later than the end of morning prayers the teacher would ask for a late note.

The class had finished morning prayers when I made my way to my seat. I didn't hear anything the teacher said. When recess came, I thought about escaping to the toilet, but I knew I was out of time. I picked out the three most popular girls and approached them first. If I told them, it would get around the class and I wouldn't have to do this again. 'There is no party this Sunday,' I told them. 'Please throw out your invitations; it's not happening.' I could feel my face burning. I hated when it did that.

All afternoon, classmates came looking for the truth. 'Why, Dassi?' they kept asking me. 'Why did you cancel your party?' I saw them whispering on the bench during last play and I knew by the way they glanced across the playground that they were talking about me. The birthday that was supposed to give me some class status was gone. Now I had dipped even lower in social standing. I tried to remind myself, *a nothing doesn't care.*

I walked home with Elly, Nicole and Isaac. We had waited for our father, but he never showed, and it was too late to beg someone for a lift. When we got home our mother was angry it had taken us so long. She had a list of chores that needed doing, and now the evening would run late.

I bathed Ben and Isaac, organised their pyjamas and set up some toys. I vacuumed the house and sorted through all the washing, putting aside the handwashing to finish later. It didn't matter that it was my birthday, I was still responsible for my chores. *It's my birthday and no one cares*, I thought to myself, but a nothing doesn't care. I wouldn't allow myself to care any longer.

Elly and Nicole, in charge of the cooking, had made my favourite dinner of chicken and couscous. I was so hungry, but my mother told me I could only have one bowl. 'You're starting to put on weight, Dassi,' she said. 'Look at Nicole, she didn't put on weight at this age. You need to eat less. You're a pretty face and nothing else.' Even on my birthday I couldn't ease the hunger.

After dinner, my mother and father presented me with a Siddur (prayer book) engraved with my name. I was truly chuffed, and I thanked them many times, so they wouldn't think I was ungrateful. I held the small book against my chest, so proud to hold something precious that was just mine. I wouldn't let the boys look at it. The Siddur had my name on it; I owned it. I knew I would pour my heart into its pages, and I begged God to make my life less painful.

That night I studied my body in the mirror. I was dressed in a floor-length nightgown, and wrapped it tight against myself so I could see my size. I never looked at my body undressed; it wasn't modest. Gazing at my covered shape in the mirror, I tried to see what my father saw. In recent months he had begun to hold me tight against his body; so tight I couldn't move. 'You're beginning to feel like your mother,' he'd whispered to me as he traced his fingers over the front of my body. 'I can feel something there.' Then he moaned for a long minute, and I wondered if he was sick. It sounded like he was in pain, and I was puzzled about why our hug was making him moan. Then my father let me go and pushed me out of his office. I hoped he wouldn't call on me tonight. The hugs were not comfortable, but when I tried to say no, he would insist.

I stepped into the shower and my stomach grumbled. After the shower, I put on a pair of tights, covered my nightie with a housecoat and crept into the kitchen. I wasn't allowed to eat without my mother's permission, but I couldn't ignore the hunger pangs any longer. I checked the cracker box where all open packets were stored, but didn't dare take one – my mother counted the crackers left. Instead, I stole two biscuits from the freezer and ate them still frozen. Four hours into my birthday and I was already sinning. I pushed the guilt into the nothing. A nothing doesn't care.

The next week I visited the Fromers, the family I helped every Tuesday. The school had recently launched a program that matched older girls with families in need. Now that

I was in Grade Six I was old enough to help a mother in the community with her young children.

Ben was six now, and the complications my mother had experienced during that pregnancy meant she would not be having any more children. All my friends had a new baby in their family every year. I was so excited to learn how to take charge of a brood of little kids.

The Fromer family surprised me with a chocolate cake covered in sprinkles in the shape of a twelve. I smiled and said thank you, and wondered why they were doing this for me. How had I fooled them into thinking I deserved to be celebrated? Did they not see the terrible girl I was?

I loved the Fromer house. Tuesday evenings were the best evenings of the week. I played with five little kids, no one ever screamed, and their mother trusted me and told me I was wonderful. I would continue visiting the Fromers every week until I was eighteen, and in a lot of ways my time there helped me to realise the meaning of family. Family didn't have to mean abuse; family could mean love and support.

Being twelve earned me a closed-door talk with my mother. 'Now that you're twelve, you will find blood in your underwear one day, and once you start it will happen every month. It's your punishment for being born a woman.' I ran to Nicole with this shocking news – did she bleed in her underwear? Why had I never seen it? I was terrified, imagining bits of my body falling out of me. Nicole showed me her pads and told me that I would need to ask Aba to put them on the shopping list, but to not let anyone else know. It was embarrassing and secretive.

With thoughts of my upcoming decay and my soul slowly turning black with sin, I tried harder to disappear. At school I was too shy to utter a peep. I never looked up when the teacher was searching for someone to answer a question, terrified she would pick me. When we had to take turns reading Hebrew text out loud, I would curl into my seat as the text danced before my eyes, which were filled with tears of shame. I was so quiet the teacher thought I couldn't read.

One day my mother told me my teacher had called. 'Your teacher thinks you need tutoring on Hebrew reading. Are you stupid, Dassi? Do I have a stupid daughter?' I had been reading since I was in kindergarten. I told my mother I knew the letters and the sounds they made, but like always, she believed the teacher. I was too dumb to know anything. 'You have nothing else going for you, Dassi. Your grades will be the only reason a matchmaker will look at you,' she told me. I knew I wasn't stupid, but unless I could read in front of the class, the teacher would assume I was.

I started reading lessons with another teacher at her home. At first, I tried to protest, but after the first lesson, I stopped objecting. Half an hour with a warm, gentle adult was worth the embarrassment of knowing that both my mother and my teacher thought I was stupid. During the lesson, my hunger pangs disappeared. The way my father touched me in the car on the way to the lesson disappeared. During the lesson, I had an adult's attention all on me. Suddenly, I loved being the girl who people believed couldn't read.

For weeks I would contemplate what I could do to make my reading tutor see the way I was drowning. I was desperate for her to notice my pain and save me from my family. Each week I tried to speak, but there were no words to explain why I needed to be saved. It was my fault. If I believed in Hashem, I wouldn't question His path for me. But before long, I had to show that I could read, and my brief sojourn with that gentle adult ended, leaving me with a deep longing for more.

Life as a twelve-year-old felt the same as life before bat mitzvah, but in some ways it was beginning to change. When I wasn't thinking about the nothing inside me, I was starting to think about my place in the world. I was proud to be Jewish and to hold the responsibility of my modesty. At school, our teacher taught us that our Neshama (soul) had more worth than the souls who bared their skin on the street. I gave up my bike willingly; riding in a skirt meant it could rise over my knees, and it was my responsibility to ensure they were always covered.

At the Shabbat table I could no longer sing if we had guests. My voice was now immodest for a man to hear. I loved singing, and I didn't understand what was wrong with it, but I accepted that this was the way it had to be.

Nicole had given me her Walkman cassette player for my birthday, and when my mother wasn't watching I would put on my headphones while I vacuumed and sing along quietly with the Miami Boys Choir – a popular Jewish choir group composed of young boys whose voices had not yet broken – about the threats in the culture that surrounded us and how we needed to show Hashem we were ready to be Torah defenders. I was a woman now, ready to stand up for my people and pass Torah on to the next generation.

When I was chosen to sing at my Grade Six graduation in front of a female-only audience, I was giddy with excitement. I worried every day that my mother wouldn't come. I wanted to show her that my teachers saw something in me that she could be proud of. Men never watched any performance in the girls' school, so my father wasn't invited. To my delight, my mother watched me sing, and I joined her eagerly at the table after my performance. 'You were hunched like an old lady, Dassi. Stand up straight; you're going to get a bump in your back. No one will want to marry you.'

47

The nothing doesn't feel sad, the nothing doesn't care.

Grade Six drew to a close. It was 1999 and all we could speak about was whether there would still be a computer room at school the next year. We had heard rumours that the computers would explode when the clocks ticked over into 2000. I wondered what it would feel like to shatter into a million pieces.

The Miami Boys Choir sang about the world ending and the possible darkness and fear setting into the streets, but how the light of the Shabbat candles would save us, and as I sang along with them, a little part of me hoped that the world would explode.

CHAPTER 5

Teenage survival

I reached under my pillow for the alarm clock and turned it off. The fluorescent hands revealed it was 5.15 a.m. I was in Year Eight, it was the last day of term one, and it was time to get up and exercise. I pulled the duvet over my head, desperate to go back two years and be eleven years old again, before my body changed, back when my mother wasn't repulsed by the way that I looked.

In the dark, I leant over the bed and washed my hands three times, then pulled on a pair of tights, zipped up a cotton housecoat (a long-skirted informal dress), and rummaged through the shoe rack for my sneakers. I was quiet, trying not to wake Elly, who slept beside me, or Isaac and Ben in the adjacent room, but the house groaned with every movement.

We had moved again, into a double-storey house on Talbot Avenue – the wealthy side of Hotham Street, as we understood it. It was an old house on a large piece of land, slated for demolition, which gave my parents room to negotiate a cheaper rent. Elly and I shared a little attic room that we entered through the boys' room. Nicole had her own bedroom on the other side of the landing, and my parents slept downstairs. In this house, we were relieved to have a closet toilet on the second floor, in the corner of the boys' bedroom.

I crept down the stairs bent double, holding my stomach. My period had arrived during the summer break, bringing debilitating pain each month. 'If you lost weight, you wouldn't be in pain,' my mother advised me. Cramps were no excuse for slacking on chores. If I had to crawl to the laundry to sort the washing, it was my fault for being overweight. It was a year before my mother revealed there were painkillers that could help, but she kept them hidden in her room and would only allow me one if she decided I deserved it.

I shuffled onto the treadmill in the small bedroom behind the dining room. The single bed that my grandmother used when she stayed over filled the rest of the space.

My paternal grandmother wasn't religious, and when she arrived from England in 1988, she made the decision to settle in Geelong. We saw her several times a year, but never longer than a day or two at a time. My mother planned each visit to the minute, envisioning a picture of the perfect family. We were coached on how to act, what to say, and when to highlight our mother's brilliance. A slip in execution meant the promise of suffering after my grandmother's departure.

I turned up the treadmill for a slow jog and set the timer for forty-five minutes.

While I ran, I punched at the curve of my hips, angry at them for not falling straight so Nicole's hand-me-downs would zip up. I ate less food than my sisters. My mother watched us eat every night and insisted Nicole dish me a smaller portion size than the rest of my siblings. 'Your sister is fat,' she announced after she caught Elly handing me a piece of bread under the table. 'I am watching carefully. Anyone who shares food with Dassi will go without food for a week.' It was the last time anyone shared their meal with me. I didn't blame them; food was scarce, and our next meal was never guaranteed.

I counted down the minutes as I sang along quietly with the Miami Boys Choir about fighting assimilation and preserving our people. I turned my mind away from the pain of my period. I would lose weight and stop being an embarrassment to my mother. Getting the matchmaker to be interested in our family was difficult enough, being a size twelve would only make it harder. When it came to marriage, the whole family was judged, and Nicole was approaching seventeen.

At 6.15 a.m. I slowed the treadmill, jumped off and went to wake Elly and Nicole before I showered. I collected my school uniform and tiptoed past my parents' bedroom to the main bathroom. I heard my mother roll over. 'Please, please don't wake up,' I whispered to myself. Every moment she slept was a peaceful minute. 'Dassi!' she yelled, just as I slowly swung the bathroom door closed. I hurried to her side. 'Massage my back and then my feet,' she instructed me. I got down on my knees beside the bed and rubbed her back. My father's bed was empty; he had left for morning prayers while I was exercising. I calculated the time left until school, and the chores I needed to complete. When my morning chores were not finished, I was kept home to complete them. I didn't want to miss the last day of term.

After an appropriate length of time, I asked my mother if I could shower. She insisted I stay for five minutes, and then another five minutes, and then another. Half an hour later, I was released to bring her a cup of water. I ran to the kitchen, heated the kettle and filled the glass with half tap water, half heated water. If the balance wasn't correct, I would be doing this again, until it was the right temperature.

My mother sipped the water and didn't complain. I was allowed to shower and do my chores. I washed in a hurry, dressed in my long-sleeved, high-necked, mid-calf, summer uniform and brushed my short hair into a ponytail. I had begged my mother to let my hair grow, but she ordered the community hairdresser to cut it even shorter. Long hair was immodest. The uniform would be passed on to Elly after today; although it still fell to mid-calf, it needed to comfortably cover my knees when I was sitting to be considered appropriate, and I expected to grow taller over winter.

Nicole and Elly had dressed and were in the kitchen setting up a tray with our mother's breakfast and wrapping a lunch bag for our father. I went to wake the boys and pick out their clothing. When they went downstairs for breakfast, I made all the beds so there was not a wrinkle to be seen. One day, I came home to find all the linen had been torn off the beds and thrown to the ground because I hadn't smoothed the sheets to my mother's satisfaction. I wouldn't make that mistake again.

I cleaned the toilet and gathered the laundry, checked that the three bedrooms were tidy and headed downstairs. It was 7.30 a.m. and I still had the clothes to sort and my mother's room to clean. My mother was still eating breakfast on a tray in bed, so I organised the laundry first. I skirted past Elly and Nicole, who were feeding the boys breakfast. 'It's not fair they get to share the kitchen duties while I have to take care of the rest of the house all by myself,' I muttered under my breath. My mother explained that she didn't trust me in the kitchen, I was too slow and clumsy. Just another way that Elly and Nicole were superior to me.

'Dassi, change my sheets now,' my mother yelled. I sighed; she liked her sheets changed every few days, which was a bigger job and meant more washing. My mother sat on her armchair, casting an eye over my work and correcting me when the pillows were not fluffed and positioned the right way. As I gathered her sheets, I heard my father's car pull into the driveway. I turned the wash on and hopped into the car. Another morning with no breakfast.

When we arrived at school, it was like all the heaviness left my body, and I could lift my shoulders again. Here, for eight hours a day, I could be myself. But who was that? It was a question I had been asking myself a lot lately. *Who was Dassi?* I didn't think about what I wanted – I knew my future. I would get married, have children and pass on the Torah to the next generation. How earnestly I prayed to God, or the secret thoughts I had about my relationship with Him, were up to me to improve. Some days, I rushed during prayer and didn't concentrate on enunciating each word. I didn't want to be the person who slipped to a lower level of holiness and was tempted to sin. Not taking prayer seriously was the first step on that slippery slope.

'Blessed are You, our God, King of the Universe, for not making me a gentile,' I murmured. I skipped the next blessing as it was exclusively recited by the men who say, 'Blessed are You, our God, King of the Universe, for not making me a woman.'

I finished one of the last morning prayers by holding my prayer book and taking three steps forward. I had to think for a moment to remember which was my right foot. The way I said the positive commandment was as important as the doing of the positive commandment. First, a small step forward with my right foot until the heel was in line with the top of the left foot, followed by a large step with my left foot and then a third small step with my right foot to bring both feet together. In class we would learn why the right foot first was important. (One should step back with their left 'weaker' foot first to emphasise the difficulty of leaving God's presence, and step forward with the right foot to show eagerness.)

I bowed to the left and then to the right in farewell to God's presence. I felt that I had prayed with my full concentration, and my heart filled with gratitude to God for giving me the ability to pray to Him.

My friends had finished praying and were studying the timetable. Our first lesson was Torah studies, followed by a double lesson of Jewish history and Jewish law before recess. Before lunch we had a Yiddish class and a lesson to complete our Passover booklet. The last classes of the day were English and maths. We usually began the day at 8.30 a.m. and finished at 4 p.m., but on Fridays, Shabbat preparation was taken into account, and we finished school at 3.15 p.m.

The religious lessons flew by. I loved delving into Jewish law and understanding the meaning behind the way we lived. I flipped through my Shabbat project. There were thirty-nine categories of laws related to Shabbat, and I enjoyed figuring out which of the day's prohibitions fit under which category.

One of my classmates put up her hand to share a story. 'On Shabbat my father asked me how we have irrefutable evidence that God exists,' she said. I sat on the edge of my seat, leaning forward, eager to hear the answer. Irrefutable evidence would shut down the doubts that had begun creeping up in my mind and put them to bed once and for all. 'Sit down,' the teacher yelled. 'How dare you ask such a question and imagine there's a need for such evidence? How dare you even suggest God does not exist?' The student collapsed in her chair and hid her face for the remainder of the lesson.

During lunch break we sat in a circle on the playground. I looked around at my friends. It was the last time I would see them for several weeks. Passover was two weeks away, and in the girls' high school, we finished the term a week earlier so that we could help our mothers prepare for the holiday. I got up and went to wash my hands in the correct way for eating bread, and mumbled the two blessings as I walked back to my friends and took a bite of my peanut butter sandwich. I hated peanut butter; I'd been eating peanut butter sandwiches for eight years, but the hunger always outweighed my distaste. I pulled at my uniform, trying to get it to cover every inch of my body, wishing I could shrink myself smaller and disappear.

It was hard to keep track of the discussion. I kept zoning out and staring into the distance; my thoughts were jumping around in a way that made it hard to focus.

'Are you okay?' one of my friends asked, snapping me back to the present.

'Bless God, Bless God,' I responded. 'How are you doing?' I asked.

'Bless God, Bless God,' she replied, then turned back to the group. Blessing God was a common way of responding to most questions, and was supposed to serve as a reminder that everything in our lives, good or bad, comes from God and is there to bring us closer to Him. I managed to piece three words together in my mind: *Gam Zu L'tovah – this too is for the best.*

I chewed on my apple without saying its blessing first. The blessing for bread covered any food I ate until I blessed God at the conclusion of my meal. I grabbed a prayer booklet from my friend and recited the long grace after meals. Some days I avoided eating bread so I wouldn't have to say the blessing, which went for several minutes.

That afternoon, the teachers had a hard time leading their lessons. 'I don't need maths to feed my kids,' one girl yelled, and everyone hooted in agreement. We played up in general studies; the respect we had for our religious teachers did not exist in maths and English. I sat in the corner picking at the black, heavy stickers that covered the pictures in the maths book. The librarian and women in the community vetted all the books the school used. Images of men and women together were covered with stickers and the images of girls and boys had their clothes turned modest with the use of a permanent marker. Some books in the library had full chapters glued together.

I wished there was some way to write down my inner turmoil, but I would be mortified if my friends read it, or my mother found it. I was terrified my friends would find out that my home life was different to theirs. I thought about all the ways my family already stood out, and not in a positive way. We had so many marks against our name. My parents were not Adass from birth, they became religious and joined the community as adults – Baal teshuva was the term used, meaning masters of repentance. We had no family in the community, as none of my parents' families lived in Melbourne, whereas most of my classmates were related to at least one other girl in the class. We had non-religious family on my father's side. My mother was darker skinned than most of the community. We were not related to any rabbi, and weren't rich enough to be respected for financially supporting a rabbi. On the totem pole of the ideal Adass community member, we ranked low. I understood that my only chance of making my way into the world was marriage. Complaining about my parents would add another mark against my already fragile name.

The school bell chimed, and the home rush began. 'Come over on Sunday,' my friend yelled as she skipped past. 'I need to help my mother,' I shouted after her, wondering why she kept inviting me over when I could never come. I often used illness to refuse an invitation or as an excuse for missing days of school; it was better than admitting I was being punished, or that the bruises had to disappear before I could be seen in public.

I found Nicole, Elly, Isaac and Ben outside the school gates. We watched the families get into their cars, counting kids vs car seats to work out who we could ask for a lift. All month we had been learning about Passover and our bags were full of material and schoolwork that we needed to complete over the term break. I almost tripped over my bag and fell face-first onto the concrete in an attempt to pursue one woman and beg for a ride. I had no energy to spend half an hour carrying mine and my brothers' bags while we shepherded their little feet home.

At 3.30 p.m. we ramped up our efforts. We had waited too long; if we walked home now, we would be beaten for arriving too late. The Ell family agreed to let us squeeze into the back of their van. Two benches lined each side, and we tightened our muscles to fit in along with the twelve other kids. I sat on the floor between their feet, and we ducked our heads to hide from any police. I had a robust fear of law enforcement; they belonged to the world beyond, and could tear us away from Torah and community.

Our mother was sitting in the armchair where we had left her. I studied her face, where her eyebrows sat, the way her mouth turned and the shine behind her eyes. She didn't appear angry. Perhaps if we did our chores well, we could bring in the holy day without added drama.

Every Friday afternoon was a whirlwind of activity. On Shabbat we did not cook, clean or work. Electricity, cars and money were just some of the things we were forbidden to use. By sundown on Friday night, when Shabbat began, the house would be spotless. We had cooked the traditional foods late into Thursday night and we used hotplates that we turned on prior to Shabbat to rewarm dishes. I took out the vacuum and began running the nozzle into the corners of the carpet.

As I was singing to myself, a loud bang made me jump. I switched off the vacuum and could hear angry shouts that travelled across the house.

My spine prickled as I walked through the kitchen and dining room. My mother stood at the bottom of the stairs, insisting Isaac bring her his drawer filled with the knick-knacks he had collected over the last few years. A teacher had complained about Isaac's behaviour, and my mother had been embarrassed.

Nine-year-old Isaac was struggling to carry the awkward piece of furniture down the steps. My heart lurched when my mother picked up the hammer she was holding, hung it over Isaac and then smashed it through the drawer.

The items flew in every direction. 'Give them to me,' she screeched. We gathered the knick-knacks and placed them in front of her. Every item met with the hammer, but the ones that wouldn't break only made her fury bigger.

We picked up the smashed pieces of our little brother's favourite things and turned on the lights we would use for Shabbat, covering the light switches with elasticated covers so we wouldn't mistakenly desecrate the day.

I toiled over my chores and had a three-minute Shabbat shower. Showers couldn't be taken on Shabbat as the mechanisms for heating water were forbidden. I changed into a long gown of velvet; weekday clothes didn't honour the Shabbat. My father returned home, showered, dressed in his Shabbat suit and hat, and left for the Shabbat evening prayers at the synagogue.

Minutes before sundown my mother emerged from her room and walked around the house to check that it had been cleaned to her standards. We followed her to the living room and stood around the small table in the corner, which held a silver tray and eleven candle holders – one candle for each family member and two for Shabbat, to represent the positive commandments and negative prohibitions of the day of rest.

My mother lit the candles with a match and quickly let it die out. The match was now an item not allowed to be handled, and would be left on the tray until tomorrow night. I looked around. The house was spotless, the tables covered in white tablecloths and Shabbat dishes, and five children stood clean and dressed in their best. To anyone who didn't know of the events that had taken place earlier, we would appear to be the perfect Jewish family inviting the holy day into their home.

My mother drew her hands around the candles and towards her face three times. Covering her eyes, she recited, 'Blessed are You, Lord our God, Ruler of the Universe, who has sanctified us with commandments, and commanded us to light Shabbat candles.' We all answered, 'Amen.' When my mother turned around, we each kissed her hand and wished her a Good Shabbat.

The hour until my father came home from the synagogue could be the quietest hour of the week. My sisters and

I set the table and then sat down and read our schoolwork, looking for a story or parable we could share about that week's portion of the Torah. When our father arrived, he and my mother retreated to their bedroom to discuss our behaviour over the week. Nicole, Elly and I dressed the salads and spooned out the food into bowls we only used for the holy day.

Some weeks we started the meal twenty minutes later, other weeks the leaves in the salad would wilt and the avocado dip would begin to turn brown as my parents discussed our sins. We sat glued to our spots, watching the door. 'Dassi, get in here,' my mother yelled. My mind raced, trying to pinpoint how I had failed this week. It turned out, the tone I had used that morning when asking to shower hadn't been respectful. I would be banned from the night's festivities and take my meal in the kitchen.

I didn't look my sisters in the eyes as I served them their food and filled their glasses. Doing all the serving, clearing and cleaning alone was part of my punishment. My mother criticised every movement, looking to my sisters for their agreement. Nicole and Elly had to agree, but later they would come to me and apologise.

In the kitchen I ate a piece of Challah (a special bread reserved for important days) and listened to the songs of Shabbat my father and brothers sang. I hummed the tunes to myself. It was lonely sitting in the dark, staring at the walls, waiting to be summoned. When the meal had ended, I washed the dishes in cold water and crawled under the table with a dustpan to sweep the crumbs off the carpet. The vacuum was forbidden on Shabbat.

I climbed up to my room, closed the door and removed the handle. The door was now effectively locked, and couldn't be opened from the outside. We were not allowed to lock our door, but the house was old and Elly and I could say it had fallen off, like it had the first time. I breathed deeply and easily; my father wouldn't be able to beckon me in the dark hours of the night.

I crawled into bed and didn't bother to peel off my tights. If my mother called for assistance, I had to be modest before I could leave my room, and she became infuriated if she had to wait for me to cover my legs. It was easier to be ready to serve immediately. I fell asleep dreaming of being nothing.

I slept until 8.30 a.m., got my brothers dressed for synagogue and walked them around the block. Isaac and Ben went to join my father in the men's section, and I walked upstairs to join the women. The women's section overlooked the men through stained-glass windows, making it difficult for the men to see us. It was immodest for a man to look at a woman, and it was our job to make sure they were not distracted by our bodies. I lost myself in the prayers, with a plea in my soul that God would trust my faith.

At home, Elly mistakenly turned off the hotplate, and the Cholent, a Sabbath dish of baked meat and vegetables, prepared on a Friday and cooked overnight, was losing its heat. 'Run and get the Shabbat Goy,' my mother told her. The Shabbat Goy was a non-Jewish neighbour who had been identified as being willing to help rectify mistakes made on Shabbat.

The neighbour entered the house. 'We need to eat our Cholent and it's getting cold,' my mother explained, looking at her face to see if she understood. One could not ask someone else to desecrate Shabbat directly, even if they were not Jewish. The neighbour took the hint and switched the hotplate back on. We had a Shabbat Goy for every house we lived in.

After the meal, I implored my mother to allow me to meet friends for a walk. I almost fell back in surprise when she agreed. I skipped down the street to meet two friends, and we walked around the block before ending up at one of their houses.

My friend's mother greeted us warmly and offered us a snack. I stared as my friend sat down in front of her mother and ate, and then left the dirty plate on the table. My eyebrows shot up and my breath caught in my throat. How did she dare to be so disrespectful to her mother? When my mother entered the room, we had to immediately stand up and ask her what she needed. I closed my eyes, unable to watch as her mother picked up the plate and placed it in the sink. I didn't understand why my friend was smiling, and not bowled over with guilt.

The sky was darkening. I bid farewell to my friends and ran home. Three stars signified the end of Shabbat, but it was customary to wait an additional hour, just to be safe. My father blessed the wine, passed around spices to smell and blew out a candle to usher out the holy day.

Nicole, Elly and I cleaned for several hours, and then begged my mother to let us watch a video of the Miami Boys Choir concert in Jerusalem, which had been given to us by one of our friends.

Watching TV and having the internet was strictly prohibited in the community. In order to be accepted into the school, my parents had to sign a waiver stating they didn't have a TV in the house, and my father had to disclose that he used the internet for work, but it was out of the house, filtered to block out lewd sites and inaccessible to the children.

The first time I had watched a moving image had been the previous year, when the Twin Towers fell in New York.

We found out about it much later than the rest of the world, as we didn't watch the news. When we heard what had happened, my mother spent days trying to get through to her family in Brooklyn. My father broke his rule against using the internet in the house and showed us a clip of the towers collapsing. While I had cried at the devastating scenes, I remember feeling amazed, too, at the way the images moved on the screen.

My mother ummed and ahhed, debating if she would be one of the members of the community that allowed their children to watch a CD. Many families forbade any moving image, even if it was Jewish. During school camp, Adass Israel School brought in Jewish stories from overseas that used a still reel projector; the photos would click over in time with the narration of the story. It was the closest we came to watching a moving image.

Eventually my mother agreed, and we squeezed around my father's computer to watch. We sang along and as I watched the choir dancing in front of various landmarks in Israel, I dreamed of the future Jewish king who would save and lead the Jewish nation. In messianic times, the deserving dead would be resurrected, and all the Jews would leave exile and live in Israel together.

When the film ended, my mother reminded us to be up by 6.30 a.m. – there were less than two weeks to Passover, and a house to prepare. Passover is an important Jewish festival of eight days that commemorates the Israelites' exodus from Egypt and the subsequent freedom from slavery. It's celebrated by eating a traditional meal on the first two nights, called the seder.

Nicole, Elly and I worked all Sunday. By 10 a.m. my back was sore, and my arms wouldn't lift. The month of Sundays past had been spent deep cleaning every room to ensure there was not a trace of chametz to be found. Chametz refers to foods with leavening agents, which are forbidden on Passover. Every item in the house had been taken out or down and wiped thoroughly, each book had been individually shaken, every surface cleaned. As we worked, my mother walked through the rooms instructing us on what to throw away. There was no space for sentimentality in our house.

Today was the kitchen changeover. I packed up the chametz food we would eat over the following week, putting it into plastic storage boxes and carrying them outside. On the covered veranda I set up a folding table and chairs; for two weeks, we would eat our meals here. From this moment, not a crumb of chametz would enter the house until the eight days of Pesach were over.

I shook my feet, brushed my clothes and lifted my foot to step inside before stepping back again. I took off my apron and shook it, jumped up and down and brushed my clothes again, more vigorously. If I carried in even a crumb of chametz, and it somehow attached itself to a Pesach food and I ingested it, my soul would die in a way that couldn't be reversed, and I would be spiritually cut off from my people forever.

Inside, Elly and Nicole were moving the dishes we used throughout the year into two cupboards in the garage. The cupboards would be sealed and sold to a non-Jewish person, so we were not liable for any chametz that survived our cleaning. My father would then buy back ownership of the cupboards after the festival.

The kitchen was ready to be koshered. My father poured boiling water over the counters and used a blowtorch on the sinks, stove and oven.

When the water had cooled, I dried it with the Pesach towels. From this point forward, even the washing would be separated into Pesach and non-Pesach clothes.

Using a roll of insulated foil and duct tape, we covered the counters and table. I traced over the stove and cut the shape of the burners through the foam-filled foil. The cupboards had their own reusable paper to line the shelves. After an hour I stood back and admired our silver kitchen. It was now Passover ready.

Nicole and I dragged the Passover boxes out of the garage. We unpacked and washed two sets of cutlery, dishes and cooking utensils – one for dairy and one for meat. During the year we had a third set of dishes for pareve foods – those that were neither dairy nor meat and could be eaten with either. For Passover, however, it was dairy or meat only.

While we unpacked and set up the kitchen, my father went shopping. The Jewish stores had koshered their own kitchens and for several weeks before Pesach they sold only kosher foods for Passover. Every year we waited excitedly to see what my father had found. In the US and Israel almost any kosher food had a Pesach version, but the Pesach foods in Australia were imported, and so choice was limited. This year we were so excited to get Pesach cereal.

Over the next week, Nicole and Elly prepped and cooked the Pesach foods, while I prepared the rest of the house for Pesach. I polished the silverware, unpacked the Pesach books and ironed my father's and brothers' white shirts for the week, including my father's Kittel. A Kittel is a white robe that men wear during high holiday services. White represented the purity we hoped to achieve through prayers on the holy days.

It was two days to Pesach and the stress in our home was palpable. I was relieved to escape the house for an afternoon to attend an orthodontist appointment in Hawthorn. As my father drove me, I gazed out the window excitedly. I rarely saw more than the eight blocks that housed the Adass Jewish community. Travelling twenty minutes across the city felt like entering a different realm. Here, people wandered aimlessly, unburdened by the upcoming holiday, enjoying their day out.

When I came home my mother was out of bed, yelling at Isaac again. For weeks or months, one of us would be deemed the rotten child, and it appeared this week it was Isaac's turn. I crept in and stood next to Elly, being careful not to look at my sisters. Exchanging so much as a glance would earn us a rant about how we were colluding to disrespect our mother. We stood like statues, scared that if we moved, her anger would find us.

My mother wagged her finger and swivelled around to face us. 'I don't have a son called Isaac anymore. Isaac does not belong in this family.' She instructed my father to take the disgusting boy and drop him somewhere far away, outside the confines of the community. As my father left with Isaac, I was sick with worry. It was dark outside, and Isaac was only ten.

My father returned home without Isaac in tow. We cried and begged our mother to change her mind, but she was impervious to our tears. Hours passed. In my mind, Isaac had been torn apart by wolves. I couldn't eat. We went to bed, but we didn't sleep. We discussed sneaking out to find him, but we didn't know where our father had taken him. Just before midnight, my mother calmed down and asked my father to pick him up. Isaac was still in the park where my father had left him; he'd hidden, shivering, behind a bench.

When we got to the end of the week of preparation, we were exhausted. My mother lit candles, and when my father came home for the evening prayers, we sat down for the first of two seders. The seder was the main part of Pesach. We followed a book called the Haggadah, which prescribed the order in which we drank, prayed, sang, discussed Jewish texts and ate. We read and discussed the Haggadah for hours; by the time we ate, it was past midnight.

We finished the seder at 2 a.m. At school we would compare notes; the longer your seder had lasted, the cooler you were.

We poured the final cup of four cups of wine for the Prophet Elijah. As I stood at the door saying the prayer that welcomed him into our home, I mouthed the very last words of the seder: 'Next year in Jerusalem'.

CHAPTER 6

Malka Leifer

It was a warm afternoon in 2002 – one of those days the sun bounced off the playground tarmac, making it hot to touch. Our Year Nine class sat in the middle of the netball court, speculating on the disappearance of our teachers. The lunchtime break had come and gone, but nobody was hustling us inside. There was a sense of something amiss in the air.

The rumours bounced between us and splintered into stories that couldn't possibly be true. Whatever was happening was happening in the staffroom. When one girl went to beg for an ice pack, she returned with instructions that the staff meeting wasn't to be disturbed.

We sat in a circle, perched atop our jumpers to shield us from the scorching surface. As Year Nines, we sat closer to the Year Tens' air of superiority and further from the antics of Years Seven and Eight. We were a close class, seventeen students in all, and teachers often remarked on the way we'd come together as a group instead of dividing into cliques.

The hours passed, and with not an authority figure in sight, our sense of daring grew. Sweltering in the afternoon sun, we found ourselves inching closer to the water fountains. *Come play with us*, the taps seemed to say. *Splash, play, cool each other down. It's the perfect day.* Water fights were strictly forbidden – wet clothes could become transparent and therefore immodest – but the lack of supervision turned to liberation, and when the first girl placed her hand over the spout and sprayed water over her friends, it took less than three seconds for the rest of the high school to join in.

I fled when the first drop hit my face and sat on the steps, watching from afar. When my friend called for reinforcements against the Year Eights I jumped up, but then glanced at my watch and reluctantly sat back down. It was 3.30 p.m. – there wasn't enough time to dry off by the end of the day. The fun wasn't worth my mother's wrath if I arrived home wet.

Minutes before the last bell rang, I noticed our principal exiting the primary school. I watched as she passed her dripping students, her head so low I'm not sure she saw them. The students, having expected her rebuke, stopped wringing out their uniforms to watch as she crossed the yard to the staff car park. She was a woman of confidence, authority and poise, and we looked at each other in amazement, wondering what could have brought about this new, defeated persona. The other teachers filed out behind her, ignoring our dampness and our questions. Some appeared to have been crying, with tissues scrunched in their hands.

There had been whispers that the principal, who'd had a secular education, was to be replaced with another more in line with the school's Hasidic values. The school was slowly moving towards the more conservative Hasidic teachings and practices.

Hasidic Jews are a subgroup of ultra-Orthodox Jews who are known for their strict adherence to traditional religious observances, and for their distinctive dress and lifestyle. Hasidic Jews practise a joyous, mystical form of Judaism and trace their spiritual roots to eighteenth-century Eastern Europe.

Litvish Jews, also known as 'Litvaks', are a branch of Ashkenazi Jews with origins in Lithuania. They are less focused on mysticism than the Hasidic Jews, and their approach to Jewish law is more traditional and conservative. Melbourne's ultra-Orthodox community is too small to have a separation of sects, so in a style quite unique to the Adass community, Litvish and Hasidic Jews live together.

The previous year, the school had brought a new teacher out from Israel. Malka Leifer had been appointed head teacher of the girls' seminary. She was a devout Hasidic woman, and the community was already abuzz about her warm and magnetic personality. I hadn't met Mrs Leifer yet, but Nicole, who was in Year Ten, had come home with stories of her Israeli quirks, and her funny pronunciation of the English words she was learning. There had been talk that she was perfect for the position.

Our principal's family lived next door to us, and my mother was on good terms with her. *Maybe I'll finally have more details than other girls in my class*, I thought to myself. I went home with a lightness in my step. Knowledge was power, in a world where I had none.

That night I was walking on eggshells around my mother. I could see by the way her eyes narrowed that she had anger she wanted to release, and I didn't want to be on the receiving end. When she called out, 'That terrible child to her room,' I knew that the child who was so bad they didn't deserve a name was me. 'That child' was a name I was called often. I had no idea what I'd done wrong, but for two hours I apologised for everything, including my existence, but it did nothing to lessen her anger. I went to bed and whispered my nightly prayers. 'Thank you, Hashem, for the bruises not being on my face.' I couldn't sleep for the pain, but at least I wouldn't be held back from school the next day to hide the stain of abuse. Thoughts of the big change at school were lost to the one thought crowding my mind: *I'm worthless and unlovable.*

The following day it was announced that Mrs Leifer had been chosen to be principal of the school. The old principal would stay on as a high school English teacher. Almost immediately, Mrs Leifer moved into an empty room in the high school building and made it her office. From that first day, everyone discussed her energy with a tone of reverence and awe. Within weeks, she had stamped her authority on the place, arriving at school before most people were up and not leaving until long after they had gone to bed. She scheduled the timetable around teachers' requests, had final say on the curriculum – Jewish and general studies, with all the paperwork passing through her office – placated parents, guided students, taught classes, and looked after her own children, ranging in age from infant to fourteen. With all that, she never complained, and made it look easy.

I was a shy girl, secure in my own group of friends, but I tended to follow, never lead. My childhood had taught me the need for observation, and I quickly picked up that this new authority figure had students she favoured.

Her special girls were allowed to miss class to assist her, run errands in her name and receive her special praise. I began to crave Mrs Leifer's compliments, and the privileges that came with being a favourite. I was desperate to be noticed.

Not long after Mrs Leifer became principal, she gave Tamar a job at the school, and for a short period we had access to our older sister in school hours, away from our mother's control. We usually saw little of Tamar and her husband, other than during Jewish holidays and the occasional weekend meal. Although they lived only a few streets away, my mother did not allow them to come over uninvited, and invitations were scarce. Before a planned visit, we were instructed on what we could or could not say, and were watched carefully for disobedience. Our phone calls were monitored, so calling her without permission was difficult. While the adults around us had mobile phones, smartphones were still a new concept, and students were forbidden to own one.

With the threat of the internet becoming more accessible, we heard stories of ultra-Orthodox men in New York gathering in their thousands to rally on the danger of allowing the filth of the online world to enter our lives. These messages were repeated among my friends, and by the adults around us. The internet was not something I had access to, so the stories of its horrors were more a curiosity to me than a threat to my religious observance.

Tamar taught Year Seven, and in between classes we managed to catch a few minutes alone with her. One morning she gave Nicole a checklist printed out from a book called *Stop Walking on Eggshells*. It was a self-help book about how to deal with a loved one who has borderline personality disorder. Nicole gathered Elly and me in Mrs Leifer's office while the principal was absent from her room. Nicole had a close connection to the principal, having become a favourite student, and use of her office for a secret meeting was granted.

We stood in a circle, hunched over the excerpt while Nicole read the items aloud. '*Her emotions can change in*

*the blink of an eye. It's hard for the emotions to change or
for her to come back down again.'*

'For sure,' Elly and I whispered, and we all looked at
each other with wide eyes.

*'You never know what mood she's going to be in when
you come home. It really stresses you out.'*

'Oh gosh, totally,' we all said together. We went down
the rest of the list, slowly shaking our heads as we ticked
off each question. When we were done, we stood back and
covered our mouths to suppress our amazement. It was the
first time we had entertained the notion that perhaps our
mother had a problem; perhaps the abuse wasn't our fault.

The idea that my mother was abusive started to take
shape in my mind. When she hurt me, I began to see it as
the result of her rage, rather than my inherent wrongness.
My utter fear of her didn't dissipate, but this realisation
allowed me to recognise and understand the source of some
of my pain. I started opening up to my friends. They already
understood that I could never hang out with them on
Sundays or after school, or participate in class get-togethers
and sleepovers. But now they knew I wasn't always 'sick',
but in fact was prohibited from joining. I still kept most of
it to myself, though, terrified the stories would circulate and
my chances of marrying out of home would be destroyed.
No one wanted a girl from an abusive home.

We finished the school year and celebrated Hanukkah,
the festival of eight nights, eight lights, in December. With
two strong friendships and the hope that I would become a
favourite of our new principal, I looked towards Year Ten
with a hint of optimism in my heart.

* * *

Summer in 2002 was extremely hot. When I walked to the kosher bakery to pick up bread for the week, I would look at the secular girls on the street in their short sleeves and shorts and wonder what it felt like to have your skin kissed by the sun. As a young child, I had been shielded from the world outside our community. At fifteen years old, I recognised we were different, but modesty had been instilled in me with a sense of superiority, and I felt proud in my high-necked shirts and long skirts, even when the sweat soaked into my seventy-denier tights and created friction sores on the backs of my ankles.

One evening our mother declared she would allow us to go to the beach. We had endured four days of close to or over 35 degrees Celsius, and the air conditioner in the house couldn't cool us down. We eagerly collected towels, sunscreen, sunhats and our cotton house dresses and placed them in bags along the front hall, ready for the next day. Outings with our mother were risky – either she would hold her good mood for the entirety of the trip and erupt when we got home, or she'd rage quietly at the beach, her face creased in a way that spelled her displeasure. If that happened, one of us would be forced to sit aside or in the car, excluded from the fun. Going to the beach was a rare treat; nobody wanted to miss out.

We packed a breakfast picnic and set our alarms for 5 a.m. When the alarm rang, I hopped out of bed and dressed in my cotton house dress. I winced as I tried to push my flip flops to sit between my toes, over my tights. As I supervised my brothers getting dressed, I felt a pang of envy. *I wish I was a boy and could wear bathers. It's not fair that they're allowed to show skin.* By the time we piled into the car, the sun was peeking over the horizon.

My father drove to Frankston Beach, about half an hour away from where we lived. He believed the beaches further from home were more likely to be empty at that time in the morning than the nearby St Kilda Beach. I bounced along to the Jewish music and imagined the feel of water wrapped around my covered legs. Before we climbed out of the car, my mother sent Nicole to scout the beach. If anyone had beaten us to the water and was dressed in a bikini, we would turn around and head home. She would not expose us, and especially not the boys, to immodesty. I heard my brothers exhale when Nicole announced that the beach was empty.

I jumped up and down in the waves close to the shore. I wanted to let the ocean embrace me, but my wet clothes would cling to me, revealing the shape of my body. With the bottom of my dress and tights soaked, I sat on the sand and built a sandcastle with Ben.

After we had been at the beach for close to an hour and the threat of beachgoers arriving intensified, my mother decided it was time to leave. That was one of two trips we made to the beach that summer.

In February 2003, I entered Year Ten at Adass Israel School. I don't remember much of that year other than the respect and awe I felt towards our principal. The girls in my class had begun to talk about whose brother they would be set up with by the matchmaker, and what speaking to a boy would be like, but my head was full of thoughts of Mrs Leifer. I thought that if somehow I could become a favourite student of hers, I would be viewed more favourably by the matchmakers. Marriageability was something we often talked about. Girls in the class above us were getting engaged, and at sixteen we knew the eyes of the community were on us.

As well as favourites, Mrs Leifer had students she disregarded. I recall her mocking one girl's mannerisms while the girl had her back turned. I felt nauseous; as I imagined being that girl, I wanted to cry. The possibility of the principal mocking me made my stomach twist. School was the only place I felt safe; I couldn't bear the idea of this space turning ugly. I was determined to be liked by her, but I didn't know if I could be likeable.

I spent weeks working up the courage to speak to Mrs Leifer, practising how I would ask her for a few minutes of her time. Her office door was open, and she regularly told us we could come to her with any problem, large or small. I envisioned asking for her help, and imagined how I would feel if the leader of our school paid attention to me. Me, the girl whose own mother had declared she wasn't worthy of existing.

One day, Mrs Leifer touched me on the shoulder and called me into her office. I stood beside her, my chin lowered and my eyes turned away. Her voice was close to a whisper. 'I know about the situation at home, Dassi. I'm here to support you, like I support Nicole.' I was enchanted. Her presence alone validated the nothingness I felt inside. *She thought about me; the principal wants to support me!* I walked out of her office with a straight back and a smile on my face.

After that conversation, I purposely walked past Mrs Leifer's office as often as I could, trying to catch her eye. She would call out to me to run an errand across to the primary school, or once even to go down the street to the boys' school. My classmates noticed, and that brought its own status. The principal's special students were worthy of respect.

At some point, I'm not sure when, I confessed to the principal that I wanted to share something I was troubled about. She encouraged me to speak up, but I was so in awe of her, I didn't share the details. Instead, Mrs Leifer arranged a private phone call with a rabbi's wife (rebbetzin) she looked up to in Israel. Safe in the knowledge that the rebbetzin lived abroad and didn't know my family, I was able to confess that my father gave me hugs that were uncomfortable.

The rebbetzin advised me to stay away from my father. I explained that disobedience was heavily punished at home, but she wasn't listening. I ended the phone call, frustrated that the rebbetzin hadn't understood me, and was further annoyed when increased attention from Mrs Leifer made me suspect the rebbetzin had shared our conversation. I was terrified of anyone finding out.

These more frequent interactions with Mrs Leifer continued through Year Ten. Before the Jewish high holidays in September, the teachers took a count of which girls would remain in school the following year. Our Year Eleven class would shrink to just eight girls, with the rest of the class going to seminaries overseas. Post–high school institutions in Israel, the UK and the USA boarded girls from across the world for up to three years, with an intent to advance their religious education. The curriculum focused on the role of a Jewish woman as mother and wife, as well as Jewish law, outlook and philosophy.

During the Jewish New Year, I stood over my prayer book in the synagogue, begging God to help my parents send me to seminary. Dalia lived in the UK with her husband Benny, and she worked as the girls' coordinator in a Manchester seminary. My mother was on good terms with Dalia that year, and entertained the idea that her oldest daughter could secure me a place at a reduced cost. The fee of $15,000 per year was prohibitive, although my parents knew it would look good on my marriageability resume. The right seminary could lead to a better offer of marriage.

The Jewish high holidays are the season of spirituality, and the New Year led into the ten days of repentance, ending with Yom Kippur – a day of atonement and the holiest day of the Jewish year. Repentance, prayer and charity are the themes of the time.

'Do you forgive me for any slight I may have made this year?' I asked my friends. They nodded and repeated the question back to me. Having asked and been asked this question by everyone I knew, I went into the day of atonement with a clear conscience.

On the evening of Sunday, 5 October, we stood around our mother as she lit candles. We had eaten the 'concluding meal' of challah dipped in honey, chicken soup and stuffed dumplings at 4 p.m. It would be our last meal until 7.30 p.m. the following night. We then followed my father, walking the 600 metres to the synagogue on Carlisle Street, Balaclava. We stepped into groups with other community members on the same route. The men wore white robes over their suits, and the women were dressed in light colours to represent purity.

I swayed over my prayer book for the next twenty-five hours, only stopping for a short sleep. 'Please, please record me in your book of life,' I begged our God. Only righteous people were written in the book of life. To be blotted out signified you would be dead by the day of atonement the following year. My head pounded and my throat itched for a glass of water, but thoughts of nourishment were chased away by the fear that I had not done enough to deserve life. I remember one year I had a migraine, so bowled over by pain that my father approached the rabbi for advice. I was given permission to take Panadol if I could swallow the tablets without water. I was so proud that I managed it.

The anxiety of the day eased as soon as the fast ended. It was time to rejoice before God and prepare for the festival of Sukkot in four days. Sukkot is a joyous time in our Jewish calendar, when we commemorate the years the Israelites spent in the desert, in simple structures, after being freed from Egypt. We sit in temporary huts (sukkahs or sukkot) outside, topped with branches and decorated with traditional posters. The men had an obligation to eat, sleep and study in the sukkah.

Each day of the eight-day holiday, we hold a palm branch flanked by willow and myrtle branches in one hand, and a yellow citron in the other.

'Blessed are You, Lord our God, King of the Universe, who has granted us life, sustained us and enabled us to reach this occasion,' we say on the first day, shaking the plants in every direction to symbolise that the divine presence is everywhere. The palm branch represents our spine, the willow leaves are our mouth and the bumpy yellow citron is our heart. We remind ourselves to use all parts of our body for good.

On the last day of the holidays, my mother sat me down and told me I was a girl she could see had an evil inside, unworthy of the effort it would take to send me to seminary. 'You're a pretty face and nothing else,' she reminded me. 'Can't even live up to the virtues of Elly and Nicole.' I searched my mind, trying to figure out what I had done wrong. I had been trying so hard. I knew she was frustrated, and I feared that I would never be able to leave the house. *Who would want to marry me?*

I returned to school dejected, concerned the matchmakers would never want to look at me. The term passed quickly, and it was soon time for the summer break. One day during the summer holidays my mother took a call. Five minutes later, she called for me to come into her bedroom. 'I have just been talking to Mrs Leifer,' she told me. My mouth dropped open, and a tremor travelled down my spine. I searched my mother's eyes for anger but saw no hint of it. 'Mrs Leifer wants to give you private lessons,' she announced, with a smile stretching across her face. I blinked repeatedly. *Was this true? Had I made it?* and I skipped out of the room. 'Private lessons start next Sunday,' my mother called after me.

I counted down the days to Sunday. Each night I went to sleep worried that the next day my mother would change her mind, but she didn't. Having her daughter receive private lessons from the principal the entire community revered was too good to pass up.

Finally, it was Sunday. I awoke at 6 a.m., showered, woke Isaac for morning prayers, put on the first wash of the day and ironed the eighteen shirts I had hand-scrubbed the previous night. I tiptoed around my mother and hurried to fulfil her demands while I watched the clock. At 10 a.m. my father drove me to school. I stepped out of the car and looked towards Mrs Leifer's office. In two minutes, I would be in a room with my idol. Quickening my pace, I crossed the staff car park, went ten steps across the yard, up two steps to the double doors and into the high school building. I stopped, listened, and heard nothing. The silence was strange. *Did Mrs Leifer forget?*

I paced up and down the hall, getting closer to her office each time. She was there, on the phone, speaking a million words a minute organising something that seemed urgent. She saw me peeking around the door, caught my eye and motioned for me to come in. I took a seat opposite her desk, conscious of how my body rested on the seat. I tried to look casual. *Don't let her see how acutely you want her attention.* I felt pained with my desperation, and panicked she would see through me to the sin my mother claimed lay within me.

Mrs Leifer ended her call and came around her desk to sit beside me. Her presence so close rendered me speechless. She pointed to a religious text and explained that we would be studying a book on one's personal Jewish morals. The book was written in Hebrew, with a smattering of Arabic words in every paragraph. I was asked to read aloud, but when I tried to voice the words, they wouldn't exit my mouth. I read Hebrew fluently, but the Arabic words were unpronounceable to me. My mind blanked. *I am such a stupid, stupid girl.* I couldn't think of the text when she looked at me. *I don't want her to regret choosing me for this privilege.* I wanted to disappear.

Mrs Leifer moved to put her arm around my shoulder. She stroked my back and my body calmed. I was not used to being touched gently. Her warmth felt loving, and I sank into it. 'Let's forget about this,' she said in a low voice. 'Let's talk about you. How are you feeling?' I couldn't respond; no words would come. No adult had ever cared how I felt. I didn't even know how I felt. Most of the time I felt numb.

She pushed for an answer, her hand rubbing circles on my back. *What do I say? What is the right thing to say?* 'I don't know,' I mumbled. My head was down, so I didn't see her face, but her tone was baffled. 'How can you not know how you are?'

I was mute. *I know there's something wrong with me; please don't give up on me.* I had never been a speaker; silence had always been my friend. My parents' abuse expected silence. Obedience is silent. Silence is safe.

Mrs Leifer moved her arm to my knees. Her touch was reassuring; I didn't want it to stop. Her hand travelled up my thigh, and even with my gaze lowered I could feel her watching me. *Does she realise what she is doing?* Overwhelmed, I kept silent. She continued to move her hand up my thigh. *This is weird, but she is Mrs Leifer; it must be okay.* I didn't know it then, but this was the start of a pattern, one that would escalate.

I went to lessons with Mrs Leifer for several weeks. I never found my words. The longer I was silent, the more Mrs Leifer touched my body. She told me I was closed, and she needed to help open me up. Help me to trust her. I slowly described our home life, and she responded with the loving words and nurturing touches I yearned for. It was like all my flaws were invisible to her. This woman, who the whole community flocked to, cared about me. *Me.* At home I was the child that couldn't be named because I was too disgusting to be human, but here in the principal's office I was someone. Here in Mrs Leifer's office, I was special.

CHAPTER 7

A new monster

As the bell for recess rang, textbooks were shut, chairs pushed back, and limbs stretched. We moved as a group to the playground. The air smelt of spring, and not a cloud was to be seen. We shouted and cheered, playing a game of cricket on the warm asphalt.

I batted the ball across to my friend, looked up to watch the yellow sphere sail past her, and saw Mrs Leifer standing by her office window overlooking the yard. My body froze. I felt sweat cover my brow, and the bat fell from my hands. I scanned the playground. *Kriah room, I can hide in the Kriah room.* I walked as fast as my legs would allow me towards the primary building.

The Kriah room was on the second floor, at the end of the hallway, in the back of the primary building. The space used fabric dividers to create four cubicles for special needs students who were taken out of class for individual tutoring. During playtime the room was empty. I checked each cubicle, chose the corner furthest from the door, sank into the chair and held my face in my hands. I imagined myself curled up under the desk, making myself as small as I felt inside. *I'm safe, I should be safe here.* I closed my eyes and tuned into the sounds around me.

Next door, a rabbi bellowed, and thirty kinder boys sang the Hebrew alphabet. Outside, the primary girls unwrapped their morning snacks. I knew the sounds of her footsteps. Heavy, assured. Powerful.

What is happening to me? Why is everything changing? I love her. Mrs Leifer was the centre of my universe. I used to be greedy for her attention, for the smallest smile or look of understanding. I needed her. With Mrs Leifer, I was special. Without her, I was nothing, and yet there I was, hiding from her.

When playtime ended I walked back to class. The Hebrew text danced in front of my eyes, making it hard to read. I watched the clock and calculated the minutes until lunchtime break. 'Dassi, what does it say?' the teacher asked. My face burned; I didn't know the answer. I hadn't heard the question. *Will she pull me out of class?* If the principal asked, her request would be obeyed. She was the boss, she did as she liked. Five minutes later, Mrs Leifer's face appeared at the classroom door. She had a quick word to the teacher and I followed her out of the room.

Her office door swung closed behind us. I sat beside her desk and lay my head down on the wooden surface. I was tired. Mrs Leifer stroked my hair gently. I used to love it when she did that. It was something a mother would do. Something my mother never did. I had felt so worthy, so important. Now I felt dirty.

I didn't want her to touch me, but she told me I needed it. She promised she loved me. *Is this love?*

Somewhere, far away, I heard Mrs Leifer asking me what was wrong. But I was a cloud, floating oblivion. Alien to the body that slumped lifeless in that room. From far above, I saw myself, a picture of passivity. Eyes that were empty and saw no colour. A frozen sack of skin and bones. I escaped to a place she could not reach.

I watched her remorseless fingers undress me. The crawl of her touch over my skin. She kissed and caressed me; her mouth tasted me. Her body was excited, and she wanted a reaction from mine, but I was not there. In that room, I did not exist. She had killed me. A silent death no one would ever know about. No one would ever believe me.

One day, months earlier, at the beginning of Year Eleven, Mrs Leifer decided I would skip class and go home with her. Ten minutes later a Tarago pulled up and we both hopped in. She sat in the front, and I climbed over the middle row to the back seats so the adults could have some privacy. As a Hasidic woman from Israel, Mrs Leifer didn't drive. Her community had discouraged women from learning to drive, declaring it immodest. During one of our Sunday lessons, Mrs Leifer had recited the schedules of the housewives in the community, including whether they worked, when they were free to drive her around. I remember being amazed at her photographic memory.

The whole community looked up to the principal, and she had a list of women who were eager to assist her. Even my mother, who rarely left the house, would be happy to help Mrs Leifer. Driving her was a privilege. I bounced in my seat and smiled to myself. I was skipping class to spend time with someone who cared about me. When I returned to school and informed the teacher I had been with Mrs Leifer, not another word would be said about my absence.

We arrived at her home in Elsternwick, a smallish, rundown three-bedroom house nestled on a long street filled with Jewish neighbours.

Mrs Leifer thanked the driver and asked her to return in two hours. *Two hours alone with Mrs Leifer! She's so busy and she gives all this time to me!* I spent all week eagerly awaiting our Sunday sessions. Mrs Leifer's house was quiet; her children were at school or creche. She called out through the rooms for her husband, paused for a response and smiled when she received none. She returned to the foyer and locked the door. I was still standing at the entrance; I wouldn't move until she invited me further into the house.

We walked to the kitchen. A vegetable soup sat on the stove. The room was cluttered; dishes were piled in the sink and grime climbed the walls. The community observed her mess when she held prayer groups for the women on the weekend, but just saw it as proof of her dedication to her position. Students would offer to clean, and she would allow them to create order in the house, but the kitchen was her domain. She took pride in being known as a good cook.

Mrs Leifer beckoned me to the table and asked if I would like a bowl of soup. I knew the flavour would be exquisite, but the dirt bothered me, so I shook my head. She pointed to the couch and instructed me to sit. I didn't speak, but I moved as instructed. She asked questions about my life, and I gave her quick responses only: *yes, no* or *I don't know.* She wondered out loud if I would ever have answers or if I would continue saying only 'I don't know'. I hated to disappoint her, but there was no language for the mess inside me, the awe I felt around her or the neediness I felt without her.

My silence was read as internal distress, and her touch was the tool to coax an answer from me. She leant forward and cradled me in her arms. *This is what love feels like,* I thought to myself. I had never known the feeling of love.

Mrs Leifer guided me to lie down. The sofa was low and shallow and had no room for her to sit beside me, so she sat on the floor. She stopped the questions; instead, her hands talked for her. She rubbed my shoulders, legs and back but I ignored it. I didn't find it weird anymore. 'You're like a daughter to me, Dassi,' she murmured. 'I love you.' I wanted to cry with relief. *Maybe I am lovable. Mrs Leifer loves me.*

The space was warm and intimate. I closed my eyes and imagined my life with her as my mother. Feeling cared for every day. Feeling worthy. My thoughts were interrupted by something cold on my back, and it took me a moment to understand that her hands were under my uniform. The muscles in my back tensed and the warm feeling disappeared. I had a million thoughts hurrying through my mind, but I could not formalise one of them. Goosebumps covered my body.

I felt her fingers over my bra strap and my neck turned a deep shade of red.

Bras were taboo. We knew they existed, but we did not speak of them. She murmured something, and I made an effort to concentrate on her words, not her hands. 'I love you, Dassi.' I was still desperate for the love she promised me, for the mother she proclaimed herself to be.

Time seemed to disappear. I was rolled over and her fingers crawled over my breasts. I cringed internally, but I concealed my discomfort. She was the principal of the school; I was confused, but I trusted her. I squeezed my eyes shut and focused on my breathing. My thoughts clambered on top of one another. *Does she understand what she is doing? Is this how she shows she is close to me?* I didn't move. If I did not acknowledge what she was doing, I could pretend it was not happening.

I heard a beep outside and Mrs Leifer jumped up. 'We've got to get back to school,' she announced in her principal voice. It was like a spell had been broken, and suddenly the Mrs Leifer I had always known reappeared, as if the previous two hours had never happened. I stood, adjusted my clothing, and followed her back to the car.

On the way back to school she chatted breezily to the driver while I sat in the back, furiously trying to work out the puzzle of her behaviour. Everyone in the community respected her, including the lead rabbi. She was a leader; women flocked to her for advice. I had never known a woman who held as much power as a man. Surely the discomfort I felt was my fault; she couldn't be anything but right. However, I also understood that I must not speak about what happened, not even to her. I must block it out and pretend it had never occurred. I needed to be able to move back into normalcy like she did.

This was a familiar game to me, a game I had played many times before. Every day I came to school and pretended everything was fine at home. This was just another secret. I trusted her. I loved her.

The months passed and the scene was repeated. Each time, she pushed the boundaries further. She touched me everywhere; there was no place on my body her hands did not reach. Each time, I walked away as if it had never occurred, and spent days convincing myself it hadn't. So effective was my dissociation that each time I was shocked when it happened again. I had no one to speak to; the only person I could ask was the same person I wanted to ask about.

I tried to build a relationship with another teacher, and spoke with her privately several times, but I could not think how to ask her if the touch was wrong. A girl's body was a secret: all of her body, from her collarbone to her feet. I didn't know the words for breast or vagina. I didn't know I had a vagina. We didn't speak about our bodies; our religion discouraged it. It was much easier to pretend it was all okay. When I walked past Mrs Leifer's office and saw the blinds closed and the door locked, I knew another girl was with her, and the jealousy I had once experienced was replaced with relief.

At school I worried about Mrs Leifer, and at home I worried about my parents and Mrs Leifer. I had no safe place anymore. I didn't sleep. I returned to the fantasy world I had created as a child, a world I had never really left, that world where I was a 'nothing', a person with no feelings. I escaped to that nothing space every night. It was the only place I could feel calm enough to sleep. Being nothing didn't hurt.

In the middle of winter 2004, I turned seventeen. That year, our class had the job of running the high school's winter camp. We were dismissed from several classes and spent weeks planning activities, prepping materials, organising the menu, and writing lists of supplies. There was a sense of sorrow that came with freedom. It would be the last big hurrah with our class of seventeen girls – by September half of them would be away at girls' seminaries overseas.

The abuse intensified. One evening at camp I was cornered by Mrs Leifer and instructed to follow her to her camp bedroom. I obeyed. It didn't matter if it meant leaving an activity I was to lead, or leaving my group to prepare a skit for the evening play by themselves. I always did as she said. Everyone did. I didn't complain and I didn't say no. I didn't know how. Life had taught me that refusal was frightening, and that the consequences of disobedience were immense. She was the principal; she was the authority.

Mrs Leifer moved me to stand before her. I was a puppet. She removed my uniform. Sometimes when she touched me, I slipped into a trance-like state, my mind travelling far away. Deep inside, I would feel endless, like I had no beginning and no end, my insides stretched for miles. When she touched Dassi, she was touching only her body, not the real Dassi. But this time, I struggled to disappear. My mind wanted to escape, but I was standing, and forced to remain present to avoid collapse. This time I was captive to her crime.

Her fingers pulled down my tights and underwear and her mouth moved to my breasts. I begged my mind to take me away, but my mind did not cooperate. I concentrated on the noises outside, the shouts of my classmates running around playing games. The room turned dark; we had been gone for a while. I wondered why nobody was looking for Mrs Leifer. *Do they know I am here with her? Can they ever imagine that on the other side of that closed door, I am half naked with her fingers inside me?*

I needed to use the bathroom, but still I was silent. I did not control the time. It wasn't over until Mrs Leifer decided it was. I no longer wanted to see my friends; I didn't have the energy to pretend. I was tired and alone.

That night, I tossed and turned. The shame ate at me. My mother had always told me I was bad, and deep down I believed her. I was terrified of someone finding out how terrible I was under my good girl demeanour. When Mrs Leifer undressed me, it was like she was peeling back my essence to uncover my badness, the badness she must have known I was concealing. *Why else would this be happening?*

I finished Year Eleven and entered Year Twelve. Halfway through Year Twelve, our class shrunk to four girls. The school didn't offer a Victorian Certificate of Education (VCE), as they felt the texts required would expose us to

the world outside of our community. Our timetable was full
of Jewish studies and Mrs Leifer, as homeroom teacher for
Years Eleven and Twelve, taught us several classes. One was
the methods of teaching. She promised us jobs as teachers in
the school if we completed her training.

I have few memories of the next two years outside of
Leifer's abuse. My mind used all its resources to numb me
from the constant fear. To face my mother's wrath, my
father's confusing hugs and then the overwhelming abuse I
suffered at the hands of my principal, I had to do everything
in my power to believe that each day I was a different
Dassi to the one that had existed the day before. I wish the
flashbacks of Leifer didn't shine as brightly as they do in the
otherwise desolate landscape of my memory.

I turned eighteen and finished Year Twelve, but in the
eyes of the community I would not be an adult until I
married. My world did not grow. The abuse did not stop.
My best friend and I both got jobs under Mrs Leifer, and
the other two girls got engaged. I went from being a student
at the school to a teacher, teaching Jewish history to the
Year Eight class. I had no qualifications but the lessons of
our principal.

CHAPTER 8

The matchmaker

I peeked through my eyelashes at the unfamiliar orange beard across the table and dared myself to look up. 'Eye contact,' Mrs Leifer had reminded me on the phone just moments earlier. 'Remember to look up.' I felt my cheeks go red. I was a young woman, dressed in a long-sleeved beige jacket, a blue-and-beige skirt and seventy-denier brown tights, sitting at a round kitchen table, on my first date. I looked up at the man sitting opposite me and then quickly down again. It felt wrong. We weren't supposed to look unrelated men in the eye.

'My name is Shua Erlich,' he began, and I was grateful it was the man's job to initiate conversation. I'd tossed and turned all night, worried that my voice would remain constrained by the years of keeping quiet in the presence of a man. At eighteen years old, I couldn't remember the last time I'd had a genuine conversation with a male that was not my father. I knew he was twenty-three years old, 180 centimetres tall, had a childhood interest in cricket, and was currently studying in a yeshivah (men's religious seminary) abroad.

The matchmaker had informed my parents that his divorced parents were Jewish but not religious, and that Shua had chosen the ultra-Orthodox life as a young teenager. The rabbis he studied under raved about his ability to understand Jewish law in a way that belied his secular upbringing. It was unusual for boys to fly home to pursue a date in February. The yeshivah frowned upon mid-semester engagements. I was told that Shua had flown home to meet another girl, and when she had turned him down the matchmaker had called my parents. A trip home mid-semester shouldn't go to waste.

I could hear my mother pacing up and down in the adjoining room. She was here to supervise our date and ensure we didn't have any physical contact. She needn't have worried. I wouldn't dream of touching him; I could barely look at him. I spent the hour looking at the laundry door behind him and the swinging pendulum on the clock above his head. Everything I did – the way I held myself, the way I dressed, the way I spoke – was designed to avoid drawing attention to myself. To avoid drawing the attention of the men who were not supposed to see us. Gazing at women was immodest. When a rabbi was invited to address us at school, they sat behind a temporary mechitza – a partition usually made from wood or cloth – to keep them from looking at us. It was a woman's responsibility to ensure the man was not tempted by her to commit an evil sin.

I knew nothing of the sin of sex; we had been taught the sin was in the man noticing us, and being distracted from learning Torah by our femininity.

My parents had spent the last few days with the community matchmaker, finding out everything they deemed important about Shua. I'd been informed of his grades, his parents' wealth and his Torah study. I wasn't asked what was important to me; my input in this process was not required.

It would be my first date. The matchmaker had called with other offers in the last few months, but my parents had turned them down. They were too far away, lived overseas and wouldn't consider a life in Melbourne; the husband was the head of the home, and he would choose where the couple lived.

I'd spent months praying to God that I would meet my husband before I turned nineteen. The older I got, the more problematic the marriage scene would be for me. We were not related to any revered rabbi and had no status in the community. I could see the black marks growing against my name: my parents hadn't grown up religious, they didn't come from money, and my mother was a dark-skinned Sephardi. Sephardi Jews, often tracing their roots to the Middle East and Africa, at times encounter racism and discrimination within Melbourne's predominantly Eastern European Ashkenazi community. Elly, due to her darker coloured skin, had often been taunted at school with the derogatory term 'shvartze' – a Yiddish racial slur for people of colour.

Good grades and youth were on my side, but the older I got, the less often the matchmaker would call. If I turned twenty without any sign of marriage, the community would assume the problem was me. This wasn't just my impression; this knowledge was as intrinsic as the way I breathed. I must get married.

I walked up the garden path with my mother on that February day in 2005 and rang Shua's mother's doorbell, knowing that inside that double-storey house in Caulfield North could be the man I was to spend the rest of my life with.

I met Shua for the first time on a Tuesday afternoon. We met four more times that week, always in his mother's kitchen, while my mother supervised our 'dates' from the adjoining living room. After the first date, I mustered the courage to look up at him and quietly answer his questions about the values I envisioned instilling in our future children. The following Saturday night, he proposed, and I said yes. I had spent less than eight hours with this man before making the commitment to spend the rest of my life with him.

I'd been told that Shua would propose that night, and he knew I would say yes. The matchmaker had checked with my parents moments before our meeting. I had been given the weekend to think about this commitment. As soon as Shabbat ended, the phone had rung: the matchmaker wanted a decision.

I could have said no. I could have said no like the girl who saw Shua before I did and turned him down. I was told that I could choose, but really, there was only the illusion of choice. If I said no to Shua, it would only be so long before I sat across the table from some other man, having the same stilted conversation.

When I had asked my teachers how I would know if this man was the right man to spend the rest of my life with, I was told that if nothing about him repulsed me enough to say no, then that was enough to say yes. The process was shrouded in secrecy; it wasn't something I could ask my friends about.

I sat across the table from Shua that Saturday night, dressed in my finest, waiting for him to begin the conversation. I looked at him carefully. Was there anything that repulsed me? He began to speak about our shared goals of building a Jewish home in God's ways. I looked harder at his orange beard and brown eyes and wondered if this was a man I could grow to love. I still didn't understand how babies were born, but I imagined bringing up a family with him. I was filled with anxiety and doubt, but also excitement. For a second, I played out the chaos that would ensue if I reneged on my previous assurance and said no, but I knew this proposal was just a formality; it had already been decided. He finished his speech. 'Will you be my wife?' he asked. 'Yes,' I said quietly without any hesitation.

Shua flew back to his yeshivah in Israel the day after our engagement. The weeks passed quickly. I went to school each morning and supervised the morning prayers. While the Year Eights prayed, I wrote. My diary entries were filled with wonder and excitement about the possibility of starting a new life with my husband and becoming a mother. But in between the excitement, there was also doubt. Would I know how to act appropriately, and be the wife and mother I had spent my life learning how to be?

Day twelve of being engaged:

Dear Diary,
Being engaged is another world, it doesn't feel like it happened to me. I feel like every minute I might wake up and find it's all been a dream. Shua told me that he feels like he has a deep strong connection to me even though we've only been engaged less than two weeks. I don't really feel that way. I have a strong feeling that Shua's haskafas (ideals) and middos (principles) are like mine and we are both striving towards the same goal. I don't really feel any strong shaykhes (connection) to him. I don't know, am I supposed to? I hope as time goes by we will eventually feel closer. Is it too much to

expect? I don't expect to feel a strong connection so soon. It will come in time.

Sometimes I have doubts. Is that normal? I've made the biggest decision of my life and I can never go back on it without repercussions – serious ones. I guess I'm scared about thinking of living my whole life with someone I barely know. I know it does take me a long time to build a solid deep relationship and eventually it will come. What I need to build a good relationship is good equal feedback from the other side. I've received my first letter, quite mushy. I feel so strange getting a letter from a man or boy who says they feel so close to me when I hardly know who he is!!!

I'm a bit confused and mixed up. I'm so used to not taking anything from my parents that when it comes to important stuff like marriage, I don't know what to take and what to discard, what to believe and what not. Anyway, although I have many thoughts flying around my head, it's late in the night and I'm finding them hard to commit to paper. So goodnight. Dassi

For the first ten weeks, our engagement was kept a secret from the community. This served two purposes. It meant Shua could travel back to his yeshivah and not be reprimanded about a mid-semester engagement, and Nicole wouldn't be humiliated by having a younger sister get engaged before her.

It was hard to hide my excitement, but with so many secrets in my life, it just felt like one more.

Nicole had been engaged to another boy the previous year, a son of our former principal, but in a move that sent the community gossips into a frenzy, Mrs Leifer had orchestrated that the engagement be broken only weeks before the wedding. The matchmaker had lined up another boy for Nicole to meet during the upcoming Passover holiday. Should she get engaged, her engagement would be announced first. My parents would wait a week and then announce my engagement.

I spent that autumn in a mixed state of excitement and worry. Once every two weeks or so, Shua would call me from Israel, but I had to be extremely careful what I said because my mother would frequently pick up the other landline and listen in. When he returned after Passover we would be allowed to meet indoors under supervision, or outdoors in public spaces, where we wouldn't dare break the no-touching rule. Touch of any sort was absolutely forbidden.

Shua is going to Manchester for Pesach, I wrote in my diary. I wish he would come here; I'm dying to announce our engagement already and it gets harder and harder every day closer to Pesach. I've been offered other shidduchim (matches) and it feels really weird that people are pushing me to go out with other boys when I'm already engaged. They just don't know. Mrs Leifer told me that I should try not to be closed and hidden with Shua. But I'm so used to it. I should just be open, but I can already see it's too hard to expect that. Already this week he asked me how was your week? I had a hard week at home as well as other things outside home. I couldn't let him know because he would ask why, and I wouldn't be able to tell him. Already I feel like I am hiding things and I'm scared to sink into that habit.

Shua came back after Passover. He was not invited over in case someone wondered why he was visiting our home. Families with young women did not invite unmarried men over. The community would find out and begin to gossip, and the secret engagement would no longer be secret.

98

My sister Dalia travelled from the UK with her family for Passover. I remember it as an exciting time; the taste of freedom was so close. Nicole got engaged just before Passover, and we announced my engagement just after.

All I remember of my engagement party is the slap I received from my mother moments before we went to my future in-laws' house, where the event was to be held. She was angry that some handwashing was still soaking in the sink. Preparing for my engagement party was not an excuse to not do as I was told. I didn't cry when my mother hit me anymore, the tears had long left me, but that night I remember them threatening to spill. It was the audacity of it. How dare she slap me just before I celebrated my engagement with the community? As I looked in the mirror to fix my mascara and cover my red cheek, I whispered to myself, 'It's only a little while until you're married, Dassi. Just a few more months and then you will be out of her control forever.'

The freedom of escaping my childhood home was threatened when Shua bluntly informed me that he had asked his rabbi if he should break off our engagement. By this time, Shua had seen enough of my mother to know the truth. An abusive home was an additional black mark against my name, and signified I was damaged goods. However, his rabbi had informed him that a broken engagement would jeopardise future matches.

Shua told me all this over a phone call which lasted an hour. I thanked him for not giving up on me, and spent most of the time convincing him I was nothing like my mother.

In some ways, over the next few months my world opened exponentially, but in other ways it stayed exactly the same. Mrs Leifer was still abusing me – preparing me for marriage, she said. These secrets terrified me; I feared that Shua might discover them and deem me unworthy of marriage. My mother's control became tighter, knowing I would be out of her orbit soon. There were endless lectures about the way I should treat her once I was a married woman. How often she expected phone calls, gifts and praise. How I needed to teach my husband to respect her, and what she thought of Shua's ability to fall in line.

At the same time, I was getting Kallah (bridal) lessons from a woman in the community, whose job, now that I was engaged, was to teach me about sex. The laws around sex were long and complicated. My mother found someone who was willing to teach me for a reduced price. I sat in my Kallah teacher's house and watched as she drew a diagram of a vagina and penis. The idea that I had a vagina absolutely blew my mind. I asked her how I would find it. She instructed me to go home, find a mirror I could stand over and examine myself.

Even after I learnt about sex, I couldn't write the word down in my diary. I left blank lines. When Mrs Leifer touched me 'down there' and put her fingers inside me I had assumed it was the same place I urinated from. The understanding that women had two openings there suddenly made so much sense. This is what Mrs Leifer must have meant when she said she was preparing me for marriage. There must be someone who prepares every girl for marriage in that way, I thought.

This is what I found in my diary, likely written shortly after my engagement.

Day ?? of my engagement
Too confused about everything, confused about life,
about my lessons for marriage, about _____. I DON'T
KNOW??????????????????? I was told yesterday about _____ I
got such a shock!!

I would need to find my vagina before my husband did. For seven days before our wedding, I would need to wrap my finger in a little white cloth called a bedikah cloth and check that I was not bleeding. Blood equalled impurity. My husband could not be with me or touch me when I was impure. Every month after my period ended, I would need to check myself morning and evening in this manner. When I reached seven days of clean bedikah cloths I would be ready to go to the mikveh and have the ritual purification with the cleansing bath.

The women's mikveh was a hushed secret among unmarried girls in the community. Men went to the mikveh regularly, and from thirteen years old the boys joined them. While the women bathed separately, men and boys bathed naked together. Unfortunately, over the years I have heard many stories of sexual abuse that occurred at the men's mikveh.

The women's mikveh house was on the corner of Furneaux Grove in Caulfield. I'd passed it many times walking home from school as a teenager, wondering what went on in there. Two days before my marriage, my mother called and booked me a room. I was instructed to arrive early, to avoid bumping into any of the married women using the mikveh that evening.

My mother drove me at dusk with a bag full of items to clean myself properly. The ritual bath would not take place until after sunset. That night would mark seven nights of checking myself to make sure I had not bled. It was all ritual; I had been on the pill for the last month. Usually, a rabbi's permission would be required, but the pill was allowed in circumstances such as this since its purpose wasn't to prevent pregnancy. I had been completely unaware that it was contraception; I was simply advised to take the pill in order to regulate my menstrual cycle and ensure a smooth wedding night.

I entered the mikveh building and found the attendant waiting for me. She took me on a tour of the facilities and explained how I needed to lock the entry door and ring the bell when I was ready. The door leading to the ritual bath would be locked from the outside, and when the bath was ready for me, she would knock first, ask if I was ready and then invite me to come in.

I locked the bathroom door and then checked that the other door was locked too. I set my bag down on the vanity and checked the room in the mirror. I kept looking at myself. I was slightly shaky, anxious with all I had to remember to ensure my dip in the mikveh was valid.

I was relieved to find a laminated sheet of paper with instructions on how to prepare myself. I cut my nails, shaved my legs, washed my hair, and cleaned myself as thoroughly as I could. If there was anything between my impure body and the mikveh water, I would need to do the ritualised dip again.

By the time I finished, it was dark outside. I looked at myself naked in the full-length mirror to ensure I hadn't missed anything. I had never seen my body reflected like this before. The head height mirror in the bathroom at home was the only one in which I had seen myself in any state of undress. I opened my towel, checked myself and then quickly covered up again. All my life, I had been taught to cover up and hide. In the locker rooms at school, changing for sports became an art form in getting changed without showing any skin. It felt weird to look at myself naked and to know that my body, which had been hidden for so long, would soon be touched by a man I barely knew.

I rang the mikveh bell, then jumped from foot to foot as I watched myself in the mirror. This was it; this was the last step before marriage. That night I had a dreamlike sense of leaving my childhood behind and stepping into my future.

The mikveh lady knocked on the door, and I lowered my towel so she could check my back. I was ready. I watched as she turned and hung my towel over the banister as I descended the six steps into the warm pool. I felt exposed, and hurried to cover myself with the clear water before she turned around. She would watch to ensure my entire body was covered in water.

'Kosher,' she announced after I had fully immersed myself for the first time. I tried to ignore the embarrassment and shame I felt. I was doing a mitzvah – a good deed that would be rewarded in the world to come. I was doing my duty as a woman. When I finished my ritual dip, I would be pure again, ready for my husband. I popped my head above the water and covered my privates while I recited the prayer after her, word by word. 'Kosher,' she said again after my second dip. 'Try again,' she said after my third dip. 'I think the top of your head was still showing.' I breathed a sigh of relief when she announced it was over. She held the towel high to cover her face as I walked out of the pool. 'Mazel tov,' she said as I walked back to my room.

I looked at myself in the mirror again. *This is where it all starts*, I told myself. *This is where I fulfil my destiny. I have just taken the first step to becoming a Jewish mother.* In that moment there was a great sense of everything falling into place. My life was finally heading in the right direction, and I felt content, knowing I was doing what I was supposed to. I was going to be okay.

CHAPTER 9

The wedding

The kitchen was silent in the muted tones of pre-dawn as I stood alone, trying to swallow a piece of toast. It was 5.52 a.m. on 11 September 2006, and the sun's rising would begin the traditional fast observed by every religious bride and groom on their wedding day. Two glasses of water and a piece of avocado toast comprised my last meal as an unmarried woman. The next time I ate, Shua and I would be breaking our fast together as a married couple.

Many mornings I had woken at this hour to eat before a fast, but the enormity of the day left me with a dry mouth and a hollow pit in my stomach. *My last morning tiptoeing around this house*, I thought to myself as I looked around at the familiar shadows. It was hard to believe that in ten hours my parents would give me to my husband, and I would no longer be their property. I breathed in a mixture of excitement and relief.

The day's schedule lay on the kitchen table. Two hours were allotted for morning prayers before a make-up appointment at 9 a.m. It usually took me forty-five minutes to recite the morning prayers, but I wanted to ensure I had enough time to pronounce each word with mindful concentration. The gates of heaven were open to the bride and groom on their wedding day, and as I went in search of my prayer book, I envisioned Shua swaying over his own in the synagogue. Today was the holiest day of our lives.

I crept back to my room to wake Elly; she would prepare the family breakfast while I used our bedroom to pray. I opened my prayer book and a list of names fell to the floor. On the top of the list, written in the traditional way, was Elly's name: Elisheva Rivka bat (daughter of) my mother's Hebrew name. There was a pang of guilt in my gut. Nicole had married four weeks prior; after today, Elly would be left to face our parents' abuse without the protection of her older sisters, and contact between us would be controlled by our mother's moods. The weight of today's direct line to God sat heavy on my shoulders. This opportunity wouldn't come again, and as I began to mouth the blessings, I vowed not to waste it.

An hour or so later, the sound of Dalia's voice filtered through the bedroom window. I finished praying and ran to greet her. Dalia had travelled from Manchester to attend my wedding, and having her there amplified the giddiness that reverberated through my body. I flung my arms around her and asked if she would accompany me to my wig appointment. With my make-up done, Dalia, my mother and I headed to meet the sheitel macher (wig maker), Chana Strasser, who lived nearby in Elsternwick.

I remember sitting on the salon chair, wincing as hundreds of bobby pins poked into my skull. I studied the strange face that stared back at me in the mirror, trying to adjust to the sight of myself in a shoulder-length brown sheitel. From that moment on, my hair was reserved solely for the eyes of my husband. When I covered my hair in accordance with Jewish law, it became a powerful declaration of modesty.

I wondered whether the wig would become a burden, or if I would enjoy not having to worry about my frizzy hair each morning. It felt bizarre that the drive here was the last time my natural hair would be seen in public.

Family photos were scheduled for noon. We arrived home with just enough time for me to put on the wedding gown my mother had borrowed from the community bridal gemach (donated dress collection). I was so relieved when we found a dress that passed my mother's approval.

The dress was made of multiple descending layers of gossamer, with crystal beads dispersed across the top layer, and had been altered to wrap modestly around my frame. The design of the dress ensured that no skin was visible through the fabric. With Elly's help, we stretched the elastic loops over the seventy pearl buttons that started under my arm and twisted around the back of the dress. I felt like a princess. A shiver ran up my spine at the idea of Shua helping me undo the buttons later that night.

Looking back at the family pictures we took on the neighbour's lawn, my face is young, but my eyes are older than my nineteen years. Beside the spring flowers, I am surrounded by my parents, siblings, niece, nephew and two fraternal aunts who travelled from Brisbane and Cairns, along with Shua's family. As per tradition, I had not seen Shua in a week. Our photos together would be taken at 5 p.m., after the marriage ceremony.

When the limousine arrived shortly after 1 p.m., I gathered my dress and carefully strode towards the silver Rolls-Royce. I climbed in and let out the breath I had unconsciously held all morning. This was it. I wasn't dreaming; in two hours I would no longer be Hadassa

Sapper. Instead, I would be Mrs Dassi Erlich. Dalia and my mother sat on either side of me, engaged in a conversation I did not hear. I clutched a prayer book in my hand and murmured promises of my faith as the car headed up Hotham Street and turned onto the Nepean Highway, towards the International in Brighton.

Brighton International was one of Melbourne's boutique wedding venues, just minutes from Brighton Beach. It was a popular choice of venue within the Adass community; its owners were accustomed to Jewish weddings and the need for community caterers to kosher the kitchen before use. Our kabalat panim (pre-marriage reception) would take place in the black-and-white tiled foyer and our chuppah (marriage ceremony) in the Georgian-styled courtyard.

The next hour seemed to pass in minutes. I sat in a throne-like Kallah (bridal) chair with my family around me. As light refreshments were served, the women of the community lined up to wish me mazel tov or ask for a blessing, and when the attention overwhelmed me, I bent over my siddur and whispered their requests to God.

Shua sat in a separate room greeting the male guests. It was tradition for men to heckle and shout at the groom while he shared interpretations of Torah texts. I strained to hear him over the singing, yelling and an occasional passionate L'chaim (to life) that carried over the chatter of two hundred people to where I sat. In less than an hour, we would be husband and wife.

There was a buzz of activity on the far side of the hall. The rabbi was completing our ketubah (marriage contract), which would be signed by two unrelated male witnesses. My signature wasn't needed. In ancient times the ketubah was meant as a protection for the wife. It acted as a replacement for the biblical mohar – the price paid by the groom to the bride, or her parents, for the marriage. In modern practice, the ketubah has no agreed monetary value, and is seldom enforced. Although the content of the ketubah is antiquated and not taken literally, according to Jewish law possessing the document is an integral part of a Jewish marriage. It is forbidden for a couple to live together without this legally binding contract.

Meanwhile, in the women's section another ritual was in process. Dressed in shades of rose pink, my mother, along with my soon-to-be mother-in-law, threw a plate against the floor. The china dish, wrapped in a pillowcase, refused to break, and with each attempt my mother's face flushed a deeper pink until it matched her dress. At the time, the significance of this ritual was lost on me. I understand now that it represents the seriousness of our commitment. Just as a broken plate cannot be repaired, a broken relationship can never be fully repaired.

At 4 p.m., a hush fell over the women and the low hum of the Jewish wedding melody, known as Od Yishama, could be heard. Across the foyer the women parted, flanking my chair; it was time for the bedeken (veiling). Od Yishama is fourteen words, but the Hebrew lyrics are sung by the men repetitively, faster and louder, while the sea of men dressed in black and white make their way to stand in front of me, led by Shua, flanked by his rabbi and our fathers.

I squeezed Nicole's hand as the procession of jumping, heaving men grew closer. I found Shua's eyes, and I was certain that beneath my make-up, my face had turned a deep red. Dressed in his traditional white robe, Shua stood before me, suddenly unsure of his task. There was a quick conversation with his rabbi and then he leant forward and covered my face. The emotions inside me clamoured for attention and I was grateful for the opaque veil to hide my tears. *There is no turning back now*, I thought to myself, and as Shua and the rabbi raised their hands above my head and prayed, I sobbed silent tears of doubt and gratitude.

The women waited for the men to leave the hall and then filed out after them. My mother touched my arms and motioned for me to get up. All I could see was the tip of my white heels, and I clutched my mother's arm as she led me outside.

Shua stood in the middle of the chuppah, and I circled him seven times, in reminiscence of the biblical figure Yehoshua circling the ancient city of Jericho before the walls fell and the Israelites were able to capture it.

The rabbi sang the first of seven benedictions, over a silver goblet filled to spilling with red wine, and then the wine cup was sipped first by Shua and then passed under the bedeken to me. With shaking hands, I took a sip and then passed the goblet back to him.

Shua reached for my finger, and I held out my right hand for the ring. I felt him slip the white gold band over my index finger – it would be moved to my left hand after the ceremony – and then in a voice loud enough for the entire congregation to hear, he said, 'HAREY AT' M'KUDESHET LI B'TABA'AT ZO K'DAT MOSHE V'YISRAEL – Behold, you are consecrated to me with this ring as my wife in keeping with the heritage of Moses and Israel.' At that moment I wanted to both laugh and cry, and I was grateful for the privacy that the veil granted me.

The remaining benedictions were shared between honoured male family members and important male members of the community. The men in the community joined in the last blessing with a loud song to thank God for the happiness of the groom and bride.

The end of the wedding ceremony was marked by the reading of the ketubah, after which Shua lifted his foot and stamped on a glass to shouts of 'Mazel tov'. The male congregation broke into joyous singing and dancing. Shua lifted my veil, and I stared up at the man who had just become my husband.

Shua reached out his arm and I placed my hand in his. His hand felt strange – it was the first time we had touched each other. As we walked hand in hand to the yichud (seclusion) room, my emotions felt too expansive to fit inside me.

Jewish law prohibits a man and woman who are not married to one another to be secluded together. Entering a room with Shua signified our newly married status, and this time together was a vital part of our Jewish marriage. The door closed, and I was with my husband unsupervised for the first time. It almost felt wrong to be alone with him. Two men stood outside to guard our privacy. We would need to be alone for at least eight minutes, but the day's schedule allowed us up to half an hour. I'd heard that some couples had consummated their marriage in their yichud room, although I was still unsure about what that really meant, or how one was supposed to do it.

I had a migraine that was threatening to ruin the short time we had together. Shua told the men outside that we needed some pain relief. I looked awkwardly at him. Did he know what we were supposed to do here?

We sat on the couch side by side. There were two bowls of chicken soup in front of us to replenish our electrolytes after the fast. Shua encouraged me to eat, but with my headache came nausea, and food did not tempt me. He lifted his arm. *Was he going to touch me?*

Shua placed his hand on my shoulder and traced his fingers down the sleeve of my white dress. *What was I supposed to do now? Should I touch him?*

I remembered the lessons Mrs Leifer had given me. I was supposed to kiss him. *How could I kiss this boy? This stranger? How did I go from this awkward side-by-side position to a lip-on-lip kiss? Why wasn't he organising it? Didn't his rabbi teach him what to do?*

He asked me how I was feeling. In a small voice, I told him I was okay. In truth, I felt like I was going to die; the pounding in my head was only growing with this awkward scene. I took the tablets that had been passed in through the smallest crack in the door by one of our guards and swallowed them gratefully, hoping they would work quickly.

Still, there was the issue of this kiss. *Would it happen? What would I tell my married friends when we gossiped about what we had got up to in the yichud room?* I was now part of their elite circle, grown up, married, ready to bear children. I could talk about what all that meant – all the talk that had been forbidden to me as an unmarried girl.

We moved to the table, and I watched Shua as he ate. I thought of all the meals we would share, sitting across from one another in a space like this. *Would it ever become more comfortable? Could I grow to love this man?* I'd been promised by my mentors that I would.

Time was running out. Soon our photographer would knock on our door. I stood up, and Shua followed suit. He stepped around the table to stand in front of me. At six foot tall, he stood a head above me. I could see his chest moving, his breath quick and shallow. He was as nervous as I was, I realised. I thought he would have been more confident. After all, he had grown up in the secular big wide world, and only recently become religious.

111

'Would you like to kiss?' he asked me. I nodded, and Shua leant down and kissed me. I wondered if he felt as shy as I did. As I kissed him back, the sense of awkwardness and the awareness that I was doing something I had been told all my life not to do overwhelmed any other feeling.

We left the room, a secret smile on our lips and a sparkle in our eye, all captured on camera as the photographer snapped picture after picture against the backdrop of the sun setting over Brighton Beach.

The rest of the night passed quickly. I was relieved that the painkillers helped, and my migraine receded to the back of my mind. The band boomed out a medley of lively Jewish music between the dinner courses. I danced on my side of the hall and Shua danced on his; only at the meal did we sit side by side, overlooking the hall divided by a mechitza (temporary partition).

The speeches seemed to go on too long. The rabbis pushed us to remember that all we did was for God, and even on this important night we must not forget Him. We were blessed to have many children who would grow in the ways of the Torah and bring nachas (Jewish pride) to their parents. At that moment, there was nothing I wanted more.

It was 2 a.m. by the time the night ended. We stepped into our temporary abode. It was Malka Leifer's home. The home she had abused me in.

Since Shua and I planned to leave Melbourne after the high holidays and set up our home in Jerusalem, we had looked around the community for a place to reside for the next month. Mrs Leifer's seventeen-year-old daughter was set to be married in Israel on the same day as my wedding, 11 September. With the entire family travelling overseas and her house empty, Mrs Leifer offered it to my parents as a place for Shua and me to stay.

112

In the week leading up to the wedding, I set up the house with Nicole and Elly's help, without once contemplating asking my parents if they could find us an alternative place to start our married life. A barrier had developed in my mind, one to separate Mrs Leifer's abuse from the rest of my life. It was similar to the barrier I had created as a young child around my father's confusing hugs and then again around my mother's abuse. I didn't consciously build these impenetrable walls; my mind created them to protect me, to allow me to move forward each day despite the trauma I faced.

The therapist I see now calls it dissociation. Back then I didn't know that it was a dissociative barrier that allowed me to climb into the same bed that Mrs Leifer had undressed me on several weeks prior, and undress myself for my new husband. I didn't think about it at all. I hadn't realised yet that I would never be abused by Mrs Leifer again. By the time she returned to Melbourne, I would be starting my life in Israel, and my mind would compartmentalise her abuse into a corner, where it would stay for several years.

Shua painstakingly undid the buttons I could not reach on my dress, and I took out the hundreds of pins holding my wig. It was time to consummate our marriage.

We made small talk, each of us covering our nerves at the task ahead. He showered quickly first, then it was my turn; the door firmly closed. I put on a long nightgown and went to sit on the edge of one of the twin beds in the room. We both recited the prayer that one must say before sex, which asks God for our children to be conceived through a holy act and not through lust.

The next thing I remember is the searing pain. 'My rabbi had said you would scream, but that I should push through and to get it over quickly,' Shua explained, as if to excuse the pain he had just subjected me to. I cried, and he quickly separated himself from me. Now that there was blood and we could no longer be together, I would need to be covered in front of him, just as I would before any other male. I quickly put on the headscarf that I had made ready and ran out of the room to clean up. Shua changed the sheets and climbed into his bed on the other side of the room.

I crawled into my bed, hiding the pain that was my rite of passage. I felt sure that God would grant me children after the pain I had just endured for His sake.

Shua and I lay and talked until early morning, each of us eager to find out everything about the other. It was the first time we had been allowed to talk unsupervised.

* * *

A few hours later I tucked the blanket around my shoulders and watched the sun create shapes on the floorboards beside the bed. It was my first morning as a married adult, and I had never felt so free. I lay back on the pillows and felt the weight of my childhood being shoved into the back of my mind. There was no space for childhood trauma in my new life with Shua. It didn't matter that I was lying on the same bed where Mrs Leifer had abused me only weeks before, or that I could still feel last night's pain. In that moment, for the first time in my life, I was an adult. A real adult.

It was 7 a.m. and I could hear the hum of Shua's morning prayers. My phone buzzed with a message from Nicole; she would be bringing over a box full of goodies and some fresh breakfast in ten minutes. I was desperate to speak to her and ask her if my pain was normal. Nicole had married her husband just over a month ago; her wedded life was only a few weeks older than mine.

114

Mrs Leifer's doorbell rang, and I jumped out of bed. I raced around the room, hurrying to cover myself in order to catch Nicole before she left. As I got down on my knees to search for the tichel (cloth hair covering) that had come off overnight, I heard Shua answering the door, thanking Nicole for the food, and telling her goodbye. While writing this book I asked Nicole if she remembered that morning, and she told me she had felt disturbed and unsettled climbing Mrs Leifer's steps to deliver us breakfast.

My attention turned to the sound of Shua walking towards the bedroom and I quickly called out to warn him that I wasn't modest. While we had consummated our marriage, blood on the first night meant I was impure and forbidden to my husband. The rules regarding how I must dress in front of men would now apply to Shua as well. Although we were newly married, we would not touch each other again until I had checked myself for seven blood-free days and purified myself with the ritualised bath at the mikveh.

I found my tichel and slipped into the bathroom for a quick shower before I dressed. Although I had a floor-length housecoat to cover my nightgown, I wasn't comfortable being semi-dressed in front of Shua. Just twenty-four hours prior, I had not been allowed in a room with Shua unsupervised; minutes from now, we would have our second meal alone as a couple.

The water washed over me, and I closed my eyes to contemplate the dizzying changes of the past day. In my mind, I watched the Dassi of yesterday getting up for the last day under her parents' roof. I could see her fervently murmuring the morning's prayers, begging God for the wedding to go ahead without a hitch. The Dassi of yesterday felt decades younger than the married woman I was that morning. Now, finally, life was mine.

CHAPTER 10

Disclosure

Chana Rabinowitz leant forward in her chair. 'Did you say it was someone at school?' she questioned me. I shifted back into the brown striped couch to widen the space between the counsellor and my overwhelming shame. Her eyes were wide and focused, waiting for my response. I fixed my gaze on the white tiles of Chana's living room-turned-therapy-office in Har Nof, Jerusalem; the same tiles that covered the floor of every Israeli apartment. It wasn't my first session. I had started seeing Chana after falling into a depression, following a year and a half of infertility that made me question my place in this world and turn to the forbidden internet for answers.

I knew the next question was coming before she asked it. 'Who?' Her forehead was furrowed, and her eyes moved from side to side as if scanning the staff at Adass Israel School. Chana had moved to Israel from Melbourne shortly before I did. My mother had introduced me to her three years ago, as the religious counsellor for my brother Isaac, who had been questioning our way of life.

'How did a man have access to you at school?' she asked, a puzzled look on her face. Having worked within the Adass community, Chana was familiar with the rigid gender separation.

I stayed silent. There was a quick, throbbing pulse in my throat, preventing me from speaking. Our previous session flashed through my mind. Somehow, my struggles with marriage and intimacy had led Chana to ask if I had been sexually abused. A slight nod and I had ended up here, in this mess.

Realising that my clenched hands were creasing the scrapbook pages I was holding, I busied myself packing them away. I had spent months creating a scrapbook of my married life, and had brought it to show Chana. She told me that the scrapbook was proof I wanted to make my marriage work.

I went through the motions, took money from my handbag, placed it on the coffee table and got up to leave. It didn't feel real. 'It wasn't a man,' I heard myself say, and then suddenly I was in a taxi home with my head in my hands, mourning what I had shared.

Chana lived ten minutes from Romema, the suburb where Shua and I had settled in Israel. Romema was a mainly ultra-Orthodox neighbourhood in northwest Jerusalem, just near the main entrance to the city. It occupied the highest hill in Jerusalem, and our one-bedroom apartment had a panoramic view of the surrounding area. It was the middle of February 2008 and the first signs of spring were beginning to sprout. Shua and I had been in Israel for sixteen months.

I dragged myself up the white tiled staircase to our apartment. Shua wouldn't be home for several hours. The lock kept playing up, and I drummed my head on the wooden door in utter distress as I struggled with it. I needed to hide, to pretend I didn't exist. Had I really said those words to the counsellor?

When I finally got the door open, I threw myself on the bed. What had I done? I curled up under my blanket and disappeared inside myself, to a place where anomalies remained frozen in the past and I hadn't uttered a sentence that could rip through the fabric of my life. When I was no longer able to detach from reality, I paced the five-metre length of our apartment, vowing to never return to therapy.

Shua arrived home for his dinner break at 7 p.m. The rigorous schedule at his rabbinical school saw him study from early morning till 10 p.m. I had spent the four hours before his return breathing deeply and burying my turmoil as deeply as I could. Nothing had happened. No one needed to know.

We didn't talk during dinner. Shua went back to the yeshivah at 8 p.m. to meet his nightly Torah study partner and I tidied up after dinner. A sharp pain in my heel brought focus and I stared at the broken bowl on the floor, wondering how it had got there. The sound of the shattering ceramic hadn't even registered. The dishes would have to wait; I was suffocating with doubt and needed a distraction.

From our porch, I gazed out over the nearby mountain and the lights of the villages. I sat on our patio swing chair, breathed in the night air and logged onto my computer. Shua didn't like me using the internet unless I was searching for work, but the lure of the world beyond my upbringing was mesmerising.

Since I first gained unsupervised access to the internet, I had begun to question our ultra-Orthodox lifestyle. Shua received a small stipend from the yeshivah and his father Henry supplemented our income. To afford anything beyond rent and basic expenses, I needed a job, and online was the best place to find one. In the last sixteen months I had worked as a babysitter, a companion to the elderly and a sales representative for an American company selling gift baskets. In between jobs and attending ulpan (Modern Hebrew language school) I still had long hours to fill in a country that was nothing like home.

Living in Israel was something of an adventure. Compared to the laid-back Australian way of life, Israel's energy was bustling, uptight and intrusive. Whether 2 a.m. or 2 p.m., life on Jerusalem's streets looked the same. Night or day, the noise and chaos never ceased. As a woman I felt relaxed walking home alone, no matter the hour, although I never got used to the many young children I would see long after dark, dragging their younger siblings through busy intersections.

In 2005–2006 there had been multiple suicide bus bombings in Jerusalem, but despite the air of vigilance and fear, Israel felt like a safe place to live. 'It feels different when you are living here,' we would tell Shua's mother when she worried about us. It wasn't unusual to see soldiers in uniform around every corner, guns casually hanging over their shoulders. I'll never forget the first time a weapon was pushed into my knee on crowded public transport. Once, the bus I was on hurtled to a stop because an unclaimed backpack had been found. Filing off the bus and waiting for the police while annoyed passengers argued with the driver felt like a natural extension to this unfamiliar culture.

Israelis are remarkably rude or refreshingly frank, depending on your perspective. I soon realised there was some flexibility around rules, and even a respect in challenging them. It's quite normal to be pushed to the back of a queue if you don't stand your ground, or to be questioned by a stranger about personal matters. With my accommodating personality and Australian manners, I didn't stand a chance in the neighbourhood makolet (grocery). If I needed to buy fresh bread or milk without Shua, I would wait for Israel's siesta time between 2–4 p.m., when the streets were as calm as they would ever be.

I learnt about Israel's red tape the hard way, while applying for a work permit. After two weeks of listening to automated messages and hold music from 9 a.m. to 6 p.m., I finally got through to an employee of the government agency and booked an appointment for the following month.

The first error I made was turning up at 1.45 p.m. for my two o'clock appointment. My second error was sitting there until the end of the day only to hear that I should try again. No matter the appointment time, it was first come, first served. My next appointment was at 1 p.m., so I turned up at nine, only to sit on a hard plastic chair for eight hours before being told that the employee booked for my appointment had called in sick. The third time, I was finally called into an office to have my passport stamped. However, I found out that after all that, I didn't have the right paperwork. Fortunately, the government worker gave me my work permit anyway.

I scanned job websites every day but there were limited options for someone who didn't speak Modern Hebrew, which was so different to the traditional Hebrew I had learnt as a child. With little else to do, I spent many hours alone, and I used them to explore things that had been previously off limits, and to find answers to questions I hadn't yet fully formulated.

I had no understanding of the internet other than that it was dangerous and forbidden. When it's so black and white, there is no opportunity for education. Viewing Facebook seemed as wicked as a porn site. And of course, people were eager to take advantage of my naivety.

With so little knowledge about sex, consent and a warped sense of my own worth it isn't surprising that sexual curiosity led me to chat rooms looking for answers.

'What do you think about blindfolds?' a man on the other side of the world asked me, and I quickly googled the role of blindfolds before I answered him. I was logged into an international chat room discussing sexual fantasies and didn't want to appear ignorant. By this time, I had been taught that the purpose of sex was to conceive, sexual pleasure was a concept I heard was possible but it wasn't something Shua and I discussed and I knew my shameful thoughts didn't have a place in our marriage. The internet provided me with a name for my fantasies, but it also made me feel like a freak. If I were a better Jewish woman, God wouldn't test me with these inclinations.

It wasn't until years and many therapists later that I would come to understand how common non-consensual fantasies can be for women, especially for those who have been abused. Back then I genuinely believed there was something inherently wrong with me.

It wasn't right to discuss these unholy thoughts with Shua. He spent hours each day studying the learnings of the Torah; he deserved a wife who was devoted to her place in this world as a Jewish mother.

The screen flashed again: 'Turn on your webcam, I want to see what you look like.' I logged off. I understood enough to know that this stranger didn't want to see a red-faced religious woman with a scarf over her hair and a blanket hugging her body. I went inside, took a sleeping pill and waited anxiously for the relief of sedation. My mind raced. Why did I keep getting pulled back to those websites? I was caught in a spiral of guilt and curiosity. Why couldn't I be different? Better? My inability to resist these websites was what had led me to see Chana Rabinowitz, and the trigger for her to ask if anyone had touched me as a child.

The week after my disclosure passed in the same manner as every other week. I had seen Chana on a Thursday, and by the following Monday I had convinced myself that life would go on as it always had. Shua got up at 7 a.m. and left the house for the day while I spent my time online 'looking for a job'. I spoke to my family back home but didn't tell Nicole how I had muttered four words that had the potential to change everything.

I suspected Mrs Leifer had abused Nicole after I witnessed her climb into my sister's bed one camp night in 2006. In the dark room we shared with our principal, I had heard the sounds of my worst fears. The next morning standing outside our cabin, no words were exchanged, but our eyes met in a way that conveyed a mutual understanding. We had not spoken about it since. The language to describe sexual abuse didn't exist in our world, and it wasn't something we could discuss. It was easy to believe it had never happened.

I didn't speak with my parents either; by this time, they had decided to disown all their children.

Just over a year after I had arrived in Israel, my parents announced to the community that they no longer had children. This parent-led estrangement had sent shock waves through the Adass community, where family is deemed integral. Several members in the community took it upon themselves to act as intermediaries, but neither my parents nor siblings were interested. Elly's engagement in the summer of 2007 was the final trigger to the family breakdown. As each of us married and started our own families, my mother's control over our lives weakened. Once Dalia and Tamar had left home, my mother wouldn't allow us to speak to them, worried their influence would undermine her absolute authority. Similarly, once Nicole and I were married, we had been blocked from Elly and had very little contact with her.

Mrs Leifer would sometimes allow Elly to call us from her office at school. Through these conversations, we understood that without the support of her sisters, life at home was deteriorating for her. My mother had threatened to turn down any marriage prospects if Elly didn't fall in line. Marriage in the Adass community was the only feasible way to leave home and Elly's way out. I was worried about Elly's close relationship with Leifer. Although we didn't have the words to explain it, Nicole and I had both warned her to stay away from the principal telling Elly she wasn't all that she seemed.

Once I was out of home, my relationship with Dalia grew. The three-hour time difference between Manchester and Israel meant that the best parts of my morning were chatting to her while she prepared for work and I cooked lunch for Shua. She had a wealth of advice about building a life as a new couple, and offered guidance on how I was supposed to generate love for a man I barely knew. Worried about our younger siblings, Dalia, who was twelve years older than me, took on a maternal role towards Elly, Isaac and Ben.

In 2007, Dalia convinced our mother to let Elly visit during the summer break to help with her two children. My mother agreed, on the condition Dalia paid for the ticket. Dalia bought Elly a one-way ticket to Manchester and then on to Israel. She had been speaking to a matchmaker who had suggested Elly meet with a Sydney boy who was studying in Israel.

Leifer was on vacation in Israel at the time, visiting family. Uninvited, she took control of the situation, appointing herself as matchmaker. Dalia and I supported Elly during her week of dating and then her engagement. News travels fast in the Jewish world, and we had to inform our parents before the engagement was announced. I remember standing with Elly, Dalia and Mrs Leifer in the hall we had booked for the engagement party. My mother was on the phone and the connection was shaky. 'What do you mean you are engaged?' she screamed. Elly quickly took the call off speakerphone and walked away to deal with our mother privately.

It wasn't weird seeing Mrs Leifer in Israel. She was still the principal of Adass and commanded the same respect as she had when she'd been the luminary of my world. The day before the engagement, Elly and I had gone shopping for jewellery with Mrs Leifer. I only threw out the silver necklace she had bought me that day several years ago when I moved home, and realised I still owned it.

My parents told Elly that if she went ahead with the engagement she was as good as dead to them. I can see Mrs Leifer's husband pacing the hall that night, screaming down the phone at my parents. People were arriving to celebrate the engagement and we were trying to placate Rabbi Leifer, embarrassed by the scene he was making. When my parents realised that we had all known about the engagement, they announced that they would not be coming to the wedding. As far as they were concerned, they no longer had children.

At fifteen years old, Ben still lived at home. My parents didn't throw him out until a year or so later, when Dalia paid for him to attend a yeshivah in the UK. My parents' parting words were that he'd better make yeshivah work, as there was no home for him to return to. They had already washed their hands of Isaac, who'd been expelled from his yeshivah in America for not conforming to the religious rules. Once again, Dalia had stepped in, arranging a flight to Israel and a place for him to stay.

Now that my parents had made a public show of their estrangement, there was no turning back. I didn't miss my hour-long conversations with my mother or the guilt she made me feel for not being the daughter she expected me to be. I'd spent the first few sessions with Chana explaining what a weight had been lifted from my shoulders, no longer having to hear what a constant disappointment I was.

Chana called me the following week, five days since I had told her that a woman at school had touched me inappropriately. The first time she called, I didn't answer, but by the third call I knew I couldn't ignore her. I agreed to another session on Thursday.

The night before, I couldn't sleep, and the day of my appointment, I couldn't eat. I must have climbed the stairs to her apartment six times before I found the courage to knock on her door. There was a sombre feel in the room and a contemplative look on her face as she ushered me in.

Chana began immediately. 'I've thought of every female teacher at the school. I can't begin to imagine who it is,' she said.

Once again, the words were stuck. I stared at the white square tiles, a battle taking place inside my head.

'I need to speak to Malka Leifer,' Chana said.

'No, don't do that,' I cried out. 'Please don't talk to anyone.'

'If the teacher still works at the school, I need to tell Mrs Leifer,' she said, firmer this time.

'It wasn't a teacher,' I managed to whisper. I paused, preparing for her disbelief. She had worked under Mrs Leifer and regarded her as highly as everyone else in the community did. Would she believe me?

Chana's eyes widened in surprise, and she leant forward, as if in anticipation.

I breathed deeply and swallowed the lump in my throat. I didn't know if my words would work, but there was something inside me that needed to tell. Something inside me that was afraid Mrs Leifer was still abusing girls under her care, and knew she needed to be stopped.

'Mrs Leifer,' I croaked, my words barely audible.

I glanced at Chana and saw a look of disbelief on her face. I knew she wouldn't believe me.

'Mrs Leifer?' she exclaimed in a loud voice. 'THE Mrs Leifer, principal of the school and head of the community?' She was shaking her head. 'This is unbelievable. How can this be?' She stared at me. 'Were there other girls too?'

I told her that I thought my sister was one of them, and found myself encouraging Chana to call her. Chana knew Nicole, she had seen her for a few sessions in Melbourne, to address her aversion to touch.

With that, I got up and left. I couldn't be in the room any longer. Somehow, I got home and once again disappeared into my mind, unable to face the fact that this secret was no longer mine.

Nicole called me later that night. 'You told Chana Rabinowitz,' she said, surprise and worry in her voice.

'I didn't feel like she believed me,' I told her.

'I know; she wanted to know if it was really true,' Nicole responded.

'What did you tell her?' I asked.

My heart was pounding and my throat was dry. I had never spoken to Nicole about what happened with

Mrs Leifer. There was still a chance that she had shut this down and told Chana it wasn't true.

The part of me that was hoping she'd shut this down was almost as strong as the part of me that just wanted to be believed.

'I told her it was true,' she confirmed. 'It feels like Chana went into panic mode. She said she needed to alert the school.'

'What's going to happen now?' I asked my sister. 'Will they believe us?'

'I don't know,' Nicole said. 'I'm so scared. What if Mrs Leifer finds out we said something?'

A few days later, Nicole called me again. She told me that the school board knew of other allegations, and that she had been advised on what to do if approached by Leifer. That was when I knew this story was no longer only mine.

CHAPTER 11

The fallout

Now that the truth was out, I had to tell my husband. I was deeply worried. It felt wrong to confess my shame, even to Shua. The Adass community discouraged exposure, and I had been raised with a reverence for silence and secrecy, but I had to tell Shua before the gossip reached him.

Over dinner at the Ramada Jerusalem hotel, I told Shua my truth. 'She touched me with her fingers, under my clothing,' I whispered, the spirited laughter of a nearby child momentarily drowning out my words. I had chosen to tell him here, over dinner, so the discussion had a defined beginning and end. I felt like I was shaping words out of the tumble inside my head. Words that my brain should not have had to create.

Shua took the news silently and did not ask me about the extent of the abuse. 'What happens now?' he asked instead, and I told him what I had gleaned from Nicole.

Nicole believed Leifer had been told that the school was aware she was molesting students. At that time, Nicole was teaching at Adass School in Melbourne. On 5 March, Leifer had pulled her out of the Grade Six classroom to ask her what she knew. Having been advised not to respond to Leifer's questions, she dutifully told the principal she did not know anything. What we truly didn't know was that immediate plans were being made to get Leifer out of Australia. By the next morning, she had fled to Israel.

The rest of my information came from Australian newspapers. 'Principal flees after "molesting schoolgirls"', the *Sydney Morning Herald* reported on 14 March. I scanned the internet daily, desperate to gauge which parts of my disclosure had crossed the ocean. I had no knowledge of the law, and was unaware that sexual abuse victims could not be outed by the press, so it was a huge relief to find no mention of my name. I was puzzled that the papers reported the story at all. I couldn't fathom why anyone beyond Adass would have any interest in our affairs and had expected the news to be tightly held by the community.

It was only when we agreed to sit down with the ABC's *Australian Story* in 2018 that my sisters and I discovered how the news got out. The documentary revealed that a concerned parent from the Adass community had called the *Jewish News*, a Melbourne newspaper, stating that the principal of the Adass girls' school had left the country abruptly, and the circumstances were murky. By the end of the week, there were news crews camped outside the school.

I was conflicted. I wanted to be in Australia to support and be supported by my siblings, but I also felt relief at being distanced from the community shame. Nicole told me that the school was in a state of chaos, and the teachers had been warned to stay away from the press. Sometime during that week, Chana Rabinowitz called to tell me that Adass Israel School were flying her to Melbourne to help deal with the community fallout. I was alone in Israel, having just made a life-changing disclosure. *What about me?* I thought but didn't say.

Community gossip reached a frenzied state. The weekend following Malka Leifer's escape, the spiritual leader of the Adass community, Rabbi Beck, addressed the congregation during his Shabbat sermon. 'Mrs Leifer should not be considered guilty of any crime as there has been no investigation. Discussing the matter would be considered loshen hora (malicious gossip),' he told the congregation.

His words had an immediate effect, and hearing about them cemented the feeling that I was wrong. Rabbi Beck had overarching authority within the community. Rumours still flew, but now they were whispered behind closed doors instead of being declared over the Shabbat table. It didn't take long for the gossip machine to spit out my name. They knew the accuser was a twenty-year-old ex-student living in Jerusalem. At the time, I was the only person who fit that description.

The rumour mill went into overdrive with questions such as why I had made the disclosure, and what precipitated my break in silence. This was the biggest story the community had faced, and with no TV, internet or radio, gossip had always been the best form of entertainment.

At one point, a friend called me to confirm a rumour that I had separated from Shua. 'He's standing right beside me in the kitchen,' I told her, and I made him call out to her when she didn't believe me.

I remember jokingly asking Shua if he would divorce me. Under Jewish law as a religious man, Shua held the obligation to 'peru v'revu' – to be fertile and increase. According to rabbinic law, if he was married ten years and his wife bore no children, he didn't need to abstain any longer from the duty of propagation. We had not yet been married two years, but I knew of one couple who had been granted a divorce for this reason. Shua's ambivalent response didn't provide me with any reassurance.

After several weeks the news cycle died down and life in Israel continued like the disclosure had never happened. Shua and I made plans to return to Australia for Elly's wedding. While we occasionally discussed the scandal, Shua never asked for further details about that period of my life, and nor did I offer any.

Elly's wedding, originally scheduled for late March, was rescheduled to June after Elly revealed that she too had been sexually abused by Malka Leifer. After becoming engaged to Kaduri, a religious man from Sydney, Elly had returned to Melbourne to live with Tamar until she was married. A week before her wedding, Elly disclosed her truth to our older sister. I cried for her pain, and out of guilt that I hadn't spoken sooner. I did not have the language to warn her, nor to describe what had occurred, even after my disclosure. The betrayal I had experienced was so deep I was not yet capable of acknowledging it. The silence of my community helped me avoid it.

Shua and I flew back to Melbourne in late March and decided to stay on for Elly's winter wedding. But I had exposed a secret, the community we resided within did not know how to deal with us, so Shua's mother Esther allowed us to live in her Caulfield North house. She and I grew close during those months. Although she was not religious, she koshered her kitchen so that we could use it.

With the long stretch in Australia looming, I looked for a job in the only place that would accept my lack of qualifications – Adass Israel School.

I accepted a job as remedial aide for Hebrew reading. I loved catching up with Nicole during recess breaks, but while the other staff were civil, it felt like the elephant in the room followed me around. Malka Leifer was not mentioned once, either in support or reprimand. What I perceived as unspoken blame became too uncomfortable to ignore, and I quit shortly after.

The weeks to the wedding passed quickly. Shua and I visited a reproductive endocrinologist to investigate why we had not fallen pregnant. I went under the knife at Cabrini Hospital for a dilation and curettage, and a laparoscopy. The surgeon advised that there was no medical reason for my infertility, adding that in the month following the operation there was a higher chance of getting pregnant. *If there is no medical reason for my infertility, I must be defective*, I thought. My long-held hatred for my body grew.

Elly's wedding was held on 12 June in the religious community of Bondi in Sydney. Sydney's Sephardi community were openly shocked by Melbourne's sexual abuse scandal, and we felt less judged there. Members of the community opened their homes to my family.

Friends of my parents rallied around them but were unable to convince them to attend Elly's wedding. Once again, our family became the talk of the town. Thankfully, in Sydney we were removed from it. Dalia and her husband Benny walked Elly down the aisle.

Although we felt like a spectacle, it was freeing to dance the night away with Dalia, Tamar, Nicole and Elly, who was a strikingly beautiful bride. My mother had shown us many times that she hated our close bond, and none of us missed her guilt hanging over us.

Shua stood by me through the drama. I tried to silence the constant worry that I would never amount to the childbearing, drama-free wife that he deserved. There were moments when I looked at him and still saw a stranger, but our time in Israel had given us the space to grow closer. At times, I really felt our growing bond. I remember making love notes out of Israeli candy across our kitchen table for him to find during his lunch breaks. I had no reference point for romantic love, but I believe that we loved each other.

The surgeon was correct, and we did fall pregnant the following month. I took a pregnancy test the day after we returned to Israel and Shua and I danced around our tiny kitchen when the test showed a positive result. The miracle of life filled me with renewed enthusiasm for religiosity. I swore off the internet and dedicated every hour of the day to repenting for my deviant thoughts, begging God to give me a chance to be a Jewish mother. I spent hours trying to purify my mind and soul, immediately punishing myself for any thought that questioned my way of life or my place in Judaism. I was desperate to prove to God that I had changed my ways and would dedicate my every minute to His service.

The loss of our baby early in the second trimester, and the crudeness of the Israeli medical system, shredded any remnants of my fragile mental health. I screamed with labour pains over the toilet, watching my identity disappear along with my fourteen-week-old foetus. After almost two years of trying, the pregnancy had symbolised hope. I had watched my classmates and sisters revel in the joy of motherhood while I cried every time my period appeared, wondering what was wrong with me. Impending motherhood had finally secured me a place in my community, in the world and, even more importantly, in the afterlife. At last, I would be the person I was destined to be – a Jewish mother.

After the miscarriage I spent weeks cowering in bed, facing the wall, unable to communicate. In his desperation to help, Shua scoured the nearby supermarkets for the only thing

I would eat – BBQ Doritos. He would drop them off after morning prayers, and I would beg him to stay at the men's seminary during his lunch break. The pressure to open my eyes and acknowledge that I was alive seemed insurmountable. I couldn't bear having a witness to my misery.

I was convinced that I had lost the baby because of my online explorations. The miscarriage was proof that my efforts to repent and refocus on my religion weren't enough. That I was not enough. God could see my soul and He knew that I was inherently defective. I didn't deserve to bring up the next generation.

Elly and her husband had followed us to Israel, and Elly visited me every day to coax me out of bed. We spent hours together outside, on the porch that overlooked Jerusalem's hills. We felt proud of ourselves when we figured out how to access Disney TV online, and with a sense of rebellion, we ate junk food and binged on *The Suite Life of Zack & Cody*.

Against the backdrop of my abject despair, those months of sisterly camaraderie with Elly were the best times I had in Israel. After Elly left Israel in September, my homesickness became even more unbearable. With our fertility issues, Shua and I needed help that only the Australian medical system could provide. It was time to go home.

We made plans to leave Israel in December after Chanukah. We spent our last months in the Holy Land doing the things that religious tourists do. We went on Kevarim tours, visiting the graves of some of the most important Jewish thinkers in history.

'Mama Rochel, help me,' I cried out at Kever Rochel (the Tomb of Rachel). Rachel Imanu was one of the three biblical matriarchs of Jewish faith, and visiting her grave was supposed to be a remedy for infertility.

As we travelled around Israel, I couldn't let go of the worry that we would bump into Malka Leifer. My poor mental health had led me back to Chana Rabinowitz, whom I had not seen since my disclosure, and she had assured me that Adass leaders were keeping tabs on Leifer's whereabouts. I took no comfort in this lacklustre reassurance. How did they think that would stop her?

Years later, Eve Finkelstein, a Melbourne doctor living in Israel, told me she was shocked at how Adass handled Leifer and had taken it upon herself to find where she was living in Israel, then informed potential employers and schools of the accusations against her.

I knew the Adass leaders had underestimated Leifer's cunning. That, combined with the willingness of Israel's religious communities to skirt around the issue, meant I couldn't wait to leave.

It was with a strange sense of relief that Shua and I finally boarded the fourteen-hour El Al flight back to Melbourne.

CHAPTER 12

Second chances

Shua and I left Israel on 31 December 2008. While our seat neighbours toasted the New Year, we nestled ourselves in our own bubble. I watched PG movies on the kids' channel while Shua stood beside me, wrapped in his prayer shawl, shuckling (rocking) out his daily prayers. The date had no significance to me; in my world, the new year had begun in September.

We arrived in Melbourne on 1 January 2009. The scorching day was a shock adjustment after the winter we had left behind; southeast Australia was about to enter a record-breaking heatwave. In the weeks to come, the Black Saturday bushfires would claim the lives of 173 Victorians.

I remember watching the inferno on TV from the safety of my mother-in-law's home. TVs are not allowed in the community, but until we found an apartment within Adass, we had access to the news. The flames were terrifying, and along with the rest of Australia, I prayed for the communities in the fires' destructive path.

We found an apartment on the corner of The Avenue and Hotham Street in East St Kilda. Returning to Australia offered a reprieve from my mental health difficulties. I shopped with my mother-in-law, Esther, looked for a job and had fun setting up home with my husband. Within both my marriage and the community, there was a blanket of silence over the era of Malka Leifer. After the turbulence of Israel, it felt like Shua and I had begun a new chapter. Melbourne was our second chance.

Shua joined a Kollel – an institute for study of the Talmud and rabbinic literature – and I interviewed for the job of assistant to the principal of Yesodei HaTorah College, Rabbi Starcher. There were limited appropriate options for a woman with no career qualifications. The job paid $14.90 per hour.

Yesodei HaTorah had been founded as a boys' school that catered to parents who were unhappy with the other religious schooling options. There were reports of poorly managed bullying within the Lubavitch Yeshiva College, and Adass boys' school, with its Hasidic teachers and Yiddish curriculum, did not suit the non-Hasidic families.

Our day developed a familiar schedule. Shua would wake at 6.30 a.m. and go to the synagogue for morning prayers. I would get up, dress, and prepare a slow cooker dinner. Shua would return at 8 a.m. and drive me to the school in Elwood for my 8.30 a.m. start, and he or his mother would pick me up at 5.30 p.m. when I finished work. I didn't have my driver's licence. Driving in Israel had seemed like a death wish to me – I couldn't imagine navigating safely in the hectic traffic, and in Melbourne after rent and bills there was no money for driving lessons.

The staff at Yesodei HaTorah College were mostly male, and used a separate staffroom to the one I worked in. I enjoyed chatting to the female non-religious staff, but their lives were vastly different to mine. The school employed several young women from the Lubavitch community, and it was the first time I had been able to connect with members of the wider Jewish community. It amazed me that as a schoolgirl I had been cautioned not to mix with them, especially when I discovered their devout religiosity, despite having gone to university.

My daily schedule rarely differed. I buried any doubts about my marriage, mental health or religion, and leant heavily into my role as a Jewish wife. When the mask of normalcy became overwhelming, I would take a sick day and bury myself in books and the TV shows I could find online, until I felt ready to face the world again as Dassi Erlich, religious wife. Every Thursday night I would cook up a Shabbat storm, and Isaac, Elly and Ben would occasionally pop in for some homemade food. Life revolved around Shabbat, Jewish holidays and family. After long days at work, I had little energy to engage in community life, and it felt easier that way.

Many of my school friends had married men from similar ultra-Orthodox communities overseas and, as was custom, lived in their husbands' hometowns. I enjoyed seeing them when they returned home to visit family, usually either at Passover or Sukkot. Those classmates still in Melbourne would organise Shabbat afternoon catch-ups, and every so often I would go along, only to leave when the talk of children became too overwhelming. I loved meeting their babies, but the absence of my own made me feel different and lacking.

Shua consulted his rabbi and was given permission to obtain medical help with our fertility. The code of Jewish Law prohibits male masturbation, as it produces wasted seed – a sin more severe than any other in the Torah, deemed equivalent to murder. To get a sperm sample, we used a non-spermicidal, perforated condom that allowed a small amount of sperm to escape the condom, which would provide a chance of pregnancy while still collecting some seed for sampling. The sperm sample, along with my fertility investigations the previous year, showed there was no medical reason we could not fall pregnant. It would take a decade more before I received a diagnosis of Polycystic Ovary Syndrome (PCOS), which finally shed light on many of my symptoms.

I diligently tracked my temperature every morning to determine when I was ovulating. Every month, I would count the seven clean days after my period ended, check myself with a white cloth each morning and evening, book a room in the community mikveh, and then stand in that green-tiled bathroom crying silent tears, knowing that once again I had failed my husband and my duty.

In September, our fertility doctor suggested we try Clomid, a medication used to stimulate hormones that support ovulation. My first month taking the pills did not result in a pregnancy, but the second month, even before the pregnancy test, my body felt different and I knew in my gut that I was pregnant.

Two days before my expected period, Shua ran out to buy an early pregnancy test. I tossed and turned all night, refusing to use the bathroom, wanting the test to have the best chance of detecting the pregnancy hormone. I watched the clock until 4.30 a.m. and when I could not wait a minute longer, I jumped out of bed and raced, test in hand, to the toilet.

Although I had read the instructions on the test box many times before, I read them again, noted the time on my watch, dipped the stick in my urine, replaced the cap and then closed my eyes to wait out the recommended five minutes. I repeatedly peeked at my watch but would not look at the test. When my watch read 4.42 a.m., I held my breath and looked at the test window. I screamed, 'Two pink lines, two pink lines!', but when Shua didn't hear me, I gingerly placed the test down on the sink and ran to wake him.

'Shua, we are pregnant, we are pregnant!' He woke up instantly and we rushed back to the bathroom together to confirm that the test still existed. We looked at the two dark pink lines and hugged each other silently, tears of gratitude streaming down our faces.

Back in the bedroom, Shua climbed into my bed. We each had our own bed due to the laws of Niddah, which stated that while I was impure, we could not touch one another. My trauma felt safer sleeping alone, so even during the two or so weeks a month that we could sleep together, I favoured my own space.

That morning we lay beside each other, caressing the miracle growing inside me with words of praise to God. At 6.30 a.m. Shua kissed me and went to the synagogue for morning prayers. I willed the clock to move forward so I could call Nicole and share my news. The fear of a miscarriage prevented me from telling anyone else.

I decided the momentous occasion called for a sick day. I lay in bed all morning whispering promises to the tiny cells inside me. 'I promise to love you and protect you,' I told my daughter. I was sure I was having a girl.

The next few months passed in a flurry of worry and excitement. After a blood test confirmed my pregnancy at six weeks, I began my pregnancy diary. I wrote about all the hopes and dreams I had for my unborn child, as well as my relief that I would finally fulfil my destiny of becoming a Jewish mother.

Thursday, 4 February 2010

Dear Diary,

You gave me such a fright today, little baby; I woke up and
I had a little brown spotting. To be truthful it was only two
spots, but still it made me so scared. I don't like being scared
like that – I love you so much and I can't wait to hold you
already. Tomorrow I will be fifteen weeks pregnant. I never
thought I would get this far, but every day I feel more and
more connected to you. I want you badly, please don't leave
me – I love you!

We went to the doctor and we heard your strong little
heartbeat which baruch Hashem (bless God) sounded fine and
calmed some of my fears, but until I hold you in my hands,
I'm going to continue worrying ... it probably won't stop then,
it'll just be about other stuff. For now, I will continue davening
(praying) for you and begging Hashem to let us keep you so
we can finally have a proper Jewish family.

I think about you a lot and dream about what you will look
like.

Shua is also excited, he is also saying tefillas (prayers)
every day so that you will be healthy, safe and grow up to be
a proper Jewish child. I can't wait to teach you mitzvot (good
deeds) and show you how to love Hashem and the Torah.

Despite crippling morning sickness, I loved being
pregnant. I researched every symptom online, which helped
alleviate my anxiety about what was normal and expected.
All my life, I had managed to push away any awareness of
bodily sensations – a survival mechanism to help me cope
with my trauma. The sense of being in tune with every
physical change was novel to me. I gave myself permission
to lean in and listen to the way life was growing inside

me. With each month that passed without any signs of miscarrying, I was able to breathe more deeply. The mother I was meant to be was within reach.

At fifteen weeks the nausea finally began to abate. One morning at work I felt something leaking. I ran into the bathroom, certain I was experiencing another miscarriage. When I calmed down enough to get my bearings, I saw that my panic was perhaps a little disproportionate; the bleeding was only slight. Still, I hid in the cupboard-like space for half an hour, texting with Shua until he confirmed that an urgent appointment had been booked with our gynaecologist.

An hour later I sat in the car, anxious and terrified and desperate to hug Shua, but the belief that I could be unclean hung between us, and we were forbidden to touch one another. Until Shua saw the blood and a judgement was made, we would act like I carried the unclean Niddah status. I didn't think the amount of blood was enough to make me unclean, but it didn't matter what I thought; according to Jewish law, women can't be judges or make Halachic (legal) rulings.

That was when I began to resent the rules of Niddah. I had enjoyed the reprieve from having to fully cover up for two weeks of the month during the hot summer, or worrying about whether I could pass something to my husband directly, instead of putting it down to ensure our fingers didn't touch. I had been taught that the forced separation from my husband was to help our marriage, to somehow make it more exciting. But at times like this, it felt like my very soul was unclean and I was being punished for being a woman.

The visit to our gynaecologist went well. Dr Wein listened to the baby's heartbeat and reassured us that everything was looking healthy.

Back at home, I changed out of my underwear so Shua could inspect it. After holding it up at every angle, he told me he wasn't sure if the spots of blood were enough to make me Niddah, and decided he would take my underwear to his rabbi for a final judgement. My underwear would be inspected under a lamp or torch light after the evening prayers.

I had been taught about this during my bridal classes but had hoped it would never have to happen. I was uncomfortable and nauseous, but I convinced myself the rabbi had seen many women's underwear and mine would be no different. *Like a doctor*, I told myself, even though the rabbi had no medical degree. All that qualified him to check my underwear was a course of study of Jewish texts and ordainment by a more senior rabbi.

Off Shua went with my underwear in his pocket, wrapped in a little plastic bag, to be inspected after evening prayer. I tried to put it out of my mind, but I couldn't let go of the image of our rabbi's face close enough to my worn underwear to smell it. I berated myself. The rabbi played a part in every moment of our lives, why was I having such trouble accepting that he reached into our most intimate moments?

Shua returned home beaming. The rabbi had declared me clean. I focused on the relief I felt and pushed away the feeling that this wasn't right. I told myself it was not my place to question it.

In February, I finally achieved a long-held dream and signed myself up to Open Universities Australia. At twenty-three years old I was considered a mature-age student and could enrol without a VCE certificate.

Now that I was pregnant, for the first time in my life I could imagine a future. I had wanted to study since I first understood that study wasn't meant for girls. I had wanted to study sociology since I first understood there was a discipline that researched human behaviour. I had begged my parents to allow me to study, but ultimately they decided that marriage was more important, and they didn't want me to begin a course of study without my future husband's approval.

I managed to complete two units in statistics and introduction to sociology, scoring distinctions in both, before my mental health began deteriorating and my anxiety and depression made it impossible to concentrate. I returned to the coping mechanism I had found in Israel – chatting online with random strangers. It filled my time and helped me push down the memories of my parents and Mrs Leifer, which crowded my mind and made it hard to see reality. I felt like two people, a pregnant Jewish wife and an uncertain, frightened and curious woman.

In my diary, I berated myself for not being able to stop the dark thoughts and focus instead on the joy of having a baby.

I couldn't understand why this was happening to me. Everything I had ever dreamed of was coming true, but still the depressive thoughts wouldn't stop. I turned to the internet and found myself cruising sites that were inappropriate for a religious woman and dangerous for someone reacting to an abusive past. I chatted to people who didn't know me, and engaged in discussions I should not have been having.

I tried to stop myself and I found a Jewish website that promised to help Jews who struggled with inappropriate internet use. Around the world, the internet had begun creeping into Jewish communities. In response, Jewish world leaders ran huge campaigns, shouting about the evils that awaited those who allowed themselves to be pulled into it. In many communities, the internet was completely banned.

I soon realised that despite the support I was receiving from connecting with other Jews who struggled with the internet, I needed more help so I looked around for a therapist. I was referred to a religious therapist in Melbourne.

The therapist was a Lubavitch man with a long white beard and sharp blue eyes. I sat in his office for weeks, heavily pregnant, unable to speak. I had no way to verbalise what was happening. Why was my joy at being pregnant marred by fear? Why did I dream about hurting myself, of needing pain to feel alive?

How could I put words to the horror that was inside me? The words were stuck in my mind, safe and untouchable.

After my initial disclosure to Chana Rabinowitz, I assumed I would never speak about the abuse again. I wasn't sure there was even a space where the words I needed to say could exist.

So I sat and stared, while the therapist spoke. I didn't know I had a voice, didn't know I *could* have a voice. I could sense his frustration, but he was patient. He asked many questions, and I always gave him one-word answers.

After several sessions, he sent me an email subtly referring to his frustration and inability to help me. If I could not speak, how could he help?

I sent an email back explaining in writing all that I could not verbalise, sparking an email exchange that spanned the length of the time I saw him.

We kept meeting in person, too. He struggled to understand that the Dassi of the emails was the same Dassi who sat in front of him. He praised my writing and encouraged it, and slowly he helped me lift those words off the page and into the counselling room. He taught me that I did have a voice. And once I found my voice, I knew that no matter what happened to me, I would never be silenced again.

Shua knew I wasn't well. All my energy went to keeping my sanity, and the myriad of Jewish laws, which seemed irrelevant to the horror inside me, started to fall away. How could I bless God for letting me wake each morning when horrors racked my sleep?

My body was supposed to be a sanctity of God, a vessel of His spirit, but I wanted to cut it off me. I tried to explain this to Shua, but he couldn't understand. He seemed to believe that if I turned to the Torah and my devotion to God, my mental health problems wouldn't exist. He agreed to my sessions with the therapist in the hope it would fix me.

The religious therapist supported me during the final tumultuous months of my pregnancy, responding to my every crisis with support and care, and somehow, I made it through my pregnancy in one piece.

At forty-one weeks and six days, I woke while it was still dark outside and breathed through the first twinges of pain. I had just experienced my first contraction.

CHAPTER 13

Lily

I shook my husband. 'Shua, I think I might be in labour.' He didn't move. *Maybe I imagined the pain*, I thought to myself. I lay back down and settled my breathing to match Shua's quiet energy. I could feel the baby shifting inside me, and I tried to visualise her nestled against my chest later that evening. My life's dream of motherhood still felt surreal, almost unbelievable.

When the second contraction rolled through my abdomen ten minutes later, I knew labour had begun. 'Shua, wake up, our baby is coming.' There was a sense of urgency in my voice now, and this time he woke instantly. Before acknowledging me, Shua leant over to wash Netilat Yadayim with the water basin beside his bed. As I watched him perform the ritualised washing of his hands, I remembered that I too must wash away the impurity of my soul leaving its vessel to visit heaven during sleep. I didn't want my daughter to be born from an unclean body.

With our hands washed, Shua and I moved into the dining room. It was 4.30 a.m.

Over the next few hours, as the sun peeked through the

bay window, we shuffled around the room, counting the minutes between contractions. I savoured the tranquillity of sharing the birthing experience with Shua before the world around us rose. There was a sense of intimacy, and I felt closer to my husband than I had in the months prior. The waves of pain grounded me in the present, and it was effortless to forget the turmoil that had marked the second half of my pregnancy. We would be parents by the day's end.

At 6.30 a.m., we called Shua's mother to announce that her new grandchild was on their way. With Esther driving over, I encouraged Shua to go to the synagogue for morning prayers. It would be the last time he would pray in a minyan for the next while, a newborn being considered acceptable justification to pray without the presence of ten men.

In the moments alone, I closed my eyes and made my own beseeching prayer to God. *Please, Hashem, let our daughter be healthy, please don't punish her for my mistakes. I promise if you give us a healthy daughter I will stop fighting against this life and be the ideal Jewish woman.* I imagined my future self thriving, a martyr, silencing my own needs when they conflicted with the needs of my religion.

By the time Shua returned at 7.30 a.m. I was holding onto the table, having called him repeatedly to ask where he was. The contractions were five minutes apart. 'Breathe,' he reminded me, but my breath felt stuck. I asked Shua to massage my back; I didn't want my mind to dissociate and slip away. I wanted to be a part of this experience, with him.

At 8 a.m., I called the maternity ward, where I was due to give birth, and the midwife told us to come in for monitoring. A sign of my struggle to believe this day would arrive meant a lack of preparation, so Shua and I hurried around the house packing a hospital bag.

Thirty minutes later we checked in at the hospital and were ushered into an empty room. The nurses told me I was two centimetres dilated. I expected to be sent home, but they asked us to wait for our obstetrician to check on me during his lunch hour. I complied with their suggestions. Unused to advocating for myself, it never occurred to me to think about the way I wanted to give birth. I hadn't participated in any of the birthing classes the doctor had recommended. I can't remember if it was Shua or myself who was uncomfortable with the classes being mixed, and the idea that I would be socialising with people outside our community but it felt not right for us then.

Shua and I camped out in our corner of the clinical space. The obstetrician's lunch visit turned into an after-work visit. The hours dragged on and the contractions came and went, but they would start and stop in a random routine. I didn't move from the bed. Having spent the majority of my childhood in shutdown, my instinct around unfamiliar pain was to be as still and small as possible.

At some point Shua's mother dropped off some food and we went back to waiting. I don't remember talking to Shua about our feelings around the birth of our first child. I knew my mental health difficulties had worried him, and I wondered if he regretted marrying me, but I was too scared to ask him. While he recited his midday prayers, I whispered promises to our daughter. 'I can't wait to meet you,' I told her. 'I promise you I will be the best mother I can be. I'm sorry that I haven't been the best, but it will all be better now.' In that moment I truly believed that once my daughter was in my arms, my mental difficulties would fall away.

At 5 p.m. the doctor announced that after a whole day of contractions, I was only three centimetres dilated. I felt like crying. He decided he would break my waters to hurry things along. Once my waters were broken, I held the Niddah status, so Shua was no longer able to touch me or see me uncovered. There was no acknowledgement of this, no mention that it didn't feel right. It was just the way it was.

Shua stood beside my head in a position that meant he couldn't see below my waist. I was wearing a hospital gown and socks, and I constantly adjusted them to ensure no skin was showing. The big needle of the epidural scared me, and I wanted a hand to hold, so I called Tamar for support. She arrived and held my hand as long as was needed. The obstetrician, assuming the epidural would mask my pain, put me on a drip to hurry my contractions.

Tamar left shortly after, certain that the epidural would do its job and I would have an uncomplicated birth, but by 10 p.m. the contractions had sped up and the medication wasn't touching the pain. I felt everything. There was a storm lashing at the windows outside, but I didn't even notice. I was in a world of misery, crying out for my sisters to be with me. I remember begging Shua to call Nicole and ask her to come urgently. I was in no state to cover myself, and he couldn't pull the covers up for risk of touching me, so he stood with his back to me while I lay writhing in pain.

Nicole had fallen pregnant several weeks after me, and we had shared every milestone of our pregnancies together. She had two young boys already, and I had turned to her for advice at every stage. Although she was weeks away from giving birth, at that moment, there was no one else I wanted by my side.

In the storm that night, Nicole slipped and fell as she hurried to see me. Unbeknownst to me, while the anaesthetist was attempting to give me a second epidural, Nicole was being monitored in a room next door. She arrived at my side just as the anaesthetist informed me that the needle had slipped and was now in my spine. To lower the risk of being paralysed, which was now significantly higher, I would need to lie on my side and move as little as possible.

I was terrified. My thoughts clambered over each other. *Was my daughter okay? I couldn't feel her. Was I going to end up in a wheelchair? Was I going to get through this alive?* I had no strength to ask; I was in a state of utter deliriousness. I lay there holding onto Nicole's hand for four hours – later, she told me I almost broke it. Due to my state of undress, Shua still had his back turned. It felt like we were existing in different worlds.

At some point my chest went numb and I struggled to breathe. The anaesthetist realised the epidural had gone up my chest instead of down. Again, I was told to lie still as they trapped me in place with more wires to monitor my falling blood pressure and breathing.

At 3.40 a.m. I began pushing, and just after 4 a.m. our daughter was born. Still immobile and on my side, the midwives placed my baby beside my chest, and I held my daughter for the first time. 'I love you,' I whispered to her. 'I will protect you with my life and make sure no one hurts you.'

I waited to feel the emotions that I had been promised would rush into every cell of my body, but all I felt was exhausted and terrified. 'I love you,' I said again to the little face in my arms, knowing that I did, but I couldn't feel it.

My body was numb. *I must be damaged beyond repair,* I thought to myself. *I will always make sure my daughter knows she is loved so she doesn't end up flawed like me.* I held her, stroked her little cheeks and promised to give her everything she needed, everything that I had needed but had never received. It was many years before I realised it was the trauma of the birth and my own childhood trauma standing in the way of me feeling anything.

I handed our baby to Shua so he too could meet our precious newborn.

The next day, the religious therapist came to visit me in hospital, and I cried to him about God punishing me with my lack of feelings. I remember him telling me to focus on the miracle I had just birthed and not lament over my failings, that the feelings of love would come in time. This wasn't about me; I had a daughter to live for now.

The week following the birth was traumatic. They left the needle in my spine for twenty-four hours, hoping it would prevent a spinal leak. My first day as a mother and I could only see, feed and hold my daughter lying on my side.

Although he still couldn't touch me, Shua moved into the hospital room and took care of the things I could not do, revelling in his new role as a father. I watched him give our daughter her first bath and tried to quieten the feelings of jealousy that arose.

The next day, I was moved onto the maternity ward and the doctor removed the needle from my spine. They warned me there was a fifty per cent chance I would have headaches from the leakage of spinal fluid around my brain and in my spine. I felt nothing the first day, but that evening when I stood up, I was bowled over by the pain. I had never felt anything like it; it was like a thousand migraines all at once.

Between the pain and the haze of the painkillers, I was unable to feel anything for my daughter, I couldn't feel anything. I was sure that this lack of feelings was a failure on my part and that it confirmed my worst fears – I was going to be like my own mother.

I didn't share these worries with Shua, afraid that he would see me differently if he knew the extent of my mental health difficulties. Until I stopped bleeding, had seven days clean and went to the mikveh, I would be Niddah and Shua would not be able to touch me. Although we slept in the same room, Shua on the floor on a mattress, the two metres between our beds felt like a chasm as long and wide as the River Nile. I only questioned our circumstances once, when I wondered how wrong it could be to hug after experiencing the miracle of birth together. *Hush, Dassi*, I told myself. *You promised to stop questioning and blindly believe. This is the right way to be.*

Shua named our daughter in the synagogue the following Monday. When a boy is born there are several traditional celebrations. When a girl is born, it is up to the family to decide if they want to celebrate it in the synagogue. Shua and I decided to provide a small buffet of sweets to the men following the morning prayers when we named our daughter Lily.

After seven days in hospital, I developed a stutter. The doctors recommended a brain scan, which would mean a contrast dye and several days of not being able to breastfeed my daughter. I knew in my gut it was the medications causing the stutter, so I refused the brain scan and signed myself out of the hospital against medical advice. I still can't believe I did that. It was the first time I had trusted my gut over the advice of authority figures.

For the next week, I dealt with the pain without the heavy medications until eventually it subsided. The stutter went away, and I was finally able to care for my daughter.

I had doubts about breastfeeding my daughter from the beginning. At first, I loved the time that was just Lily and me, knowing that I was giving her something only I could provide. I would cuddle her in my arms and burp her over my shoulder, determinedly pushing away the memories of Leifer sucking on my breast for hours. But as the months passed, it became harder and harder to push those memories down.

The community has a beautiful ritual of providing meals for a new mother. Twice a day for two weeks after I came home from hospital, I would receive a box filled with a hot meal and other delights. Not having to worry about cooking while I was exhausted and starving from breastfeeding was an absolute blessing.

The therapist was right – the feelings of love did come. As the weeks passed, I fell more and more in love with my daughter. This love felt strange; it was unlike anything I had ever experienced. I read every parenting book I could get hold of. I doubted myself constantly, wanting to be the best mother I could be. I worried that I would repeat patterns of intergenerational trauma, and studied my interactions with Lily constantly, but I put on a calm face and tried to ensure she couldn't sense my agitation.

The months melted into one another in the way life with a newborn does. Shua and I settled into a rhythm of caring for our daughter. Lily slept little and ate a lot, and we took turns holding her through the night. When I was too tired to lift my arms and pick Lily up from the crib between our beds, Shua would get up and put her beside me so I could breastfeed. I didn't leave the house for the first few weeks, reluctant to leave the warm, safe world we had created together.

But by the time Lily was four months old, the lack of sleep made it harder to keep my promise to be the perfect Jewish woman. I had been taught that religion was black and white, so it followed that I believed if I didn't do everything perfectly, I may as well not do anything. If I couldn't spend forty-five minutes on morning prayers, what was the use of saying all the other prayers throughout the day? With this line of thinking, I quickly sunk into believing that although God had granted me a child, He had abandoned me to my darkest demons, and I would never be who I was supposed to be.

Shua and I had many arguments about my lapses in religious practice, and I felt that he had appointed himself as protector of my spirituality. He would stand outside the bathroom waiting for me to finish so he could check if I was washing my hands in the appropriate way, and then following me around until I made the blessing that thanked God for my bowels working. I missed the calmness and closeness we had experienced together after Lily's birth.

Towards the end of my pregnancy Elly had divorced her husband and had been ostracised from the community. Isaac and Ben had both returned from abroad and were living a secular lifestyle. For the first time, all my siblings except Dalia were living in Melbourne, and we began to see more of each other, shedding our childhood trauma bonds and building our adult connections.

I was still twenty-three, and at times I yearned for a life of spontaneity. I lived vicariously through my siblings' stories of adventure, but Shua felt they were a bad influence. He told me he didn't want them visiting our house. I ignored him, inviting them over while he was at the synagogue and rushing them out before he came home.

Around the same time, Elly began dating a young man from the wider Jewish community. Several months into their relationship, she disclosed to him about Leifer. Elly knew what had happened wasn't right, but her boyfriend had to explain to her the extent of how wrong it was, and that what she had experienced was abuse. He gently encouraged her to go to the police.

I had never thought going to the police was an option. The religious therapist had referred me to the South Eastern Centre Against Sexual Assault, and I had begun seeing a sexual assault counsellor, Mary Mass, during my pregnancy. When Mary suggested going to the police, I had immediately shut her down. My job as an Adass woman was to forget and keep quiet. When Elly told me she had gone to the police, I ruminated over her decision and realised she had done the right thing, but I wasn't ready to do the same. I remembered how my disclosure to Chana Rabinowitz had shaken up the community, and I was scared. As these thoughts swirled within me, I began to question my religion. How could going to the police be the wrong thing? How could silence that allowed a predator to continue their abuse be the right thing?

The more I strayed from the religious path, the more insistent Shua became. I resented his assumption of authority. I had seen marriage as my ticket out of a controlling home, and I felt bitter towards Shua for what I saw as him trying to take my freedom. I was no longer a teenager; I was a mother, responsible for another life. For the first time, I decided that I would not allow someone else to hold my actions over me. I was sick of being told what to do and how to do it. I needed Shua to see me for who I was, not for who he felt I should be.

I was still breastfeeding Lily, and as the summer of 2010 dragged on, the nightmares and flashbacks that were triggered by breastfeeding got to the point where sleep was impossible. My mental health deteriorated further, and the decision to go to the police was tearing me apart. I began to wonder if life was worth living at all. The chasm between Shua and I grew. I withdrew emotionally from our relationship, and the further I drifted from Shua, the more I looked on the internet and outside of our marriage for the sense of adventure I was missing.

Shua's mother was insistent that I breastfeed until Lily was six months old, but despite wanting to give Lily the best start in life, I knew that having her mother alive was more important. I stopped breastfeeding when she was five months old and made the decision to return to work at Yesodei HaTorah College, hoping the space from Shua would save my mind and our marriage.

I remember standing in front of the mirror one morning before work, putting on a sheitel (wig) that Elly had passed on to me after her divorce. Since Elly had left the community, she had made the decision to stop wearing her wig. The sheitel was made of beautiful hair and flowed down to the middle of my back. It was the first sheitel I had that went past my shoulders, and Shua wasn't impressed.

'It's not modest,' he told me. I said that I was the one wearing the wig and that I believed it was fine. 'You can't change Jewish law to suit you,' Shua would respond. I knew Jewish law on wig lengths differed according to which rabbi you asked. 'It's modest enough for me. The decision to wear this is between me and God, not you and me,' I would say, and around and around we would go with no end to our disagreement.

I went back to therapy and the therapist recommended I write Shua a letter. I explained that I knew he loved me, but I needed to be loved in a different way. I needed his understanding and tolerance, not to be rebuked for the Jewish laws I was not keeping to his standards. Shua insisted that just as it was his duty to ensure I had the best care if I was physically ill, he must do everything in his power to fix me if I was spiritually ill. No matter how many times I asked him to allow my spirituality to be between myself and God, he could not do that. In his eyes, embracing a more liberal definition of Jewish law meant I was killing my very soul.

In desperation, Shua turned to his rabbi, who suggested he could ask for a p'sak – a ruling on how to proceed with our marriage from a renowned Gaon, a brilliant Jewish scholar overseas.

To ask for a p'sak is to present a rabbi with a question and then abide by the decision he makes, whether or not you agree with his advice.

Shua turned to the rabbi overseas and, knowing only our names and the fact that I was struggling with religion, the Gaon declared we should divorce.

I didn't want a divorce, I wanted understanding and empathy. I got neither.

I decided to call Shua's local rabbi in Melbourne and speak to him myself. Traditionally, the husband went to the rabbi on behalf of the wife, but I was determined to have this conversation myself.

When my sister Tamar and her husband had approached the same rabbi several months prior for some understanding on my behalf, explaining to him that I had been abused by Malka Leifer his response had been, 'What's the big deal? It was just a woman.' Knowing this, I didn't have a lot of hope, but I also knew that ultimately Shua would abide by his rabbi's advice. Besides, I had nothing to lose. My life was hanging in the balance.

'How can you advise Shua to ask a rabbi overseas, who knows nothing but our names, to make a life-altering decision?' I asked him. The rabbi was shocked by my question. 'This is a great rabbi who is very learned,' he told me. Raising my voice, I told him that no matter how much

Torah one learns, that doesn't give them the capacity to make vital decisions for two people across the world, based only on their names.

My audacity surprised me. I was rebelling against the male-dominated world I lived in without even understanding why I was so frustrated with it. I told Shua I refused to divorce just because some rabbi overseas told us to. At that point I wanted to fight to save our marriage, not give up on it. Shua agreed to stay, in the hope that fixing my mental health issues would also fix me.

The environment at home was acrimonious. We had arguments, not conversations. It didn't matter what I thought about Jewish law; there was a right and a wrong, and I was wrong. We both knew to keep our voices low and not argue in front of Lily. She was a bright baby, full of natural curiosity, and her giggles were the only moments of joy in our household.

Four months after birth, my period returned, and the discussion of birth control came up. I knew I was in no position to even think about another pregnancy, but we needed permission from the rabbi in order to use contraception. I asked Shua to speak to his rabbi, but he didn't agree that birth control was the way to go and refused to seek permission on my behalf. In that case, I told him, I would make it impossible for us to get pregnant again.

As the wife, it was my duty to provide Shua with intimacy. I had been taught in Kallah classes that ideally that should happen twice a week. Being intimate over Shabbat was an extra good deed that would be rewarded in the world to come, and it was suggested that the other night should be a Tuesday. I knew if I didn't go to the mikveh I would be breaching wifely duties, but not getting pregnant felt more important to me.

I had been at work for a month when I realised that putting on a fake face to the world was crushing me. Underneath the smile I presented to the staff at work, I was fighting a constant voice in my head that told me I shouldn't be alive, that I didn't deserve to live.

I didn't dare look into the bathroom mirror at work, frightened of the image that would stare back at me. I didn't recognise myself. Who was this woman who finally had the baby she had dreamed about and still couldn't push down the trauma that was overwhelming her?

One morning, I couldn't shut out the images of death. I could see scenes of my childhood, and felt a strong sense that I should not have survived. I raced around the school in an attempt to distract myself, but instead of heading towards the staffroom, I felt pulled towards the road, drawn by fantasies of jumping in front of a passing car.

I left work on a Monday morning and never returned. I knew there was no more ignoring it – I needed help. Esther booked me in to visit Shua's family GP, who put me on valium with the expectation I would see him every three days until I could see the psychiatrist he referred me to.

The next week was torture. Each morning when I got up, I had no idea if I would still be alive at the end of the day. Holding and playing with Lily was the only reason I got up every day. By the end of the week, I was able to see the psychiatrist, who determined that a hospital admission was necessary. Despite having top hospital cover, my insurance wouldn't cover it.

Again, I turned to the religious therapist for help. Days after Leifer had left the country, the school had sent out a letter to past students, promising to help cover the cost of therapy. The therapist wrote to Adass Israel School asking them to cover a two-week admission. The school refused.

I couldn't guarantee my safety. The idea of ending my life crowded my mind in every moment. I was meeting strangers I'd been chatting to on the internet hoping they would kill me. Shua was staying home from Kollel – not to look after Lily but to babysit me.

After another week of this hell, my father-in-law Henry paid for my admission into a psychiatric clinic. Two weeks before Passover, on 8 April 2011, I was admitted to the mother and baby unit in the Albert Road psychiatric clinic.

CHAPTER 14

Albert Road

The doors of the hospital opened, and I pushed Lily's pram inside. Shua walked beside us, lugging my suitcase. When I stepped inside the foyer, I had no idea that my life would never be the same again.

The entrance of the hospital was framed by several white columns and had six steps leading up to the reception desk. I looked around for the locked metal doors that I had pictured in my mind, the padded cells, but the office-like space with its beige and white colour scheme was nothing like my expectations. 'Your name?' the receptionist asked. 'Dassi,' I responded. She didn't hear me. I forced myself to say it louder: 'Dassi.'

I shifted my weight from one foot to another as I waited for her to find my name on the admission list. 'The intake coordinator will be right down,' she informed me. I stood beside the counter, unsure what to do. I straightened my top, my skirt, my wig, and then I straightened them again. When I noticed the receptionist watching me, I stuffed my hands into my pockets and clenched them around a tissue. Lily whined; she was teething and uncomfortable, and

I sighed with a mixture of worry and relief. I could hide behind the baby bag in search of a snack.

Moments later, the intake coordinator arrived and led us to a room behind the desk. I followed her in a haze. Shua provided most of the answers as she created my file, while Lily bounced on his knee. The intake coordinator took my pulse and blood pressure and then pulled out a camera. 'A picture for your medical file,' she explained to me, 'to ensure we are dispensing medication to the right person. Look up, face this way.' The camera flashed; I didn't smile. The whole idea of sitting in this box-like room being admitted into a psychiatric unit astounded me. Sweat covered my forehead, and under the table my leg wouldn't stop bouncing. I couldn't believe I was here.

When the therapist had first brought up the possibility of a mental health stay, I had baulked at the idea. Growing up, I had rarely heard the term 'mental illness', and on the few occasions I had, the words were spoken in hushed tones, clearly something to be ashamed of. I remember my mother speaking to the matchmaker about a potential match who had experienced mental illness. 'He'll never get married,' she told me. 'Not when everyone knows he takes medications every day.' I only knew enough to somehow believe he was to blame.

I imagined psychiatric hospitals as the insane asylums of the 1950s, full of people with lost minds needing help to find their sanity. Locked behind bars, force-fed medication until they were deemed safe to be part of society. I wasn't insane, I was fully cognisant; I just didn't see the point in being alive anymore. If I could not be a religious mother, I was better off dead.

My upbringing had left no room to consider that being a good mother meant more than my ability to teach our children religious values. My self-worth as Lily's mother was intrinsically tied to raising her as a religious Jewish girl. If I could not bring her up in the way God intended, she was better off without me.

As a teenager, I had participated in many fundraising drives for men and women around the world who were fighting for sole custody against a partner who had abandoned community ways. Now I was in the same position, contemplating doubts about my religion. When my psychiatrist reminded me that I couldn't kill myself because I had a daughter, I stayed silent. Although Jewish, he wasn't religious; I didn't expect him to understand.

It was late Friday afternoon when I was first shown to my room in the mother and baby ward. I studied the space I would occupy for the next two weeks. Non-opening windows looked out over St Kilda Road, and a cot stood against the window beside a double bed, dresser and change table. The shower in the bathroom had no curtain, and I later learnt that the strange shower head was designed to be suicide resistant.

Shua lifted my suitcase onto the bed, and I stood silently as the nurse went through my belongings. Each item of clothing was unfolded and refolded as the nurse searched for anything I could use to hurt myself. I was supposed to watch her do this, a sign of my consent, but I looked away when she got to my underwear, and gritted my teeth until it was over. The nurse handed me several forms to fill out and explained that the staff would need to note where I was every fifteen minutes. As per hospital policy, I was on quarter-hourly watch for the first forty-eight hours.

When she left the room, I began to unpack. Shabbat would start in less than an hour, which presented several difficulties. The electric doors at the entrance of the building could not be used, nor the lift that took us to the second-floor ward. We would not be able to warm our pre-packaged kosher meals, and without a Shabbat timer for the lights, they would need to stay either on or off for the next twenty-five hours.

Shua spoke to his rabbi and was told he could leave through the electric doors to attend a minyan if he followed someone out, and the nursing staff would unlock the fire escape at predetermined times. I spoke to Esther, and she raced to bring us some food that didn't need to be warmed.

At 6.30 p.m. I turned the lights on and off and murmured the Shabbat Blessing. With the bathroom light as our lamp, I watched the shadows lengthen over the bed and imagined the women in my community circling their hands over warm flames, ushering in a weekend of calm and tranquillity. There was no Shabbat atmosphere here; it felt wrong. The hospital had considered allowing us to light Shabbat candles, but ultimately decided their safety policy trumped our ritual. Shua's rabbi had reassured him that a light quickly turned on and off could be used in an emergency.

Shua spent twenty minutes working out which wall faced east, in the direction of Jerusalem, then stood in front of the back wall mouthing his evening prayers. He would walk the fifty minutes to his synagogue in the morning. I tiptoed around him, sorting Lily's clothes and setting up an inflatable mattress. As I had not been to the mikveh I was Niddah, so we were forbidden to touch one another or share a bed. The hospital allowed partners to spend the night, and Shua had chosen to stay the weekend.

Shua finished praying and we ate our meal on the floor. We didn't speak; there were no words for eating schnitzel over a towel on the floor, with the bathroom acting as our source of light. I was eager to finish and close my eyes. Although my family was with me, I felt alone, stranded in this strange alternate reality. While Shua settled Lily, I crawled around picking up breadcrumbs, desperate to ignore the horrors hiding in my mind.

Lily woke regularly through the night, and without electricity there was no way to warm a bottle. I waited for the nurse to check in so I could hint that having a microwave turned on would be useful. I couldn't ask them directly to desecrate Shabbat on my behalf, but if they understood what I needed, I wouldn't be sinning. I didn't care about sinning – I was struggling to find a reason to live, and the myriad of laws governing this day felt onerous – but Shua was there, and I wouldn't disrespect his space too. The nurses understood my convoluted hint and returned to my room with a warm bottle for Lily.

The next day passed slowly. The windows provided the only vent to the world outside our room. I stood with Lily in my arms, watching life as it passed us by. Although I was only six kilometres from home, I rarely left the block of streets that housed my community. Bustling St Kilda Road felt like another country. Lily was antsy. I played with her on the bed, the floor and then the bed again. I suggested opening the door and venturing beyond our ten square metres, but Shua wasn't comfortable because he didn't want me to mix with non-Jewish people on the holy day. When Lily napped, I hid under my blanket and counted the hours till the day of rest would end. When the sky turned dark and the three stars signalling the end of Shabbat appeared, I breathed a sigh of relief.

The next morning, I woke up with a start. All night, my mind had been trying to convince me that Shabbat in the clinic had been a dream. As I waited in line outside the medication room for my morning dose of antidepressants, I realised the nurses had stretched protocol the previous day by bringing my meds to my room. I appreciated their kindness in allowing me to acclimatise to this strange new world. The other patients, still in their pyjamas, joked with the staff. Fully dressed with a headscarf covering my hair, I felt completely out of place. I gulped down my medication and hurried back to the safety of my room.

I emerged late in the afternoon and met the other five women and their babies in the unit. On my request, Shua had packed his mattress and left. I needed time alone in a safe space to bond with Lily and deal with my trauma. Shua would spend time with Lily every day, picking her up after the morning program ended at midday, and dropping her back before the afternoon program began at four.

I spent the first week adjusting to living in a space separate to my community. Once I was allowed out of the unit unsupervised, I enjoyed walking around the nearby Albert Park Lake. While the sun rose, I would push Lily on the swing and delight in her giggles as the swans paraded around the pram, trying to steal the crumbs she had left behind. I was shy and confused around the other mums – sometimes it felt like we were speaking a different language – so that hour alone with Lily was the highlight of my mornings.

Speaking with those five families was the first time I had glimpsed life outside the Adass community, and it was their first time conversing with a religious Jew. I had grown up surrounded by people who acted and behaved like I did. I would catch the other women staring at my head covering, too shy to ask, but once they understood I was happy to answer their questions, they bombarded me. I explained that my hair was only for my husband, but when I changed into a wig, they looked at me confused. Their curiosity paved the way to friendship, but also opened my eyes to the way others lived.

Behind the smile I presented to the staff and the other mums, I was hounded by thoughts about giving up on life. I would look into Lily's eyes and imagine her growing up without a mother and immediately feel guilty. The struggle between life and death was overwhelming, and I dissociated to numb the feelings. It was easier to make plans to die when I didn't care about anything.

When Shua asked if I was abiding by Halacha (Jewish rules), I would steer the discussion elsewhere. I didn't want to hurt him. My first taste of non-kosher food – an Arnott's biscuit – had passed as a non-event; even the fear of God's punishment didn't evoke feelings. I kept this a secret from Shua. Why did the present matter if I didn't have a future? Every day that passed, it was harder to keep up the facade of a pious woman. Rituals began to slip further.

During my second week, two women from the Adass community were admitted into the ward. I was shocked to learn that they had both suffered from mental health issues for many years, and this was not their first time in a psychiatric hospital. With gossip such a strong part of the community, it surprised me that I had never heard about them. The women asked that I warn them before my family came to visit so they could hide in their room, terrified that news of their admission would make it back to friends and family.

I decided it was time to demystify mental health in my community. While in Israel I had learnt about Facebook and had set up a private account to stay in contact with Dalia overseas. My friend list had grown with Elly, Isaac and Ben's contacts now that they had left the community. I posted a picture of my room, tagging Albert Road Clinic. I knew the information would make its way back to Adass and it did, fairly quickly. I felt little for anything, but that small act of rebellion tasted sweet.

As an unexpected benefit of this exposure, I was added to the list of community members in hospital, and each morning a box of pastries from the kosher bakery was delivered to my ward. Although I had started eating non-kosher, I still primarily ate the packaged, plane-style kosher food that the hospital offered, so these fresh treats were a welcome addition to our limited diet.

One evening I sat in the playroom when another mum's partner entered the room. I felt awkward about sharing a space with an unrelated male so I stood to leave, but the mums convinced me to stay. Half an hour later, I was sitting on the couch having what would have appeared to most people to be a normal conversation, except the entire experience was far outside my norm. When the man found out I didn't know a thing about football, he spent half an hour trying to make me understand. I still didn't get it. *Don't be weird*, I kept telling myself, *speak like you would to any other acquaintance*. It was my first casual conversation with a man who was not my husband.

Afterwards, I went to my room and stared in the mirror. I saw the way I appeared to the mums: headscarf on my head, skirt covering my knees, thick tights and a modest top. The way I dressed no longer reflected the way I behaved. I had been brought up with a presumption of superiority, told that non-Jewish people were drunks and drug addicts needing something to fill their empty lives. But here, all I saw were mums – loving, kind and honest, struggling like me. The us versus them mentality was beginning to recede.

I tore off the headscarf I was wearing as an alternative to a wig and studied the woman looking back at me. My thoughts were almost crushing in their intensity. Did this feel more like me? Would my marriage survive if I went wig free? Did covering my hair really make me a better person? I contemplated this for several minutes, exploring the idea that everything I had been brought up with wasn't as absolute as I believed. Questioning my beliefs brought a strong sense of danger, but instead of feeling scared, I felt an eagerness to push it further.

I went to walk out of my room, but just before I opened the door I turned and pulled my headscarf back on. The risk was too great; the two religious women might tell their husbands and then Shua would find out. I would need to find less obvious ways to experiment with this idea that there could be flexibility with my beliefs.

The mums gently teased me about my lack of general knowledge. One of them, Georgia, became a lifelong friend, and to this day still laughs about my ignorance of Australian culture. Not only did the mums help me create a bucket list of experiences I must try, they also helped me tick off several firsts.

I remember the shocked face of one mum when she learnt I had never tasted fast food. We sat on the floor in the lounge, and she spoke about McDonald's as though my life would be transformed if I only tasted my first burger. It was almost midnight; the rest of the mums were sleeping, and I didn't need to worry about anyone else watching. I was curious, and not just about the burger. The little girl inside me was excited to experience food from a drive-through.

Across the road from the hospital the golden arches gleamed enticingly, and despite curfew, the mum was determined to make her way across. Dressed in her pyjamas and carrying a cigarette to avoid arousing suspicion, she snuck past the nurses and out the front door. Twenty minutes later she returned, and with a glint in her eyes handed me a small burger wrapped in paper.

As I held the package, my heart beat a little faster. Non-kosher biscuits or cereal could almost be justified, but non-kosher meat was taking sinning to another level. I crossed my legs, sat upright and carefully unwrapped the burger. The mum sat down next to me, wanting to see my face as I took my first bite. I don't know what I was expecting, but the burger was cold and disgusting, and I had to stop myself from spitting it out. I choked it down and we laughed at her audacity. I didn't have the heart to tell her it was one of the driest things I had ever tasted.

Time in hospital settled into a routine. Pesach was approaching but, still struggling with self-harm and suicidal urges, I wasn't ready to leave. I felt overwhelmed with the idea of needing to prepare my house for Pesach, to cover my kitchen and cook the traditional foods. I was beginning to question if I could ever see myself going home again.

Because foods with chametz (leavening agents) are forbidden on Passover, living in a space that housed them presented a problem. Shua discussed this with his rabbi, and it was ruled that I was permitted to stay in the hospital as long as my room was chametz-free. Armed with a flashlight on Pesach eve, Shua inspected every corner of the bedroom and bathroom and then drove us to Tamar's house for the seder – the traditional meal of the first night of Passover. The hospital gave me an exemption to attend, provided I was back before morning.

Tamar's house was bustling with family – religious or not, my sister and her husband invited all the siblings to celebrate together. I loved being together with all my siblings. A long table covered in white was set with all our seder needs, and a plate with the six symbolic foods sat at the head. I settled Lily in my niece's bedroom, and we sat down to begin the traditional meal.

As I was pouring the first of the four cups of wine, I noticed that some had dripped on the tablecloth, and I excused myself to grab a dishcloth. As I was dancing back to the table, I felt compelled by a strange sense to still myself at the entrance of the room. For several minutes I stood by the door and watched my family. I saw my brother-in-law raise his cup for a blessing, and my nieces and nephews following along with their picture Haggadahs. Around the table my siblings answered Amen. The person I was here, back in the thick of religious observance, would have slaved over the kitchen cooking Pesach foods all week, just as my sister had done. The Dassi I was that morning had walked around the lake, oblivious to the pressures of the holiday. That Dassi had felt free. Which version was me? I brushed aside the thought; it was too risky to entertain.

The seder finished at 1.30 a.m. and I walked back to the hospital with Shua. The halls in the clinic were devoid of life; a stark difference to the world I had left behind. I crawled into bed and forced my mind to quiet, but all night I tossed with life-altering deliberations. In the early hours of the morning, I realised the truth: God had put me in hospital to test my devotion and I was failing.

When the two religious women in the hospital invited me to join them for the second Pesach seder the next evening, I was grateful for the chance to pass God's test and observe His will away from the community. But paper plates on a laminated tabletop didn't lend themselves to a holiday atmosphere, and I struggled to stay present with my observance. Again, for another night I tossed with questions and couldn't sleep.

The second morning of Pesach dawned, and I groggily made my way to the kitchen to prepare a bottle for Lily. One of the mums had just made breakfast, and the room smelt of coffee and toast. I stared at the toaster and the loaf of bread beside it; that multigrain rye could be the answer to all my problems. One bite of bread would mean the punishment of Kareth – the extinction of one's soul and the denial of a share in the world to come. At school, I had been taught that God tested Jewish people by putting them through suffering in order to reward us in the world to come. If I no longer had a soul, God would not care enough to test me.

I got up from the table and walked slowly to the counter. I was being tested a lot; according to my understanding of God, He cared too much. I was in hospital, suicidal, self-harming and struggling with whether I should talk to the police. I picked up the loaf of bread and held it, weighing the choice I was about to make. One piece of bread meant an immediate disbarment of my soul; maybe I would no longer be worthy of God's 'merciful' punishments. Very carefully, I undid the clip on the bread bag and took out a slice. Immediately, I dropped it onto the benchtop. With my heart racing, I picked it up again. *Am I really going to do this?* I thought to myself. *Will a dying soul be painful?*

I dared myself to take a bite, and as my shaking hands lifted the bread to my mouth I knew there was no turning back. That one bite stuck in my throat while I hurriedly hid the rest of the piece in the bin, astounded by my actions. I leant against the counter and waited. I don't know what I was expecting – perhaps a miraculous lifting of my depression now that God no longer cared enough to test me, or a sudden strike of lightning that would instantly kill me – but there was nothing. I felt exactly the same as I had twenty minutes earlier.

I didn't tell the other religious women what I had done. I was embarrassed and discouraged. But when I look back, I realise that piece of bread marked the beginning of a journey for me. Only a few days later, I decided it was time to talk to the police.

CHAPTER 15

Self-harm

I sat in a sterile interview room at Moorabbin police station, in Melbourne's southeastern suburbs. 'Please start,' the policewoman told me.

'My name is Dassi,' I said, then stopped. I could feel panic pulsating in my throat. What did I say next? It felt like the lessons of my childhood had strangled my voice. I took a breath, calmed myself and thought, *If my younger sister had the courage to speak out, I can do it too.*

'She touched me down there,' I said. My words sounded foreign to me. I couldn't believe they were coming out of my mouth.

The police officer looked up and asked me, 'Did you mean your vagina?'

I silently nodded, and a red flush coloured my face. I knew I needed to use the correct term. I said the word slowly: 'v a g i n a'.

I felt vulgar and crude uttering the word out loud. I breathed deeply and reminded myself why I was doing this. I was a 23-year-old new mother living in a psychiatric hospital because of this abuse. I needed my life to be more than a perpetual struggle against my abusive past. I would not allow Leifer to hurt anyone else. I must speak up.

Detective Danielle Newton was patient in the face of my discomfort. She focused on the computer screen and typed as I spoke. I wondered how she was making sense of my disjointed disclosures. I looked around the room in search of distraction, but there was none to be found in the small space. A computer, a desk, two chairs, the police officer and me. The walls were white and empty, and a lone light bulb cast shadows across the room. A window opened into a long quiet hallway; there was no natural light.

Detective Newton shifted, seemingly trying to get comfortable on the hard office chair. She was visibly pregnant. Her first child, she informed me. I imagined her as the epitome of normality and success. A powerful career, a stable marriage, approaching motherhood with unbridled excitement. A perfect life in a home with a white picket fence. I envied her; she was everything I was not.

Against my will, I returned to the space I struggled every day to evade, and my head filled with pictures of Leifer's abuse. I heard my breath quicken and felt powerless to stop it overwhelming me. The police officer interjected, and her voice reeled me back to the present.

'Start at the beginning,' she requested.

'Where was the beginning?' I wondered aloud.

'Your history, please,' she prompted.

And so, I began my story.

As I spoke, I could hear my stilted sentences, and the fear behind them. Leifer's image crowded my mind. My father had touched me, my mother had hurt me. I had thought Mrs Leifer would save me. I had loved and trusted her, but she had betrayed me too. I still couldn't make sense of that betrayal. Could my broken words bring justice to the warped world she had created?

The police officer was gentle with me. 'Tell me about your community,' she suggested, and I launched into a lengthy explanation.

I watched the detective's reaction as I spoke. Her face mirrored the perplexity I'd seen at the psychiatric clinic when I'd tried to explain the community to other patients. I fidgeted with my wedding ring and struggled to control my anxiety. I must persist with this.

'Mrs Leifer,' I began.

The officer interrupted, asking me to be clear about who I was referring to.

'Malka Leifer,' I stuttered. Even now it felt uncomfortable discarding her title, as though somehow it discredited her power. The same power she had used to abuse me.

I looked closely at the police officer's face, attempting to read her. Did she think I was foolish for believing in Leifer's love? My therapist told me I wasn't to blame, but I was filled with disgust at my own stupidity.

After two hours I broke down, overwhelmed and devoid of words. The police officer was sympathetic, and we scheduled another time to meet.

Shua picked me up and I returned to the clinic. We didn't speak in the car; there was nothing to say. He dropped me off and drove away. The nurses asked me how I was, but I could only think of one thing. As soon as I could, I fled to my room and groped at the plumbing beneath the sink. My secret was tucked somewhere between those pipes, and I was desperate to get to it. Every nerve in my body was on high alert, my ears straining for the sound of potential disturbance.

The tread of a staff member patrolling the hall drew near, and a nurse's voice came through the door, gently inquiring about my state of mind. Clinic policy required staff to note my position every half hour. 'Breathe,' I reminded myself. I needed to contain the adrenaline surging through me. 'Just jumping in for a quick shower,' I yelled out, and I turned the water on to mask my fear of being found out. The nurse, apparently accepting my comment at face value, moved away.

My hands found what they were seeking. My eyes fixed on the razor in my palm, and I shifted the blade, watching it gleam as it caught the bathroom light. Exhilaration flooded me, immersing my body in a whirl of euphoria. My anxiety was pushed into the remote corners of my mind and forgotten. I felt guilty like a disobedient child, coupled with a pride in my deception at smuggling the blade inside. Secrecy was a crucial part of this scene.

All day, the demons in my head had been baying for my blood. Now, they relaxed, anticipating their red reward.

Sharps were prohibited in the mother and baby clinic. One could earn the privilege by showing staff they could be trusted with the razors, but I had not earned that privilege. Quite the opposite – I had self-harmed two days ago, and my hiding place had been found. But I had figured out a new place to hide my blades. Initially, I had no intention of using them; the comfort lay purely in their presence. Without them, I felt adrift in a world of pain, filled with shame and self-blame for Leifer's abuse, robbed of my only potential coping mechanism.

During Lily's waking hours, I suppressed my gnawing anxiety. Caring for my daughter, feeding her, bathing her, giggling at her charm. I played the lead role in a show of sanity, performing for an audience of one. But as bedtime drew near, the demons grew louder. The medication could no longer hold them, and I was on the maximum dose.

The wail of a nearby patient punctuated my thoughts, and I began to worry about the passage of time. Prolonged periods of seclusion would raise suspicion among the staff. I needed to move. I tucked the blade into my sleeve, snug against my skin.

Titanic was playing on the TV in the lounge. The previous week, the other mums had initiated 'movie nights', intrigued by my ignorance of the cinematic world. I was being given an education on the classics.

The frivolous banter as we watched the film belied our surroundings and the inner struggles we all faced. By all appearances, we were a circle of mums sharing laughter while our children slept.

All evening, my fingers obsessively skimmed the blade in my sleeve. The sensation brought relief, but my mind silently berated me. I was there, in hospital, for help. *Take advantage of the coping mechanisms you are learning*, my mind urged me.

The therapeutic groups I attended each day coached me to find solace from overwhelming emotion elsewhere. In my mind, I revised the steps: seek support, engage distraction, readjust my focus. It appeared simple. I intended to follow those steps – soon. Later. Communicating with the nurses meant confessing to the secret in my sleeve, and I wasn't ready for that. Not yet.

My body heaved against its physical constraints, frustrated with the struggle to repress the anxiety I had battled for months. I searched for a nurse, and she suggested a PRN – medication dispensed on an as-needed basis. The doctor had prescribed Seroquel, used at low doses to alleviate agitation, but my chart revealed that the day's limit had already been reached. My treating psychiatrist was contacted, and he authorised an additional dose. I sat as directed, within eyesight of the staff, aching for a drug-induced peace. On the table, adult colouring books offered an exercise in mindfulness.

The poise promised by the medication betrayed me. I was so tired of fighting myself. I needed to find effective distraction. I went to my room and turned on my computer – perhaps I could write these feelings out. Moments later I found myself searching for support online, and discovered a world where my cravings were shared by many. On these forums, I wasn't crazy. The other users didn't know me, but they also didn't judge me. The internet normalised my urges and enchanted my obsessions. 'It is YOUR body, YOUR choice,' they shouted on the self-harm chat groups, and I agreed. I was in control. I would do whatever I chose. It was MY body.

I now had justification for abandoning hospital rules. *My body, my decision*, played repetitively in my mind, inciting me to act. I crept into the bedroom through a cracked door to shield my sleeping daughter from the light and noise in the hall. As I tiptoed towards the bathroom, my ears picked up her snores. The gentle noise immediately soothed my panic, and I moved towards her cot. As I watched Lily's chest rise and fall, my breathing slowed to match her peaceful rhythm. Part of me wished she would wake – feeding, cuddling and resettling her were all powerful adversaries of the noise clogging my head.

I slipped into the bathroom. 'Only one minute,' I told myself. 'A last moment of choice before relinquishing my blades to the nurse.'

I unwrapped the blades and discovered empowerment. Tranquillity fell over me; this was the magic I needed. The psychiatrist had suggested I snap a rubber band against my wrist, but he didn't understand: it wasn't the pain I craved, it was the power.

I slid a blade over my skin and my nerves jumped to attention. Blood pulsated through my arm, drawn towards the friction. My body felt so alive. I brushed again, soft with the sharp edge. The blade went up and down, tracing old scars. Tiny spots of blood appeared, and I quickly wiped them away. A bliss unlike any other filled me. This was control. This was choice. This was me. I told myself this was enough, and it was time to stop, but delusion captivated me.

Crimson warmth flowed down my arm and pooled on the shower floor beneath me. I tracked the stream to an alien wound splitting the skin above my elbow, and was transfixed by the intensity of colour. Although I saw mutilation, I did not imagine it as mine. When did this happen? How did it happen? This could not be my doing. I felt nothing. The moment had passed quietly, without me.

I revelled in the dissociation and floated above my body, watching the blood run down an arm that wasn't mine. I was merely a spectator in this play of violence. I existed beyond reality. I felt safe in this world, isolated and untouchable.

The peace survived another minute before truth began to tug at me. I fought gravity, clinging to my weightless freedom. I needed to remain adrift and invisible. But panic and guilt dragged me back to the present. I slowly took in my actions, and the cycle of self-hatred was instantly set in motion.

I looked around the bathroom, absorbing the wreckage of my inner struggle, and admonished myself. *Look at yourself, Dassi, the stupidity you created. What have you done?* I didn't want to accept responsibility.

I did this?

I did this. Shock seized my body; this horror was a part of me.

The wound throbbed, and self-loathing swelled to feed the sting. I was stupid, so stupid. I deserved misery, punishment, pain.

I washed away the blood, desperate to obliterate this vileness that seeped from me, but the flow was stubborn and wouldn't stop. I needed medical attention; this one was impossible to hide.

I left my sanctuary to seek help. I felt small and vulnerable in the halls. The sound of approaching footsteps broke through my shame. I didn't have words for the nurse, but he didn't need any; self-harm painted my sleeve. I understood that transgressions like this generated additional paperwork, and I accepted his sigh of disapproval. We moved into a sterilised space; the white walls highlighted the shame that coloured my face.

The routine was familiar. Self-harm required photographs and measurements preceding treatment. In my mind's eye I saw the psychiatrist receiving my report, saw his disappointment. My body distorted with contempt for my existence. I lowered my eyes, unable to stomach my reflection in the nurse's gaze. I was a portrait of disgrace.

The nurse was silent as he prepared a trauma kit and unwrapped the wound. I felt nauseated on his behalf, unworthy of gentle touch. He peered up at me, a strange look, not the usual reaction, then disappeared, returning with the unit manager. Her face presented a similar worry.

The two staff members spoke above me. I understood that stitches were necessary, and the clinic was not authorised to provide such treatment. The nurse informed me that I would need a transfer to the Alfred Hospital and asked of my history there. I told him this was the first time I had cut deep enough to need stitches.

It was 8.30 p.m. In my room, Lily slept, unaware of the

commotion her mother was causing. Hospital transfers were tedious to arrange, and a non-fatal injury would delay the service by hours. Family provided an alternative, so the staff called my siblings for a chaperone, as I was not trusted alone. Elly arrived and the staff entrusted me to her care. The nurses promised to look after Lily until I returned. Elly drove me to the Emergency Department while my humiliation reached new heights. All this turmoil for one moment. I wished I could turn back time.

The clock moved slowly in the waiting room. The chairs held no comfort, and their rigidity exacerbated the night's crawl. Hours passed under harsh lights and the constant whine of wheels and hectic steps. Every so often, Elly contacted the clinic to report an update. She was patient with me, despite having to attend work early the next morning. Conversation distracted us, and I told her why we were there. As siblings, all seven of us shared an incredible bond, built through trauma and against forces intent on breaking us. I felt safe with Elly.

At 4 a.m. my sister escorted me back into psychiatric care following my treatment. The night staff checked the doctor's work. I hurried towards solitude, desperate for sleep, but in the dark of my room, the demons in my head confronted me. I hid under my bed sheets and begged for privacy. The voices circled my head. *You're a failure, a bad mother, Lily deserves better.* I prayed for the local anaesthetic to fade; I needed pain. Pain brought focus; pain controlled the never-ending noise. The calls to self-harm again crowded any hope of peace, but guilt prevented a repeat of the night's events.

Lily woke as the sun rose and my show of sanity began. A late therapy session earned me 'the talk' from my treating psychiatrist. He too had been affected by my situation, with late-night calls and updates. He warned me that another incident would earn me a transfer to a public psychiatric unit as a non-voluntary patient. Private care only provided a place for those who desired help. I had heard the horror stories, and I knew the threat was real. I nodded my head, agreeing with him. Next time, I promised to ask for help. There in that room with him, I had the strength to silence the doubts in my head.

I continued to struggle with self-harm throughout my admission. Giving my police statement had brought up overwhelming feelings I didn't yet know how to process.

I continued disclosing to the police to complete the first of six statements. I wrote the parts I could not verbalise. As I signed each page of the fourteen-page report, I knew that my story was no longer mine to control. I tamped down the growing fear inside me. I had survived the abuse; I would survive this too. There was no turning back now.

I placed my trust in Detective Danielle Newton and the Moorabbin sexual offences and child abuse investigation team. I hoped the Australian criminal justice system could make sure Malka Leifer would never hurt anyone else. I had done what I could; it was out of my hands. Now I had to face the consequences.

CHAPTER 16

Jewish divorce

A stuffy room in the back of a building and six men dressed in suits. Black jackets, pants, and trench coats made of silk, with white socks of cotton pulled up over the cuffs. Outside, the sun had skipped over the synagogue windows and left the room to its sombre mission. It was 23 November 2011. Three rabbis sat at the table, along with two witnesses and a scribe. The fees had been paid, documents prepared and my Jewish divorce was underway.

I stood alone in that room of men beside a man who no longer felt like home. My knees were shaking, and I could hear my heartbeat in my ears. *Are you also wondering how we got here, Shua?* My mind turned over the decisions of the past year, trying to identify which one had pivoted our future onto this course.

Six months earlier, I was a married woman completing my first admission in the Albert Park psychiatric clinic. After five weeks, I had left the mother and baby unit feeling like a different woman. A new bond with my daughter had been woven through the emotional detachment that had blanketed my life since childhood. I could feel my love for her radiating through me, and the chaos that had once engulfed my inner world had finally dispersed. I was now armed with a range of coping mechanisms that didn't involve harming myself.

Shua had supported my decision to report Malka Leifer, but having grown up outside Adass, he struggled to understand the secrecy that governed our community, and why the burden of that silence challenged my confidence in our way of life. We still argued often about religious practice. My psychiatrist referred us to a marriage therapist, but those sessions only served to highlight our fundamentally different world views. Neither of us could see a way forward.

One afternoon towards the end of my admission, Shua picked Lily up for a few hours. While they were gone, I sat on the floor and imagined packing up my clothes, Lily's toys, her favourite blanket, and returning home. There was a heaviness in my chest. I didn't want to pretend to care about religious practice in order to keep the peace. I wasn't ready to go home, but I no longer needed the safety the hospital provided. When Shua returned, I sat him down to talk about our future.

Later that evening I met with my psychiatrist to discuss discharge planning. 'I spoke to Shua earlier today and we have decided to trial a separation,' I told the doctor. The words spooled out slowly, as though they had only become real now that I'd spoken them aloud. I watched the doctor for his reaction and his face looked uneasy.

'Will Shua move in with one of his parents?' the psychiatrist asked. Although he was Jewish, he was not religious, and lived in a different world to the one I lived in. Shua moving into one of his parents' houses so I could return home with Lily had never been discussed. The separation was my fault. Finding somewhere to live was my responsibility.

'Until you find a place, there is no discharge plan, Dassi. I cannot release you without a fixed address.' His eyes searched mine, gauging the impact of his words, but there in the hospital I was warm, sheltered and fed. It was hard to confront the notion of not having a home. The decision to separate had felt right, but I hadn't considered what would happen next.

I watched him walk out of the room, folder in hand with my discharge papers stacked on top. There was a big red line across the box labelled 'homeless'.

Homeless, I thought to myself as I lay on the bed. *I am homeless.* The thought was simultaneously captivating and terrifying. Freeing and overwhelming. I reached for my phone. *I can call Shua and tell him it was all a mistake*, I told myself. *Homeless. I'm not homeless.* I pressed his name but put the phone down before connecting the call. I knew I wasn't making a mistake.

I rolled onto my side and looked around the room. Everything I now owned could fit into the single suitcase standing against the window. I had no money – Shua regulated our finances, and the bank accounts were in his name. *He probably knows I can't do this.*

Later, I sat beside Lily's cot, staring at her little fingers curled against her chest. 'Am I doing the right thing?' I asked myself aloud. I wondered about the impact my decision would have on Lily. In sixteen years, would the matchmakers look at her and see my mistakes? Lily's marriageable self was always in my view. That was the way I had been seen all my childhood, and it never occurred to me to look at my daughter in any other way.

I took a deep breath. 'I'm doing the right thing,' I whispered to her. 'I'm doing the right thing. I promise to give you a world where reporting abuse isn't punished but encouraged.'

Later that evening I sat with the mums in the lounge and told them about the separation. They could see the way my face creased and the fear in my eyes. One mum promised to reach out to a Jewish friend of hers to see if she could help. The next morning she bounced over to me with a note in her hand and handed it to me. There was a mobile number written on the paper. 'Rachel is happy for you to call her,' she told me.

I waited for Shua to pick Lily up. Now that we had decided to separate, there seemed to be a wall between us. We couldn't look each other in the eyes, and we exchanged the barest number of words to communicate how Lily was tracking. I kissed my daughter goodbye and escaped to my room. I had several hours alone and intended to spend the time finding a place to live.

First on the list – calling Rachel. My jaw dropped when she told me that she too had grown up around the Adass community. I listened to her journey of moving away from ultra-Orthodoxy and concentrated on the wealth of knowledge she shared, including how to direct parenting payments from the Australian Government into a bank account of my own.

It was my first conversation with a woman who had left the community. Her confidence gave rise to mine. *If she could make it, I can too.* Growing up, I had never heard of her. I could think of only two such names that had been passed around my friends in hushed tones, knowing we were not supposed to speak about these taboo individuals. I wondered how many more Rachels had been hidden from us.

With the promise of some parenting funds to come, I asked my nurse if we could sit down for a chat about finding a place to live. I didn't know where to start. The nurse suggested a couple of websites to look at, but everything but shared houses were beyond my budget. The parenting payment was around $350 a week, and I needed that to cover rent, nappies, formula and food. The shared houses didn't look like the right place for a nine-month-old baby. I had no idea where I was going to go.

Elly, Isaac and Ben lived together and I knew if I was desperate I could sleep there, but they were young and carefree, and every night their friends gathered at their house for dinner and drinks. It was no place to put a fretting baby to sleep. Tamar and Nicole could offer me a couch, but they both lived in small apartments with four little kids each. That wasn't a feasible solution either.

Looking back, I wonder why I didn't ask Shua's father Henry and his wife Marilyn for help, or Henry's sister Freda and her partner Peter. I'd had very little to do with my father-in-law, his wife or sister during our marriage; they were not religious, and our worlds didn't mix. I had seen Henry and Marilyn occasionally with Shua, but I hadn't seen Freda since she attended our wedding.

But during my hospitalisation Henry, Marilyn, Freda and Peter all visited me regularly, and I built a relationship with them independently from Shua. They were beautiful people who supported my decision to go to the police. Henry, who had once worked as a lawyer, had encouraged me to speak to a friend of his about taking out a case against Adass Israel School, but I wasn't ready to hear it. The shame was still too overwhelming.

My relationship with Henry and Marilyn was incredibly supportive, but it was still new, so it never occurred to me to seek their help. I had always been taught not to take up space, punished for being a burden on my parents. I was terrified of being too much, and asking for help felt like placing a burden upon them that wasn't theirs to carry.

Elly had left the Adass community two years prior and formed a new group of friends made up mostly of young adults who had left other Jewish religious communities. One was another single mother with a two-year-old daughter, and she agreed to rent me half a bedroom on a temporary basis. Lily and I would share her bedroom, as her daughter had the other room. It was enough to take back to the psychiatrist and resume discharge planning.

With the promise of a place to transition out of inpatient care, my psychiatrist signed me up to a dialectical behaviour therapy (DBT) program at the hospital, which ran twice a week. The program would continue to teach me how to understand my triggers for self-harming, and to change my behaviour so I could engage in less destructive coping mechanisms. I would continue seeing my psychiatrist as an outpatient once a fortnight, and would also visit the marriage therapist with Shua.

I left the hospital unrecognisable from the woman who had gone in. The world looked different beyond those glass doors. Excitement and fear lurked around every corner; there was a void of possibility where one had never existed before. The certainty about how to live had been smashed apart, and now life was open to interpretation.

The impact of moving apart from the community and my marriage still hadn't hit me. I hadn't given up on the idea of living with Shua. I lived in the rented half bedroom separated from him but we both continued to see our marriage therapist. I was still hoping we could find a way to stay together for our daughter's sake. My fear of the big world beyond our community also pushed me to continue trying, despite knowing that unless I could be the wife he'd been promised, it wasn't going to work.

Alongside the DBT program and seeing my psychiatrist,

I also continued seeing my religious therapist. With his help, I wrote to Shua asking what he would need from me in order to stay married. I noted down everything that he wanted. It made me think there was no future for us. Shua would never accept that my relationship with religion was mine, not his.

If I wanted to make our marriage work I was told I needed to modify my behaviour and appearance. He made it clear there was a lot that had to change, and the following were just some of what I needed to do:

- I had to make my blessings over food in a loud voice so others would easily hear them.
- I had to wear a skirt long enough so both my knees stayed covered no matter what I was doing. The skirt could not have a split.
- I had to make sure the neckline of my clothing was above my collarbone, and that it closed all around my neck so I was completely covered by clothing.
- I could only wear a sheitel (wig) that was clearly a sheitel, and I should never cover the fringe.
- My tights could not be transparent so you could see my legs.
- I couldn't wear make-up or clothing that was colourful or eye-catching in any way.
- I could not wear nail polish.
- I had to make sure I was always covered if I was in front of Shua while Niddah.
- I couldn't socialise with men or go to bars, clubs or non-kosher restaurants and could only attend religious gatherings and not parties.
- I had to only take prescribed drugs and could never drink to excess.

- I couldn't accept food from anyone who was not Jewish but even then they had to be religious, even if the food was kosher.
- I had to always maintain the Adass modesty standards and I couldn't associate with women who did not do the same.
- I had to limit the TV shows I watched and the non-Jewish music I listened to, but I was told I should work towards cutting this out completely.
- I had to monitor what I read and not read commercial novels, especially romance.
- I had to make sure I prepared dinner every night, and lunch as well if I could.
- It was my responsibility to make sure the house was clean and tidy.
- I had a curfew of 11 p.m. unless my husband gave me permission to be out later.
- I had to agree to have more children and not use contraceptives.
- I had to tell my husband everything, allow him access to my emails and phone and never talk about private matters without approval from him beforehand.

Shua's demands were extensive but despite my fears that our future together was over, I was willing to try one more thing. Our therapist recommended that we try to live together for a few days to see how it went.

Late Friday afternoon before Shabbat, I moved back into our family home. I cooked the Shabbat meals like I always had, then watched as Shua settled Lily, and said goodbye when he left for evening prayer.

I sat on the couch and for a second, I let myself believe that I had made it, that I was home. The past few months had been a dream, a step away from my reality; this was where I should be. Together, we would put the trauma of the past year behind us. I would find the joy in religion again and we would move forward together, as the religious couple and parents we were supposed to be.

But by Saturday morning the dream began to fall apart. Without access to my phone, I had no lifeline out of this world, and I was feeling very trapped.

I remember sitting on the floor of our bedroom with Shua, backs against our beds, separated, as I had not gone to the mikveh, and talking about our marriage.

It was a civil conversation. There was still the memory of the love we had for one another, but we could both see that there was no use pushing.

'I can't live a religious life, Shua, not like this, but I don't want Lily to have divorced parents.'

'I can't be married to a non-religious woman.'

'I won't drop religion, I'll just follow a different, more Modern Orthodox practice.'

'I need a wife who abides by the rules of this community and sees the world the same way I do.'

'I understand.'

And that was it, that was the end of our marriage. We sat apart until the sky turned dark, and then I left our house for the last time.

I went back into the world, back into my rented half-bedroom in St Kilda, weighed down by the realisation that my marriage was over. Whether I was ready or not, I would need to forge my own path now. The weight of the decision felt heavier; I could no longer trick myself into believing this was a game. There was no normal to fall back on.

Several weeks later, my housing situation fell apart and I was readmitted into hospital with a resurgence of self-harm and suicidal ideation. I had been drunk on the idea of freedom and wanted to try everything that was on offer. I didn't know about dating and couldn't understand the danger that online dating could bring. My vulnerability, my childhood and the ongoing trauma from Leifer's abuse meant deep down I believed I was born to be abused.

The men I met were sometimes decades older than me and many saw my naivety as a weakness and too often played out the patterns of my abusive childhood. Somehow, somewhere, in my fantasies turned real, I believed I would find my redemption.

This time when they hurt me, I was bigger. I could show myself that I could take it, that it wouldn't destroy me. But it did destroy me – in ways that I would not understand for another decade.

This time when they hurt me, I had the ability to run, but I never ran.

Not hurting never occurred to me.

I remember the shock I experienced one therapy session when I explained that these men weren't abusing me, they were only abusing my body, and my therapist looked at me strangely and then explained that I *was* my body. It's still something I struggle to understand.

The abuse I had suffered during my childhood had taught me to separate from my body, to believe it was not mine, in order to survive.

There had never been boundaries. My body had always belonged to someone else; boundaries didn't exist.

It would take me years to be aware of boundaries, to understand them, and then many more years to recognise that I had the right to enforce them.

As I write this now, I cry for the woman who was once in hospital, escaping the men who were so eager to mistreat her. The woman who didn't think care and affection were possible, and was unable to imagine what a healthy relationship might look like.

* * *

The six weeks of my second hospitalisation passed quickly. I used the resources there to find a new place to live with a Chabad family who were happy to rent me a room, and Shua and I worked with a rabbi to iron out a parenting plan. It was like I had an internal switch – when I was with Lily, her needs were all that mattered, and I belonged solely to the role of mother. When Lily was with Shua, I belonged to everyone else.

Dissociation allowed me to live two completely different lives, and the people who saw me in one life had no idea about the other; an extension of the legacy of my youth.

Shua wouldn't find out about my other life until a year later, when a Jewish mentor I had spoken to about these struggles sent him copies of our online chats. He didn't understand the dissociation, and refused to believe that I hadn't or wouldn't put Lily in harm's way, hadn't used my real name, and met the person I was dating far from home. I had never shared that I was a mother, careful to ensure that the life where I was being abused had no connection with the other.

By the time Shua found out, I had sworn off dating, recognising my inability to see red flags. But he wouldn't believe me. Although that hurt, the part of me that worked constantly to be a good mother understood it.

While in hospital, I talked to the nurses and the psychiatrist about my failure to escape these dynamics, and even though it would take me a lot longer to absorb their lessons, I was able to end a relationship with a man who didn't hear me when I said no.

Lily had been admitted into the hospital with me, and Shua and I continued to meet with the rabbi. I wouldn't engage in divorce talk until we had both signed a parenting plan. Once that was sorted, the rabbi booked our Jewish divorce.

I arrived at the synagogue with Elly at 4 p.m. and noted Shua's car parked across the street. As the man, his presence had been required hours earlier than mine. Elly looked at me as we knocked on the door. 'This is it, Dassi,' she whispered while we waited for admittance.

The Adass Israel synagogue of Melbourne sat on the corner of Oak Grove and Glen Eira Avenue in Ripponlea, and spanned several suburban blocks. Most mornings, evenings and weekends the glass doors were thrown open and groups of young boys could be found swinging on the bannisters or lounging on the steps as they waited for their fathers to finish prayers. At 4 p.m. on a Tuesday, however, the street was empty. I squeezed Elly's hand; the quiet felt ominous.

At the synagogue entrance, a man dressed in black shook his head and told Elly she must remain outside – her short sleeves and neckline revealed skin that was unsuitable for the holy walls. I had been instructed to show up alone, but I had refused. The Gett is part of a patriarchal tradition that ties a woman to the man she married until she is freed by receiving a piece of paper in front of the rabbinical court. I would not walk into a room paid to watch the dissolution of my marriage alone.

In Jewish communities around the world, agunot, or chained women whose husbands refuse to grant a Gett are a significant concern. This issue affects both genders, but it particularly impacts women. The chained woman cannot remarry and in Jewish law any child she has, without a Jewish divorce, is considered illegitimate.

This Gett was a pivotal moment, and one I knew would change the course of my life. By divorcing my husband, I was also divorcing our way of life.

After a short, whispered argument, a decision was made – Elly was permitted inside, but would need to remain in the foyer. I bit my lip to withhold my frustration and walked towards the end of my marriage alone.

The room felt airless. The rabbi checked the spelling of my name and I confirmed the Hebrew letters for him.

'Are you doing this of your own free will, Hadassa?' he asked.

Would life go back to normal if I said no?

'Yes,' I said loudly. Twice, the rabbi repeated his question.

I lifted my hands for inspection; nothing could come between the document and my hands. Shua stood facing me, his eyes down as he mouthed each word carefully. 'By giving you this Gett, and by you, Hadassa Erlich, receiving this document, our marriage will end.' I tried to catch his eye, to smile, to laugh at the ridiculousness of what we were doing, but it was as if our four years of marriage had been erased and I was standing across from a stranger.

I held out my arms as instructed and waited as Shua folded the Gett and dropped it into my hands. I cupped my hands around it, raised the piece of paper and showed the room my ownership by placing it under my arm. I stepped away from the man who was no longer my husband and gave the document to the rabbi.

'The marriage between Shua and Hadassa is over,' the rabbi announced.

I had fulfilled my obligations. I walked out of the room untethered to anyone. I was my own woman now.

CHAPTER 17

Beyond the community

Holding my breath, I listened to the noise of the house. I could hear the men arriving home from the synagogue, and the preparation for the Friday evening meal. I was grateful that the Chabad family I was living with were unaware of how I filled my weekends. I worried constantly they would find out.

My hand trembled as I touched my phone torch and tucked the light partly beneath my blanket. The scent of the evening's cooking drifted up the stairs to my bedroom, but I was too preoccupied to think of my hunger. An email had appeared on my phone, and I knew it was from M, written all in caps for emphasis. We had dated for four weeks and then, while in hospital, I had told him I wouldn't be seeing him anymore. It had been three days since we had last spoken, and now he was threatening to post 'those photos' all over the internet. My chest felt cramped, and my heart was racing. It was all my fault for leading him on. *I am pathetic.*

My body hated Friday nights. My mind didn't dwell on the memories of my mother at her worst, or the quiet hours that belonged to my father, but my body remembered. The panic surged up my throat, threatening to strangle me. I glanced at the clock: 8.30 p.m. The only way to will the hours away was to sleep. I found the sleeping pill packet beneath my bed and filled my water bottle in the bathroom before gulping one down. A way to forget, at least for a while.

The sleeping pill lulled me through to late Saturday morning, my nightmares softened by the foggy haze. I checked the clock, it was 11 a.m. I reached for my phone, but there was nothing. Dalia, Tamar and Nicole kept Shabbat and had their phones off. Elly, Isaac and Ben were out of range, camping at a New Year's event. I didn't know anyone else, and didn't believe anyone would want to know me. I had no plans, no commitments, nowhere to go. I went to the bathroom, filled up my water bottle, and took my last two sleeping pills. *Please, let me sleep until Shabbat is over.*

As I was drifting off, my host knocked on my door. 'Dassi, are you in there?' she called out. 'Would you like to join us for the meal?' I felt my chest tense up – I had already desecrated Shabbat by using my phone. *Was I a hypocrite if I still joined them?* Guilt prickled at my skin, and I was unable to answer. Dropping all religion seemed too extreme, but picking the parts that meant something to me didn't seem right either. I felt like a fraud. All I wanted was for the voice to go away.

My breath came in short, shallow gasps. I tucked the blanket up over my head, trying to shut out the voice in my mind, the one that kept repeating, *You're stupid, stupid, stupid. You're nauseating. Who would ever want to be near you?* I held my breath until I heard her footsteps recede.

I had received another threatening email: *I CAN DO SOMETHING HORRIBLE TO YOU IF I REALLY WANT TO.* I lay in bed, hunched in on myself, too scared to move, wishing I could just disappear.

I had taken two sleeping pills the Saturday before and slept my way through the weekend. Now I hoped the sleeping pills would keep me from responding to M and meeting up with him. I felt that I deserved the pain he would inflict. I switched my phone off, tried to force my muscles to relax, and waited for my inner critic to tire. Sleep was my only refuge. My anxiety about M faded away while I slept.

I can barely recall the beginning of 2012. In January I signed up for a nursing diploma, and was accepted into Navitas University. It was the only wise decision I made during the early months of that year. I ceased taking my antidepressants, discontinued therapy and completely surrendered to my inner critic. I simply lacked the strength to resist it. I was a failure.

In my diary, I wrote of my despair and my conviction that nothing would ever improve, no matter what steps I took. I refused to bring heartache to my family, so I was readying them for a life without me. I was back to where I had been before my hospital admissions. I felt myself sinking further and further, and I knew I could not be the mother Lily deserved.

Dear Diary,
I'm beginning to forget why I need to be in Lily's life. It is hard for me to believe she needs a mother like me when I see the things I am doing and the level I have sunk down to. I feel like I am preparing myself and her for life without me.

The parenting plan I had worked out with Shua meant Lily had equal time with both of us. Since I wasn't keeping Shabbat, I agreed for Shua to have Lily each week on Friday until Sunday afternoon. Sunday would turn into Monday or Tuesday; some weeks it was Wednesday before I picked

Lily up. I spent days in bed hiding from other people, but mostly from myself. I believed I was disgusting. I couldn't bear myself; how could I force my daughter to bear me?

The guilt of leaving religion weighed on me like a cement block, crushing me with the fear that I was trying to be something I wasn't meant to be. I was trying to figure out how to make my own decisions, even simple ones like creating a daily routine, but my mind was telling me I should have trusted God's plan for me. I felt so stupid for thinking I could take control of my life, for believing I could make it in this new world. I felt like I was a mistake. I couldn't work out how to be.

Motherhood was the most significant element of my life, but I grappled with the idea that being a good mother meant letting my child grow up religious with her father and separating her from all that was broken in me.

My self-worth had been tied to my devotion to God's rules; without that, I felt I was nothing. I could not see the value I could bring to my daughter's life. Maybe Lily was better off without a mother like me.

By mid-January, I felt defeated and once again had no desire to keep myself safe. I reconnected with my psychiatrist and was admitted back into hospital. I wanted to take Lily with me, so I contacted Shua through his mother. The rabbi had told us at the conclusion of the Gett ceremony that we could no longer communicate directly. I thought it was ridiculous. But Esther told me Shua didn't think it was appropriate to take our eighteen-month-old daughter into the mother and baby unit. I felt despair, but some part of me still wanted to survive – not for myself, but for Lily. When I said goodbye to her, I promised her I would find a way to live.

A storm raged within me. I remember curling up under the desk in my room with my hands over my ears, trying to drown out the tormentor in my head. *You are a terrible mother, useless, you don't deserve to live.* The noise was relentless. I felt like I was burning up with the shame of existing. I was desperate to cut myself, anything for some peace. I went to find a nurse. *I can't shut you up, but I will not let you win,* I whispered to myself. The nurse took me to a private space for a chat and helped me get out of my head.

My final admission to the hospital lasted a full six weeks. Esther would drive Lily to the clinic twice a week for forty-minute visits. I started a new course of antidepressants and joined therapy groups, slowly learning to accept the parts of myself that wanted to live. I knew that the inner bully would never truly go away, but I was beginning to understand my own resilience and self-worth. With each passing day, I felt my strength and determination come back, and I was eager to be discharged so I could have more time with Lily.

Housing was an issue. One of the Chabad family's adult sons was returning from overseas, meaning I needed somewhere else to live. It would not be appropriate for me, as a single woman, to stay in the same house as the unmarried son. Again, a red check was made on the box labelled 'homeless' while I searched for a residence within my means.

Despite being hospitalised, I was determined to start my nursing degree in February. I had a strong desire to help others and care for those in need, and I had seen the positive impact nursing could have on people at their most vulnerable. As a mature student, I was required to prove my competence by taking a maths and English test. With the help of YouTube, I was able to successfully pass the maths test, which boosted my confidence even further.

I agonised over what to wear on my first day of university. I stood in front of the mirror for twenty minutes, having already changed clothes twice, then bounced from one foot to the other as I studied my third outfit, a short denim skirt and long-sleeved T-shirt. I had removed my wig on the day of my Jewish divorce, on the advice of a rabbi. It had felt strange to step into the world with a bare head, yet it clearly marked my transition from being married to being divorced. I looked at myself again in the mirror. *Do I look normal? Will I fit in?*

The nurse for the morning shift came in to introduce herself. 'I'm going to university!' I shouted at her. I lowered my voice; the ward was still quiet. 'I'm going to university!' I high-fived her as I skipped out of the room, dragging my nursing manuals in my wheelie backpack. I had studied the tram routes from St Kilda Road to the campus on Bourke Street carefully; I didn't want to be late.

It took me several weeks to find my place in the class. I had grown up in a different world to my classmates, and they seemed intrigued by it. I was worried that I was too different to fit in, but I soon found friends among other mature-age students, and gradually I learnt social norms through our interactions. I felt a sense of belonging.

During my admission I asked to be referred to another therapist to work on my parenting, and I began seeing someone solely to discuss mothering and how to break the cycle of intergenerational trauma.

Despite these efforts, the monster in my head still refused to die. 'Love yourself,' my therapist said, 'your child needs you.' But I couldn't help but feel that, no matter how hard I tried, the darkness in me was still there. I told her of the darkness and the doubts, of my parents' hate and my own sense of inherent wrongness. Gradually, through our sessions I began to understand how vital I was to my daughter, and I worked to become the mother I wished I'd had, the mother I had needed.

When I left the hospital in early March, I was in a much better mental space. I set up residence in a small, one-bedroom flat I had found above a sandwich shop in Caulfield, and on Monday evening I went to pick up Lily per the parenting schedule we had agreed on the year prior. The night was a little unsettled, but I knew it would take Lily a little while to get used to the change of schedule. I dropped Lily off again on Wednesday morning and hopped on a tram to university, feeling somewhat secure. But later that day I received an email from Shua that shattered my newfound confidence. The email stated I could no longer have Lily overnight and that he would not give her back to me at all. He also told me not to bother going to the police or come near him or his mother and suggested I contact a lawyer.

I stepped off the tram and trudged towards Shua's house. I pounded on the door, desperate to see my daughter. When his mother informed me that he wouldn't come to the door, I felt as though I had been kicked in the stomach. I stumbled back home, not even watching where I was going. *Failure*, the voice inside my head repeated. *Lily is better off without you.* But I wasn't ready to give up. All night in my kitchen, I shouted out loud, 'No! I am her mother; I deserve to be her mother!' I refused to accept defeat. I refused to let the darkness win.

The next morning, I called my lawyers. Henry, my former father-in-law, had introduced me to a barrister to explore the possibility of pursuing a civil case against Leifer and Adass Israel School. In a civil case, the outcome relies on the 'balance of probabilities', a different standard than the 'beyond reasonable doubt' used in a criminal court. Despite mounting medical bills, I was hesitant to take this step. I still blamed myself and the shame was toxic. But when the lawyers mentioned they could assist in negotiating parenting arrangements with Shua, funded by potential civil case winnings, I decided to move forward.

I felt no sense of determination about committing to the case against the school at this time, it was a decision born out of desperation. It seemed the only way to access legal help for the complex parenting situation I faced.

My lawyers spoke to Shua's lawyers and a resolution was reached. Shua would allow me to see Lily, but I was not permitted to keep her overnight. I felt I had no choice but to agree, and so began our first communication through legal representatives. Over the next four years, all our exchanges were conducted in this way, and they grew increasingly bitter. We were instructed to attend mediation, overseen by our respective lawyers.

The two months until mediation settled into a routine. Monday, Wednesday and Friday I attended university. Sunday, Tuesday and Thursday I spent the day with Lily. The hours on each day were decided by Shua. Thoughts about giving up continued to hound me, but the struggle made me more determined to create a life for myself and my daughter.

My four sisters were a wonderful support. We created a WhatsApp group called the '5 Sisters' where we shared the daily happenings in our lives. Lily was a bright, inquisitive child, and as autumn turned cold that year I felt a hint of optimism for the future. But, as quickly as I felt that glimmer, the darkness of self-hatred came crashing back, telling me I didn't deserve to be happy.

I kept my doubts hidden from Lily, but I could feel the weight of self-hatred pressing down on me. It seemed to ooze out of every pore, and I was convinced it was written all over my body. I doubted my new friendships. I was no match for the consuming hate that slowly drained me of my strength. I battled it every day, but it would be a long time before I truly believed there wasn't anything fundamentally bad about me.

Mediation failed. We continued to disagree through our lawyers. Unbeknown to me, Shua had been sent online chats from a man I thought I could trust. The chats described the relationships I had been involved in, my struggles of shame and guilt, and my wishes for death or for someone to kill me. My lawyer was worried. I explained that the chats were months old. I had changed, and wouldn't stop working on myself, but she knew this would be used against me.

It was decided that until I received psychiatric clearance, time with my daughter would be supervised.

For legal reasons nothing more can be said about this. The fight had left me. *Everyone can see the darkness inside you. You are worthless. Lily is better without you.*

The next morning, I woke up on autopilot. I took my nursing books and walked to the train station.

My daughter is better off without me.

It is better if I am dead.

Friday, 22 June 2012 began like any other Friday that year. Except on that particular Friday, I was on the edge of a train platform, about to choose life.

When I decided not to jump in front of the train that wintry day, I also made the decision to stop seeing death as an option. I had made a promise to myself. It was time to do the work.

The next six months were among the most difficult of my life. Tamar, Nicole, Henry and Freda were all approved as my supervisors. I was only allowed to see my daughter for two hours, five days a week. I yearned for moments of peace with her, away from the hustle of nieces and nephews, but until I could prove myself as a mother, I had no other option.

Through those supervised visits with Henry, Freda and Marilyn, I built a beautiful relationship with that side of Shua's family that continues today. Even years later, Henry, Marilyn, Peter and Freda continued to support me, regularly inviting Lily and me to their home for catch-ups and dinners. It feels like a safe haven, and a chance to be part of the family – something I cherish to this day.

5 Sisters WhatsApp group

11/10/2012 9:46 a.m.

Dassi: It's just crazy how my daughter's future can be decided in these two hours of talking to a stranger who doesn't know me yet will assess my competence as a mother. Going into the appointment now.

11/10/2012 12:06 p.m.

Nicole Mobile: My stomach is churning now wow.

11/10/2012 12:07 p.m.

Dassi: The psychiatrist said he sees lots of patients and he thinks I've come very far and worked really hard to be where I am now.

12/10/2012 9.08 a.m.

Dassi: I have so much going on at uni and I can't concentrate, and now on top of it – need to move because the sandwich bar was bought by someone else.

Saving up every penny for driving lessons.

I think my body is reacting to the stress, uni, moving, won't have internet for 2 weeks. How will I do assignments?

Can't sleep wondering what's going to happen Monday, if supervision will be lifted.

Just so stressed, I can't wait for the next 3 weeks to be over!!

The psychiatrist signed off on my competency as a mother, and Lily and I began to slowly but surely embark on a new journey together. It would take six or seven months but by the end of 2012, I was granted unsupervised time with my daughter. I gradually gained more self-assurance as a parent, and sought guidance from my therapist on how best to help my daughter adjust to the reality of living between two households.

Assignments, assessments and affidavits are how I remember 2013. The days were divided between writing papers for my nursing course, attending multiple therapeutic assessments for my civil case or parenting issues, and dealing with my lawyers.

I struggled. Consistency and concentration were a constant battle. Old coping mechanisms were difficult to ignore, and I knew that my personal growth wouldn't be an easy journey. Often, I found myself in a pit of despair, but each time I emerged, I felt better equipped to make the climb.

Shua had taken over the government parenting payments. Unable to find suitable housing on my study allowance, I applied for government housing, and was eventually granted a subsidised apartment in Glen Iris. I was still struggling to make ends meet, but my brother Ben, who was in a more comfortable financial position, would take me to the store twice a month to get groceries. My siblings faced their own struggles, yet they still found it within themselves to offer me support. My strength was in part theirs.

I recall the first time Isaac, Ben, Elly and I went out to dinner together. We went to an Indian restaurant on Carlisle Street, a place we wouldn't have even noticed during our childhood, so accustomed were we to ignoring un-kosher life. It was the first of many such nights together around the dinner table. The sheer joy of being able to explore and taste different foods, all so new and electrifying. The laughter and chatter as we visited different restaurants around Melbourne. We tried every cuisine we could find, every dish we had never heard of before. So many firsts. It was a tradition that would continue every month for years.

My lawyers advised me to go to VOCAT and apply for victims of crime assistance, which granted me a sum of money that I used to buy a car. Isaac and I found an old Toyota from the 90s at a second-hand car sale. Although it had seen far too many years to be called second-hand, it cost just under $4000 and allowed me to take another step towards independence. Driving that car home was a moment of pride and joy.

A week after gaining my driver's licence, I set off to an aged care nursing placement forty-five minutes away. It was the dark side of the morning, and the GPS promised a shortcut if I turned off the highway. Ten minutes later, I found myself on a road that wound around a mountain with only the reflectors to guide my way. Cliff-side driving hadn't been covered in my driving lessons. I sat hunched over the steering wheel with my eyes glued to the road, sweating far too much for a cold June morning. On the radio, ABBA was belting out one of their hits from the late 1970s – 'Chiquitita'. The lyrics were about the sun's ability to lift your spirits and as if by magic, the sun began to rise. I was enamoured, my posture relaxed, and I turned the music up loud, humming along all the way down the mountain. It was my first exposure to the Swedish supergroup since I had left the community, and it brought back memories of Dalia and Tamar singing to me as a little child. For the next two months, Lily and I woke to ABBA music and danced our way through the morning.

Music opened the door to movement, and I started training with Dave Milla at his gym, For Fit Sake. While stress forced me to live in my thoughts, working out gave me a healthy way to reconnect with my body. It became something I would return to each time I lost myself in my head during difficult periods. Each time, Dave would welcome me back without judgement and meet me where I was.

With my aged care certificate in my pocket, I signed up with a nursing agency and began taking shifts while Lily was with her dad. I quickly grew accustomed to the shifts I was doing, serving as a carer for those in need. Every day was different, from helping an elderly man with his morning routine to accompanying a woman to her doctor's appointment. It was a fulfilling experience. A routine established itself, and after some time I was confident enough to consider entering the world of dating.

A few months into 2013 I met a young man named Marc, a kind man. We fell in love and, despite everything that was going on, the world looked rosier. After the abusive relationships of the previous year, I finally let myself be vulnerable and opened my heart to love. I had spent so long putting up walls to protect myself thinking all I deserved was abuse, shielding my heart from further pain, that I didn't understand what it felt like to be open and trusting. Love felt like a new beginning.

Six months into a whirlwind romance, I finally introduced Marc to Lily. I met his family, and he met mine. His parents asked about my parents, and I offered the explanation I had learnt to tell people – that their absence was due to religiosity – rather than the truth. Lily turned three, we adopted two bunnies, and she started kinder. There were moments of warmth and laughter and love that helped us through the turmoil.

Dassi Mobile to 5 Sisters:
The song 'I Want to Marry You' by Bruno Mars is on the radio,
Lily tells me she wants to marry Marc. I told her she is too
little; she tells me don't worry Marc will wait until I am bigger.
I asked her who will marry Ima and she responded, Ima, I give
you permission to marry my rabbits!

All the while, Malka Leifer was still hiding out somewhere in Israel.

I told Marc about my decision to report the abuse to the police. He assured me that he would be present in any way I needed him to be throughout the process.

Nicole had maintained contact with the police throughout the year of investigation following our police statements in 2011. The detective told her he was confident there was sufficient evidence to apply for Leifer to be extradited to face court in Australia. In 2012, after swearing our statements in front of a magistrate we were told the Australian Government would soon send the request to Israel. It took months to navigate the bureaucracy in Canberra but finally, early in 2013 an extradition request for Leifer's return was sent. Nicole regularly checked with the police for news from Israel, but they had none to give her. We had all assumed that an extradition would soon be granted. We assumed wrong.

By mid 2014, the extradition request had been in Israel for over a year, three years since I had given my police statement and months since we'd heard anything. I'd more or less given up on the idea of Leifer ever returning to Australia. Dalia begged us to fly over to Manchester for her son's bar mitzvah, so I got a weekend job, borrowed some money, and sat down with Elly to plan a trip to Europe. I was desperate to broaden my horizons, and I wasn't about to spend all that money on a ticket without doing something else while on that side of the world.

Elly and I somehow managed to organise a backpacker's trip on a shoestring budget, through Italy, Greece and Spain, culminating in the UK for our nephew's thirteenth birthday. I would be away for a month.

It was my first time leaving Lily. I informed my lawyers, university, work, therapists and Shua. With the stars aligned, I sat down with Lily and created a scrapbook of pictures with a calendar for her to tick off each day. Each day that week we read a book called *The Invisible String* which told the story of a string made of love that connected people no matter the distance. Marc promised to stay at my place and care for our two bunnies.

On 15 August 2014, Elly and I left for our summer in Europe. A day later, we checked into a six-bed dorm in Athens, Greece, locked our passports in the hostel safe and changed into clothes suitable for the heat. We spent the day walking the culture of the old city, ignorant of the history, yet eager to soak up all we could see. That evening we perched on our backpacks in between the bunk beds, eating crackers and cheese on paper plates and chatting to a retired couple from Sydney on the opposite side of the room. It was the start of an adventure that would create lifelong memories. We still laugh about the fact that some days we had to decide which was more important, food or water. We couldn't afford both.

That first night, as the hours drew close to morning, I tossed and turned, too excited to sleep. I climbed down the bunk to Elly's bed, squeezed in next to her and whispered in her ear, 'Did you ever imagine three years ago that we would be here?' She looked around the dorm with the eyes of her childhood at the couple sharing a bed, our pile of non-kosher snacks, and the bikinis hanging over the door. The scene was far beyond the imagination of our younger selves. 'Never. Who would have thought this is where we would one day be,' she whispered as a smile stretched across her face.

But three days later, our trip came to a halt. While we were on a plane to Italy, our sisters were sending us tons of messages and posting article after article on our WhatsApp group.

Melbourne Jewish school's ex-principal arrested in Israel on sex assault charges. That was the headline in *The Guardian* on 18 August 2014.

Elly and I huddled into a private room in the hostel that we promised to pay for later while we downloaded Skype. 'Why aren't you answering?' we badgered Nicole repeatedly, not realising in our shock that it was 4 a.m. in Australia. *Everyone is saying we should be happy, it's good news,* I wrote while we waited for her to answer, *and it is, but we are woefully unprepared, and I'm angry it mentions three sisters. Where is our privacy?* Nicole had spoken to the police, but it was she who informed them of Leifer's arrest and they had no information to give her.

When we hung up, neither Elly nor I moved. We sat on the floor in stunned silence. Finally, I slowly got up, moved to the front desk and heard myself asking for the price of the private room. I handed over the money we had put aside for the following week and found my way back to Elly.

'Why aren't we relieved?' she asked me. An hour ago, we had been explorers, free and happy; now, though our names had not been published, the media across the world was calling us the three sister victims. The news had hit us like a brick. We considered returning to Australia but decided to delay the decision until morning.

The next morning, we set off at sunrise on a walk through the historic centre of Rome. It was going to be a warm day; already the sun felt like it was hugging my body. I flicked some water at Elly, and she opened her flask and flicked some back at me. We giggled and decided ice cream was the perfect breakfast. 'Let's continue our trip,' I told Elly. I didn't want our adventure to end. In Rome, we weren't victims of Malka Leifer. In Rome, we were tourists, and I loved being a tourist.

We wouldn't let the gossip that was trickling through the Jewish communities ruin our trip. Instead, we drank pina coladas on the beaches of Barcelona.

Two weeks later we arrived in Manchester, sun-kissed and relaxed.

I hadn't seen Dalia since she visited Australia when Lily was a newborn. Elly and I followed her around, helping out where we could, as she cooked and scrubbed and got everything ready for the bar mitzvah. We never stopped talking. Her kids found it funny when our stubbornness clashed; we would have to stop and place bets on who would be the winner. Our arguments were the kind that ended in laughter and pillow fights and big fat slices of cheesecake. So many moments of perfect happiness.

A week later, we waved Dalia goodbye. We would see her again three weeks later, when she arrived in Australia to continue the bar mitzvah celebrations – Dalia's son had asked that his birthday gift be a trip to see his cousins in Australia. All the way home, Elly and I spoke about how much fun it would be having the five sisters together again.

CHAPTER 18

Dalia

The day after Rosh Hashanah, the Jewish New Year, quickly turned into the worst day of my life.

Rosh Hashanah marks the beginning of the high holidays. It is the one holiday when many Jews, both religious and secular, gather in synagogues around the world to pray for a successful year ahead, and to celebrate God's creation of the world.

Rosh Hashanah 2014 was the first year I decided to skip celebrations with my family, opting to ignore the significance of the day and continue working. I was still figuring out my connection to Judaism, and didn't want to be restricted by the long list of laws that dictated what I could or couldn't do during the two-day festival.

This year, Lily was with her father for Rosh Hashanah, and, needing the money from my aged-care shifts, I chose to prioritise my needs over those of a religion that had demanded so much from me.

Over the last few months there had been some tension developing in my relationship with Marc, and the night before, we'd had our first argument. I had gone to sleep angry and alone. When my phone rang at 4.57 a.m. I thought it was Marc calling. As a chef, he regularly worked the first shift, and early calls were not unusual.

It wasn't Marc. The missed call had been from Tamar. It took a moment for my brain to recalibrate. A phone call at this time could only mean an emergency. I immediately began to calculate how quickly I could get dressed, run over and babysit if she or one of her kids were sick.

Tamar's number flashed on the screen again. It was 4.59 a.m., and this time I picked up. Straight away, I could hear horror in her voice.

'Dassi, wake up, I need to tell you something.' I wanted to beg her not to utter whatever words were coming. I sensed the pain that was about to hit me, and I knew I couldn't take it.

'Dassi,' she said, 'I don't know how to say this, but Dalia is dead.'

'Dalia who?' I yelled at her, not wanting to acknowledge she meant our Dalia, our loved and cherished older sister.

'Dalia our sister,' she confirmed. 'They tried to save her, but Dalia, our Dalia is gone.'

The sound that escaped my mouth was unlike any sound I had heard; a guttural howl that originated in a place I hadn't known existed, deep within my body. I pleaded with Tamar to take back her words. The pain was ricocheting through every nerve in my body and my soul was burning. Dalia, my protector, my advisor, the sister I looked up to and aspired to be, was gone. How did the world continue to turn without her in it? How was I alive in the same moment she was gone?

We needed to tell the rest of our siblings, Tamar told me. I was suddenly jealous of my brothers and sisters, that they still lay sleeping, unburdened by this trauma. I wished I could save them from it, but I knew I couldn't protect them.

Tamar asked if I could quiet my tears while we rang Elly. Until that moment, I hadn't realised how deeply and loudly I had been sobbing. I couldn't remember the last time I'd cried; the dissociation I used to survive my childhood had long stolen the tears from me.

I don't recall the phone call with Elly. She was living with our brothers, and had to wake Isaac and Ben to tell them. I remember tipping over my washing basket to find yesterday's clothing and realising that from that moment on, everything in my life would be divided into before we lost Dalia and after.

I probably shouldn't have been driving in the state I was in. It was only when I got to Tamar's house that I looked down and saw there were no shoes on my feet. I was desperate to be with my siblings, but still none of us had been able to get hold of Nicole.

Nicole was in Sydney visiting her in-laws for the high holidays. We had tried every line we could find to get a hold of her but without success. We rang other families in Sydney at 6 a.m., hoping an early riser may be able to go over and wake her. I felt deep desperation to reach into her sleep and shake her into this new horrific reality.

Elly, Tamar, Isaac, Ben and I huddled together in Tamar's driveway, pouring our shared grief into the space between us. In between our tears, reality began to dawn: someone needed to tell our parents that their oldest daughter had died on an operating table over Rosh Hashanah.

Having been estranged from our parents for many years, we didn't know where they lived, or how to contact them. A year ago, we heard through community gossip that my parents had moved to a place in South Caulfield. If we could guess the synagogue my father belonged to, maybe his rabbi would have the information we needed. There was a sense of urgency; it was now 6.30 a.m. and my father was an early riser. We knew if he made it to synagogue for morning prayers, the worldwide Jewish gossip machine might deliver the news before we could.

Multiple phone calls followed until we found a rabbi who could help us. We didn't feel it was right to share why we needed to speak to our parents, but he could hear the pain in our voices. The rabbi didn't have an exact address for our parents, but he knew the name of their street, and we agreed to meet him there.

Somewhere in our grief-stricken brains we remembered which car my father owned. Isaac, Tamar and I drove up and down the street, peering into driveways, trying to match a car to our childhood memories. It boggles my mind that only an hour after finding out our sister died, we were cruising a quiet Caulfield street, playing detective.

We found the car parked on the street against the nature strip between two houses. The rabbi thought it was house number 44, but it could easily have been house 46. Tamar and I hadn't seen our parents for years and here we were on their doorstep. The sun was still rising on the worst day of my life; I couldn't fathom how it had come to this.

The rabbi knocked loudly on the door of house number 46; he thought my parents' shock would be lessened if he were the first to call out. Finally, we heard the slow shuffle of someone just waking, asking who it was. It was my father's voice. The rabbi spoke loudly through the wooden door, letting my parents know that two of their daughters and their son were here and had something urgent to tell them.

'What is it?' my father shouted. The rabbi spoke again, telling him it wasn't appropriate to be shouting from the street.

My mother called out that she needed to make herself modest before we could come in. My parents knew we wouldn't come to them unless it was urgent, but still she made us wait fifteen long minutes before she opened the door to us.

We stood there, our faces red and our eyes haunted, while my parents asked us why we were there. 'It's Dalia,' Tamar said. Before we could say anything more, my mother screamed 'No,' and slammed the door in our faces.

The rabbi spoke gently but firmly, trying to convince them to let us in, but I could see my mother didn't want to know more.

I couldn't empathise with my mother's grief. She had made the choice to cut herself off from all her children; it had been seven years since she had seen or spoken to Dalia. In the pain of that moment, compared to mine, her grief seemed unauthentic. *You are not deserving of this grief*, I thought.

My father opened the door and showed us towards the dining room, where we sat awkwardly in a house devoid of any childhood memories. There were no photos of us on the walls. It was as if in their picture of family life we had never existed.

'Come sit next to me,' my mother beckoned. I didn't want to be in her presence, but I reverted to the little obedient child and obliged. We told them what we knew.

Just after Elly and I left the UK, Dalia had experienced some chest pains. She was put on angina medication and was waiting for the doctor's clearance to fly.

Three days ago, she had told us she was back in hospital for some heart-related investigations. We were slightly worried, but Dalia was only thirty-nine. Her two older children were teenagers and the youngest had just turned three.

Dalia worked as a religious principal in a Hasidic school and was under a lot of pressure. Although she was not Hasidic, her family belonged to the ultra-Orthodox community, where reputation is everything.

During our last phone call, she told me that two men had visited her from Israel on behalf of Leifer to threaten her place in the close-knit community. They warned that if she didn't convince her sisters to withdraw their police statements, her family could be ostracised. Her job, her husband's job, the children's schooling and their marriage prospects were all on the line.

The two men met with her boss, and were pressuring him to fire her. Dalia turned to her rabbi for support, but he didn't want to get involved. Regardless, she promised to always support me. 'If I have to leave Manchester and start again somewhere they can't find me, I'll do that, Dassi,' she said, and I believed her. She would never ask me to drop the charges against Leifer. I had been furious that Leifer's lackeys were using their self-righteous power to hurt my sister. I worried this was a sign of things to come, and of the lengths they were prepared to go to in order to silence us.

Dalia's last message on our WhatsApp group expressed how lonely she felt in hospital without family on the most important Jewish holiday of the year. Between time differences, work and Rosh Hashanah, I had missed the last call. How I wished I could have had that call with her.

It was twenty-four hours after Dalia died before her husband phoned Tamar to tell her. Jewish laws regarding the use of technology on Rosh Hashanah meant he couldn't call us until the holiday was over.

* * *

Dalia had been booked in for a routine angiogram – a low-risk investigative procedure performed at an outpatient clinic. During the procedure, the main artery feeding her heart had ruptured, and by the time she was hurried back to hospital her body had endured one cardiac arrest after another. I've read through the medical reports, trying to work out how long she was conscious and if there was a point when she'd have known she was dying. I wish I'd been there to hold her hand and promise to be there for her children. I couldn't bear the thought of Dalia all alone in the back of a racing ambulance, the life slowly leaving her. The double bypass had not been enough to save her.

In my mind I was screaming at the injustice of losing my beloved sister, but there in front of my mother, my face was still and my body motionless, that instinctive protective mechanism I had learnt as a child.

Tamar stayed with my parents while Isaac took me back to where Elly had gathered with Ben. They had reached Nicole and she was on her way back to Melbourne. Elly and I discussed who would travel overseas for the funeral. Although I had just returned from abroad and worried about leaving Lily again so soon, due to medical reasons, Elly wasn't able to travel. I needed to be there for Dalia's children. Ben made the decision to travel with me.

It was now 8 a.m. The morning had taken on a surreal feel.

I had to keep repeating to myself, *Dalia is dead, Dalia, my Dalia is dead.* I wanted to scream it at the people on the street: *Dalia, my sister, is dead.*

Ben and I walked through the airport like two civil, polite adults, buying coffees and waiting at the assigned gate. I couldn't comprehend how the world seemed to be going on as normal. How could people smile? Did they not know?

Every moment that passed was another moment when I existed and Dalia did not.

Somewhere on the long flight I realised that until that point, I had still held onto a magical belief that God wouldn't do this to me, to our family. God had tested us with so much trauma already, surely He wouldn't take away someone so precious to us. I couldn't accept that Dalia was dead while my abusers went on living.

While Ben chatted to our seatmates, I sunk into my grief. We flew first to Israel, where Dalia was to be buried, and would then continue on to England when the service was over.

The ultra-Orthodox knew death, and Dalia's community organised everything.

According to religious tradition, as soon as I touched down in Israel I needed to tear my clothing as a visible sign of my loss. I had packed a black jumper to put over my dress for this purpose. Two Hasidic men were to pick us up from the airport and drive us straight to the cemetery.

I don't remember ripping my clothes, but I do remember the wife of one of the Hasidic men briskly marching up to me and pinning my clothing. My torn jumper exposed a little collarbone; it was not appropriate for an ultra-Orthodox gathering.

The entire funeral procession waited for us as the men drove frantically through Jerusalem's peak-hour traffic. The drivers chatted to Ben, but they were not allowed to engage with me, a woman. I was grateful for the silence. We were on the way to bury our sister; traffic and small talk felt highly inappropriate.

We landed in Israel at 3 p.m. and by 4.30 p.m. we arrived at the cemetery. I was ushered past the crowd into the building where my sister lay. I could see my niece in a room with large glass windows. I rushed to give her a hug. I was shocked to see my sister lying on a low metal gurney, wrapped in white sheets, her face covered. I wanted to shake Dalia, beg her to open her eyes, but with broken English and urgent hand gestures, the men told me I was forbidden to touch her.

They left me in the room for a few private moments, but I could see them watching, their eyes following me. I was angry at this intrusion into my final moments with Dalia, and the rigid laws that dictated my mourning.

I held my pain close. I was there for Dalia's children, and I needed to set aside my own grief to hold theirs. I placed the phone beside Dalia's ear while my siblings in Melbourne had their final words with her. The men hurried me; time was now of the essence. According to Jewish law, one needed to bury a body immediately, and that had already been delayed to accommodate our flight from Australia.

The rest of the service passed in a blur. I stood with my niece behind a lace curtain that divided the women from the men and listened to the rabbi, tears streaming silently down my face. Several men spoke about my sister. Their speeches sounded empty, focusing on Dalia's religiosity but devoid of her love and spirit. I wanted to tell the mourners about my sister's beautiful soul and the loving way she mothered her children, but my role here was only to observe, I couldn't make a scene. The rituals to help a soul reach heaven were performed only by men.

The sun sank behind the glowing stone of Jerusalem's ancient walls. With my arm around my niece, we watched the funeral procession pass us and take Dalia to her grave. She was to be buried in the oldest and holiest cemetery in Israel, on the Mount of Olives next to Jerusalem's old city. I watched my nephew descend the mountain with my brother to throw the dirt that would cover his mother's body. I wished I could reach out and hug him.

In the eyes of the law my nephew, just turned thirteen, was no longer a child. As the oldest son, the responsibility to lead the group of men in prayer rested on his shoulders.

It was agonising to leave my sister in Israel and return to her home in Manchester without her. The walls in her house screamed her name, and the bedroom still smelt of her. At times I caught myself acting like a three-year-old, checking under beds or behind the doors, hoping to find her. Maybe if I opened the door just one more time, she would be there.

The week following a death, the family sits Shiva. For seven days we suspend daily living needs and personal comfort to sit solely with our grief. The mirrors in the house are covered and the torn garments are worn the whole period. The community rallied around, visiting the mourners at home, bringing food and condolences.

Dalia's mother-in-law sat on a low chair in the dining room downstairs and greeted the women who came to pay their respects. For the whole week, I camped out upstairs with my nephew and niece in Dalia's bedroom, emerging only to find food. We dragged out every photo we could find, and I told them everything I could about what their mother was like growing up. It tore at me that we were speaking of her in the past tense.

On the fourth day of this strange week, Dalia's boss visited and asked to see me. We sat in the kitchen and he spoke slowly without looking at me. 'I would never have fired your sister. The men pressured me, but I did not support them,' he told me, and I could see why Dalia respected him. I wanted him to fill me with stories of the Dalia only he was privy to, but the conversation had finished. Men and women did not mix.

The Shiva period ended on Yom Kippur, a 25-hour fast and the holiest day of the Jewish year. I wondered if Dalia could see us, if she was watching the slow way we went through the motions of preparing her house for the holiday. I so badly wanted to believe in an afterlife.

I hadn't fasted for four years, but Dalia would have, so that year I fasted for her. As I sat crying in the attic, listening to the men singing in the synagogue next door, I wondered what sin had brought us to this.

I needed to get back home to Lily. Ben stayed on with Dalia's children and I flew back to Melbourne alone. Having been cocooned in Dalia's bedroom for ten days, the world seemed a foreign place without her.

Her medical issues resolved, Elly flew to England. Nicole and Tamar filled me in on the tension of sitting Shiva with my mother and Isaac with my father. There had been hope that the week would close the rift with our parents, but it had only served to strengthen it. I was grateful that I'd been away and removed from the drama.

We renamed the '5 Sisters' WhatsApp group 'Devastating Loss'. Dalia's number was still active. Over the next few weeks, as my sisters and I sent each other messages of grief, a small part of me wanted to believe Dalia was still reading.

CHAPTER 19

Living with grief

It was my first school morning routine with Lily since I returned from sitting Shiva in Manchester. As I prepared for the day, all I could think was that the last time I had packed Lily's lunch box my sister was alive.

I had been back in Melbourne for three days and still couldn't shake my surprise that the world looked the same as it had before I left. How could my plants, bunnies and even furniture exist in the same way they had always done when Dalia lay six feet underground, covered in dirt and a circle of rocks?

Marc had been looking after Flopsy and Cottontail, our one-year-old bunnies, while I was abroad. We had barely communicated in the past few weeks. Relationships were hard for me at the best of times and now, with this irrevocable loss, I couldn't keep up. I struggled with intimacy and trust. Although cognitively I knew Marc was a good guy, the hurt and betrayal I had suffered in childhood meant I couldn't believe it. I knew I needed to end our relationship; it wasn't fair on him.

I dropped Lily off at kindergarten and was pulling away

when a police officer tapped on my window. I was about to receive my first fine. I hadn't been holding my phone, but it lay on the passenger seat on speakerphone – something I hadn't realised was prohibited for P-plate drivers.

Through tears, I gave the officer my details. I was distressed and embarrassed. I wanted to explain that I had just buried my sister, that I was still trying to figure out how to balance mothering with my overwhelming grief, but the officer wasn't interested. In the morning hurry, Lily's lunch box had been forgotten. I was rushing to work and had been calling Shua to see if he could get to kindergarten before snack time. Shua had assured me his mother would organise a fresh lunch. At some point within a year of our divorce I had simply ceased communicating to Shua through his mother and began communicating directly with him. I thought the rabbi's advice to always communicate about our daughter through a third person demonstrated a complete lack of understanding about parenting. Shua eventually followed suit.

Sometimes I marvelled at the complexities of my relationship with Lily's father. Shua had proclaimed to believe that having no mother was better than having a non-religious mother. Yet here, on a Wednesday morning, two weeks after Dalia was buried, I was calling to ask if he could make lunch and take it down to Lily's kinder and I knew he would do it.

Although we each thought the other should love Lily differently, at the end of the day I knew that he was doing what he believed was best for her, just as I was. If only there was a way to bridge the gulf between our parenting values.

The police officer handed over a ticket with a $400 fine, and I wondered how on earth I was going to pay it. Christmas was approaching; perhaps I could pick up a few shifts at public holiday rates.

Being Jewish, I didn't celebrate Christmas the way it seemed most people did. Growing up, even the word 'Christmas' was considered dirty. If it had to be said, it was called X-mas. Last year I had celebrated with friends, but it had felt very strange.

Despite my disastrous start to the day, I managed to get to work on time and care for the elderly lady I looked after each morning. I worked there seven days a week, from 9 a.m. to 11.30 a.m. On Tuesdays and Thursdays, I took an additional lunchtime shift that ended just before school pick-up, but the rest of the week I was finished by midday. I needed time without Lily to attend therapy, endless meetings with lawyers and medical specialists. Over the past three years, the parenting issues with Shua had moved forward and my schedule with Lily had evolved to now include overnight visits and equal time with both of us.

I had worried about working seven mornings a week and giving up the chance of ever sleeping in, but the schedule had provided a much-needed routine.

The part-time work also allowed me to manage the flashbacks and night terrors I struggled with every day. *I'm only at work for three hours*, I would tell myself in the morning after another night of broken sleep. *I will deal with that anxiety later, in therapy.* Knowing there was a safe space I could process my fears helped me put them aside and get through the next few hours.

The previous night, I'd had a terrible nightmare. I had woken in paralysing panic, my mind half aware of the present and half stuck in a vivid, terrifying nightmare. I could feel the terror pulsating in my veins and hear my heartbeat thumping in my ears. I desperately wanted to open my eyes and search the darkness for something that would drag me into the present, but I had no control over my body;

it had betrayed me. I was supposed to be safe in bed, but I was stuck there for several long, terrifying minutes, trapped between reality and a living nightmare.

When I was finally able to get up, I walked around the house, orienting myself to my surroundings. This was my home, I told myself. I was safe, I could run if I needed to. I checked the windows and doors, then went into Lily's bedroom and sat beside her bed, watching her sleep. Her soft breathing calmed me. Knowing the adrenaline coursing through my body meant I wouldn't get back to sleep, I counted the hours till morning, and the safety that came with sunshine.

'Night terrors with sleep paralysis,' my therapist would write in her notes, and I would repeat those words to the specialists I was required to see who wrote reports for my parenting matters or the civil case.

Those five words did nothing to capture the moments of pure terror that haunted my sleep, that had me scared to go to bed for fear it would happen again. Five words in a long list of symptoms that the court would hear without truly understanding the debilitating effect they could have on someone's life.

Still in a fog from my sleepless night and difficult morning, I finished work at 11.30 a.m. and went to therapy. As I drove, I played songs about the tragedy of loss, turning up the volume to chase out the bright spring sun and new life blossoming on the streets. My heart felt tired and heavy. I had thought my usual post-traumatic stress disorder symptoms would be suspended by my grief for Dalia, as if somehow the younger parts of myself that had lived through the abuse would know I was grieving and not disturb me. My therapist explained that PTSD didn't work like that; I didn't have a choice about when the trauma chose to take me back to my childhood pain. Even in the midst of this irreversible loss, my trauma didn't disappear. Having to continually discuss the abuse with court-appointed assessors wasn't helping either.

My civil trial against Malka Leifer and the Adass Israel School was nearing its conclusion. My lawyers had repeatedly assured me that 95 per cent of cases settled without going to trial, but we had tried mediation twice now. The school was refusing to even settle for an amount that would cover legal costs and my medical needs; a trial was looking increasingly likely. If the case did go to trial, I was looking at a final decision about my parenting of Lily in March and a civil trial in April. The year 2015 was shaping up to be a hectic year.

I couldn't wait to live a life not shadowed by the demands of legal cases. In order to prove that I could safely parent Lily, I needed to prove I was mentally well and able to be a good, sane, safe mother for my child. Meanwhile, in the civil courts I needed to show that the sexual abuse had affected me in ways I would never be able to completely move on from.

The juxtaposition of these conflicting demands was exhausting. Over the past four years I had worked hard to identify which parts of my life I could 'heal' and 'fix' and which parts I had to accept and learn to manage.

Now, I needed to work out how to take care of myself so those parts wouldn't negatively affect my parenting.

'Living with duality', my friend Dassi Herszberg described this as when I shared my frustrations with her. Dassi had also grown up in the Adass community; older than me, she had left years before I did. A previous therapist had put us in touch, and we'd been firm friends ever since.

Dassi could relate to the black-and-white way of life we had grown up with, and understood the search to find colour. One way of being was not mutually exclusive of another. Living with severe PTSD did not mean I couldn't be a good mother.

One of the things I learnt to accept was that my flashbacks and nightmares would never fully go away, but that I was better able to manage them when I was less stressed. When they did happen, I could ground myself so they wouldn't throw me off for days.

I worked hard in therapy to intimately understand myself and learn how to avoid triggers within my control. How to listen to my body, stand up for myself and construct boundaries around my mental health.

When I first started therapy, I hadn't felt worthy of receiving help. I was self-harming and suicidal, but determined to push through for my daughter. Now, I was doing it for me. I deserved to live. As a young girl I never imagined a future. Now that I could see one, I wanted to do more than just survive.

I learnt to track my thoughts and recognise if it was just an off day or if it was the beginning of a depression. If it was the latter, I then put a plan in place to get the help I needed and ensure it didn't progress into a dark spiral of despair.

It was hard work – it still is – but I knew that I had grown from it, and that as a person I was stronger for it. I also believed I was a better parent for it.

I was constantly self-monitoring, I needed to, but I didn't think that was a bad thing. I thought very carefully about the way I parented my daughter; how every action of mine caused a reaction in her. More than that, I learnt to be in the moment and cherish the time we had together.

The rest of 2014 passed in a blur. I travelled back to Israel with Nicole, Elly and Tamar to meet Dalia's family. Together, we travelled to the cemetery to witness the unveiling of her tombstone. The sight of the elegant marble tablet with her name etched upon it stirred a deep longing in my gut. I knew that I was, slowly, coming to terms with her passing, but I still wished so much that I could bring her back. As is Jewish tradition, we each placed a small stone atop her grave.

I broke up with Marc in November. I couldn't see the future he was hoping for – I was scared to move forward, and I knew it wasn't fair to stay in a relationship if I wasn't ready to take that leap. Despite feeling sad, I was resolute in my decision. I worked my way through the summer break and spent the beginning of 2015 preparing for the upcoming changes in my life.

In March, Lily went under the knife for the second time in her young life. The first time had been only months earlier. It was the most complicated of three surgeries she would need for her double duplex kidneys which she had been diagnosed with in utero. While Lily faced minimal health issues, the surgeries were required to prevent more serious complications in the future.

We spent the day before surgery reading hospital picture books we had borrowed from the library, so by the time Lily was admitted early the next morning, dressed in her favourite bunny pyjamas, she was ready for an adventure.

Shua and I must have made an interesting picture for the nurses. Me, on one side of the room enjoying non-kosher cafe food, and Shua on the other with a stack of religious books, quietly murmuring his prayers.

We were one month out from a decision on Lily's parenting orders, but for those five days in Cabrini Hospital, Shua and I lived together in a strange suspended reality, working together amicably to comfort Lily. In the dark hours of the night, relieving Lily's pain was the only thing that mattered to us both.

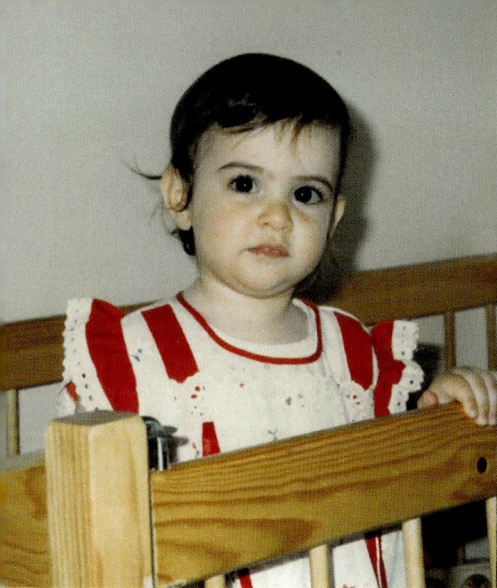

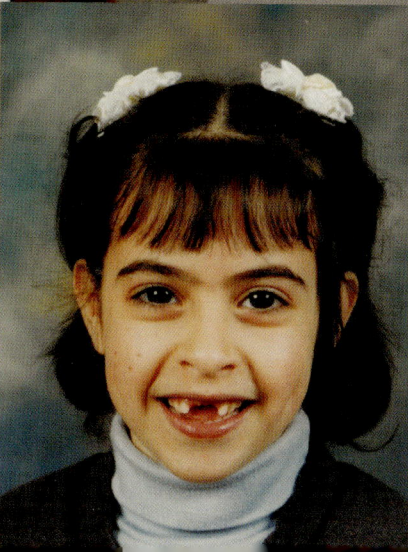

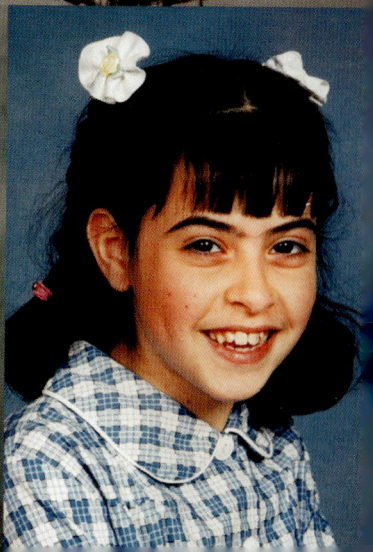

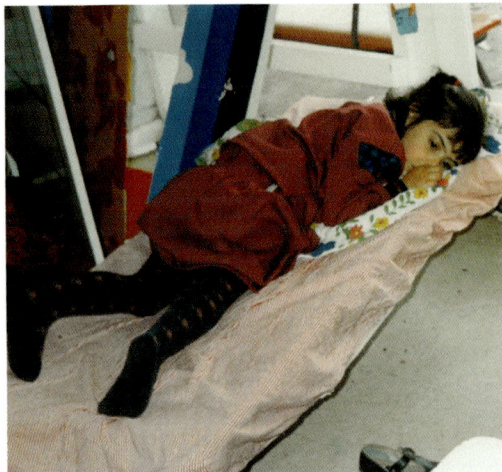

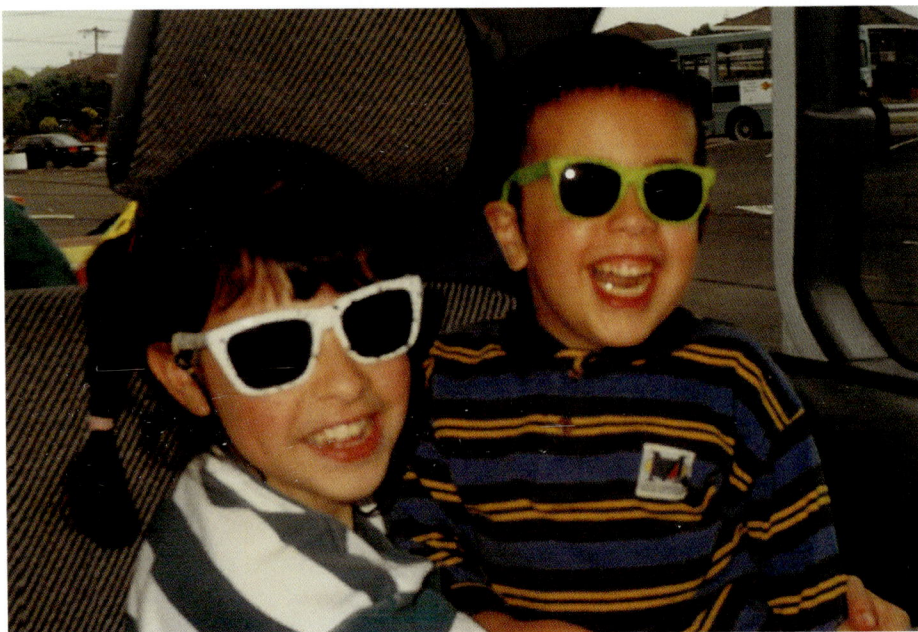

The thing is, we never know the home life of a child. Despite everything, outwardly I was a happy child (I knew I would be punished if I didn't smile). No one knew the truth, except my siblings: Dalia, Tamar, Elly, Nicole, Ben and Isaac. With Dalia and Tamar out of our home, Nicole, Elly and I had to look out for each other. We would watch each other's backs, and together we would survive. I would keep the monster away from my brothers, I would make sure they were fed, and I would pray every day that my mother would love me.

Me and Elly.

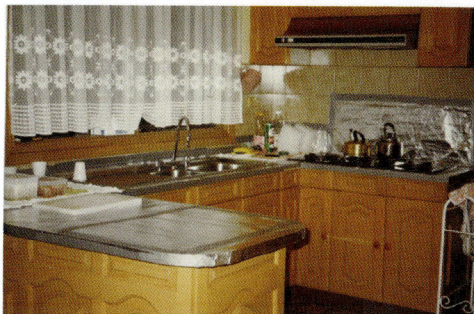

Our kitchen prepared for Passover. Using a roll of insulated foil and duct tape, we covered the counters and table. I traced over the stove and cut the shape of the burners through the foam-filled foil. The cupboards had their own reusable paper to line the shelves. It would take us days to prepare but I remember standing back and admiring our silver kitchen. It was now Passover ready.

Feeding the birds with my sister Dalia behind me. Once Dalia and Tamar had left home, my mother wouldn't allow us to speak to them; she was worried their influence would undermine her absolute authority. But Dalia always found a way to let us know she was there for us.

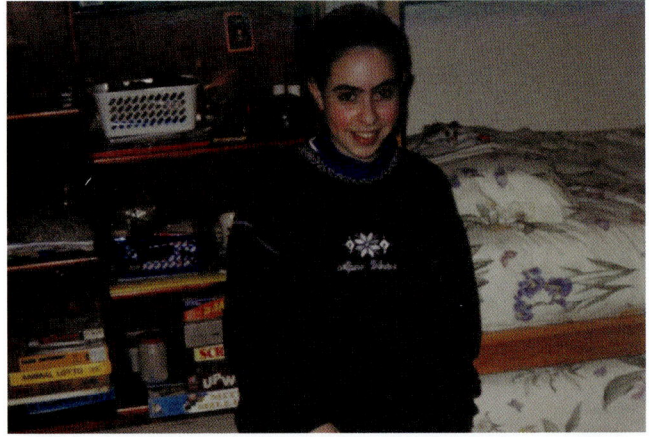

Here I am in my bedroom packing for camp, and then lighting candles at camp. Until I was fifteen, school was a refuge for me. But one person changed that. I always did as she said. Everyone did. I didn't complain and I didn't say no. I didn't know how. Life had taught me that refusal was frightening, and that the consequences of disobedience were immense. She was the principal; she was the authority.

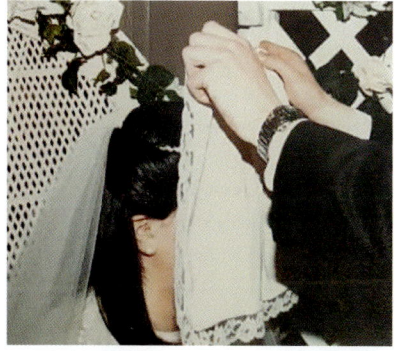

I turned eighteen and finished Year Twelve, but in the eyes of our community I would not be an adult until I married. It was a matchmaker's job to find me a husband and they had presented offers, but my parents had turned them down. I was worried it was taking too long. The older I got, the more problematic the marriage scene would be for me. Good grades and youth were on my side, but as time went on, the less often the matchmaker would call. And then, after five supervised meetings with Shua, I was engaged. I look back at the pictures we took on the neighbour's lawn on my wedding day, and see my face is young, but my eyes are older than my nineteen years.

Fighting for justice for myself and my sisters would see the three of us step outside our comfort zones and have to address our anxieties to talk to politicians, lawyers and activists. Any media we did was not just to call for our abuser to return to Australia to face Australian courts, it was also to show other survivors of sexual abuse that they should not be shamed into silence.

Outside Adass Israel School with Ted Baillieu and David Southwick. LOUD fence is a wonderful organisation that ties ribbons around institutions where sexual abuse has occurred, conveying messages of support to victims, their loved ones and the community. These red ribbons draped through the Adass Israel School gate stayed there throughout Melbourne's first Covid lockdown, while the school was closed.

At a press conference with Josh Burns at the Glen Eira Town Hall just after an Israeli court found Malka Leifer had been 'impersonating someone with mental illness' and was fit to stand trial. My abuser was being extradited to Australia to finally face justice. The uncertainty and stress continued until the actual day she landed back in the country. Only then did I know the truth of what happened would finally be revealed to a court.

Without my sisters, and my brothers'
support, I don't know if I could have stood
strong for the fifteen years it took for my
abuser to be found guilty. Her actions are
still reverberating through my life,
and I now need to focus on healing myself.

One night, as I sang lullabies to Lily, I realised the last time we'd all been in a hospital room together was when I had just given birth.

I could never have imagined this picture four and a half years earlier.

For a moment I allowed myself to dream of the way I had imagined life to be, all of us one happy family, but despite the difficulty of the journey, I knew I was where I needed to be.

Finally, Shua and I reached a parenting settlement in April. The final family evaluation had been released and it was what I had hoped for.

I had always wanted Shua to be a part of Lily's life and never intended for him to be stripped of his legal parental rights. For so long, time with our daughter had been controlled by others, and finally the system was giving me back the right to help decide what was best for Lily's future.

Two friends, Dassi and Danni, and my sister Tamar accompanied me to my last day of legal proceedings. I recall waiting to be waved through security and then standing nervously beside Shua's lawyers at the lift, a barrister who loved swearing and encouraged me to do the same, Dassi hurrying off to find Nurofen for my impending migraine, lawyers scurrying between meeting rooms, fine-tuning our parenting schedule down to hours and minutes, and the long hours watching the clock, trying to work out if I would still make school pick-up.

When the mediation finally concluded, Shua and I had arrived at a schedule that we could both agree to.

With the legal proceedings behind me I felt more hopeful about everything. Now it was time to turn my attention to the civil case.

CHAPTER 20

Erlich v Malka Leifer and Adass Israel School

On 5 May 2015, as a cold front swept through Melbourne, Tamar and I stood outside the Owen Dixon Chambers, studying the rain, trying to time our two-minute run across to the Supreme Court of Victoria. It was the inaugural day of a civil trial that had been four years in the making – Erlich v Malka Leifer and Adass Israel School. Avoiding frizzy hair was vital.

Walking ahead of us, the senior counsel, Dyson Hore-Lacy SC, and barrister David Seeman clutched their court wigs to their heads while their black robes billowed around them as they traversed the wind tunnel of William Street. Behind them, Nick Mazzeo, the solicitor, and Tom McCredie, his junior, dragged trolleys spilling over with folders of rubber-banded pages – the history of my life in black and white. Mediation with the school had failed twice, so now it was time a judge heard the case. My team of lawyers had assured me they were primed for a battle.

At a break in the rain, Tamar and I hastened across the

road. The highest court in Victoria commanded an aura of grandeur, and as we climbed the staircase, which was flanked by bronze lions, nerves danced in my stomach. After passing through security, we turned off our phones and followed the lawyers to our assigned courtroom. The atmosphere inside the court was sombre and serious. Voices were muted by carpeted walls and there was a sense that the building itself was burdened by the weight of the stories it had witnessed. I thought about my impending time on the stand and a heaviness settled between my shoulders at the thought of describing my abuse to a room full of strangers.

On the first day of the two-week trial, before Justice Jack Rush, my lawyers outlined my case. I had suffered psychiatric injury due to the abuse of my former principal at Adass Israel School. The school had failed in their duty of care to protect me. The case we put forward was that the school was vicariously liable for Malka Leifer's conduct, as not only was Leifer employed by the school, she was, in effect of the law, 'the will and mind of the school'.

The lawyers for the school's insurance company laid out their defence. Malka Leifer, they claimed, was not the principal of the school. They argued that Leifer was a head teacher of Jewish studies, and while Jewish studies took place on school grounds, they were not a part of the school, but rather, were organised by the community.

Adass Israel School did not employ Leifer, the Adass community did, and a community is not an institution but a sum of individuals. A community is not a legal entity and therefore cannot be sued, they claimed. The defence further argued that they did not act on behalf of the community and therefore the case would need to be adjourned.

Tamar, Elly, Nicole, Dassi, Freda, Peter and their son Alex sat beside me. I was grateful for the presence of my support team; it took all my effort to conceal my shock at the untruths the defence proposed to prove. I didn't want to make a spectacle of myself in front of the reporters in the courtroom. I knew they weren't allowed to reference me by name, but I could feel their eyes following me, watching my reactions.

One moment on the first day made me sit up straighter. Weeks prior, a person from Israel wishing to remain anonymous due to fear of repercussion, had sent a secret recording of Leifer's husband to Nick Mazzeo. I had been ushered into my lawyer's office and handed the transcript, which contained some previously unknown details of how Leifer and her family had fled the country. I hadn't been able to keep still or breathe deeply with the magnitude of this new information, but I had kept it quiet. The defence were unaware of the recording until that morning, and they fought to have it thrown out of evidence. Ultimately, the judge allowed it into evidence. I left the court with a bounce in my step and a hope that the trial wouldn't be adjourned like it had been the previous year, when the defence managed to delay it with legal disputes.

On the second day of the trial, Justice Rush declared the case would proceed. My lawyers formally opened their case and called their first witness. It was time for me to take the stand.

I had risen early after a night of broken sleep; the terrors had visited me every time I closed my eyes. That morning, I stood in front of the mirror watching my lips shape the word 'vagina'. *Vagina, vagina, vagina.* Even then, it was still a word I found hard to say, and I had to remind myself not to refer to it as 'down there'.

My senior counsel Mr Hore-Lacy guided me through the evidence, and I told a room full of men how Mrs Leifer had violated me with her fingers. The weight of my shame, a lifetime's worth, felt heavy, and yet through it all I couldn't help but think of my younger self and how proud she would be, seeing me stand up for myself. I explained the vulnerabilities that kept me in Mrs Leifer's grip, the religious culture I had grown up within and the absolute control she had over the school. Later, Justice Rush would note in his report that he had seen my emotional disconnect – a stoic demeanour, but also great vulnerability.

Dyson Hore-Lacy told the court that they had received a further box of documents through the discovery process with approximately 150 pages of evidence, notably one that showed Adass Israel School as Leifer's nominated employer in the documents from the Department of Immigration, Multicultural and Indigenous Affairs. If the defence claimed she had not been employed by the school, it looked like the school had misled the Immigration Department.

Unbeknownst to me, that evening my barrister David Seeman was walking around Caulfield Park when he received a strange phone call. 'Follow the money,' said the caller, who refused to identify themselves. 'The money will identify who paid Leifer to leave the country.'

On the third day of the trial, I watched my lawyers ask the court for leave to serve a subpoena on an account held with the Bank of Queensland. The account had been used to pay for the tickets that allowed Leifer and her family to flee the country; they wanted the name of the individual attached to that account. Justice Rush granted the request. Then it was my turn to take the witness stand again, to face further questioning and cross-examination.

A wave of relief swept over me as Christopher Blanden, the defence barrister, made it clear he had no intention of questioning my experiences of abuse. I answered his questions truthfully, but I could sense he was trying to downplay the damage done to my mental health. I battled the urge to stand up and declare how the abuse had irrevocably altered my future, to tell them how often I lay awake at night, wondering how my life would have been different if I'd only had one loving person in my childhood to support me, instead of yet another adult who abused me.

Finally, I was dismissed from the stand. As I left the courtroom I sent a look of strength to Nicole as she made her way inside to front the judge. Elly's turn would come later. We had never exchanged specifics of our abuse, and once we had given our statements we had been asked by the police not to discuss it.

Meanwhile, my lawyers toiled away, tendering reams of documents that offered proof of Leifer's employment at the school, including her contract, payslips and visa application.

On the fourth day, the truth behind Leifer's escape from justice began to surface.

Nick informed me he had called six travel agents in the vicinity of the school until they identified the agent responsible for issuing Leifer's ticket out of Australia.

The travel agent took the stand and told the court that at 9 or 10 p.m. on 5 March 2008, she received a frantic call from one of her employees, who also happened to be the wife of Meir Ernst, a member of the school board. The board had convened the previous evening at a prestigious community member's house with the intent to confront Leifer about the sexual abuse allegations. Ernst's wife asked for tickets to Israel for an 'urgent compassionate need' and, without any hesitation, the agent issued tickets for one adult and four children on the first flight en route to Israel out of Australia that very night.

Meir Ernst was summoned to the witness stand. Finding him and serving him his subpoena had been no easy task. My lawyer, Nick, had told me how he'd sat outside the board member's house for two evenings, keeping watch for any signs of movement. On the second night, just as it seemed that no one was home, a car pulled up and a figure rushed inside. Nick leapt to his feet and managed to catch Mr Ernst just moments before he left the country.

Meir Ernst stood before the court, recalling the moment he first learnt of the allegations against Leifer. It had been dusk, the light fading fast, when the president of the school board, Yitchok Benedikt, had approached him outside Ripponlea train station. Benedikt told Ernst that the gravity of the allegations demanded an urgent meeting of the board; Leifer must be removed from her position.

Two and a half hours later, the board gathered, including three rabbis, a barrister, a psychologist, a prominent community figure and two head teachers. On a loudspeaker call, they implored Mrs Leifer to join them. When she refused, they challenged her on the allegations. Meir told the court that she yelled and screamed, and denied everything.

Meir Ernst confirmed that he had called his wife to organise the tickets, but how they had been paid for – thousands of dollars worth – remained a mystery. He simply could not remember, even though, as he confirmed to the court, it was an unusual occurrence, not something that happened every day of the week. Nor could he recall what had driven him to make that call to his wife, or the discussion about Leifer leaving. It was all a blur. The decision, it seemed, had been made collectively by those present that night.

As details of the help Leifer received to flee the jurisdiction unfolded on the stand, I could feel a stone pressing against my chest. The knots in my stomach twisted tighter and tighter. I didn't sleep much that week.

On day five, the defence began their case, claiming the evidence would demonstrate that Leifer had elected to leave the country of her own accord. Under the terms of her contract, the community was responsible for her and her family's tickets.

Current principal of Adass Israel School Professor Israel Herszberg was their first witness. He spent the entire day in court, arguing that Leifer wasn't employed by the school but by the congregation, though the defence failed to provide a single payslip to substantiate this. However, Herszberg did confirm the tickets were paid for by a company owned by the president of the school board, and that the school reimbursed the company. Bank records confirmed as much. It was an exasperating day that required occasional visits to the restroom to quietly scream and release my pent-up frustration.

On day six, the subpoena from the Bank of Queensland was returned and submitted into evidence. Mrs Etty Spigelman, head teacher of general studies, was called to the stand.

Mrs Spigelman told the court about her time working with Leifer, insisting she never had any cause for concern when it came to the woman's character. She said she had seen the close connection between Mrs Leifer and myself, and remembered Leifer taking certain girls into her office and closing the door, but she said the principal would talk to her about it afterwards, so she thought nothing of it. Despite the paperwork that labelled her assistant principal under Leifer's name, Mrs Spigelman suggested they ran the school together, on an equal footing.

The night Leifer fled the country, Mrs Spigelman received a phone call summoning her to the meeting of the school board. She was deeply shocked to learn of the allegations. The following day, she went to see Leifer, to tell her goodbye, disbelief and shock a heavy burden in her heart. Leifer told her of her urgent departure, claiming that 'if she wasn't running the school, there was no reason for her to stay in Australia'.

I'd thought I couldn't be more shocked, but what followed a few hours later left me a mess for several days.

A senior teacher, Mrs Sharon Bromberg, took the stand. She described how Leifer was a huge part of the community, explaining that her position as headmistress bled into her role as a respected community figure.

Then Mrs Bromberg revealed that Mrs Casen, a psychologist who worked in the Adass community, had called her back in August 2007 – seven whole months before my disclosure – to mention that Leifer was crossing boundaries with girls. Mrs Bromberg had approached Leifer about this, but Leifer had told her not to worry; she had spoken to the rabbinical council and everything was in order.

Seven months.

Seven months earlier. I felt the guilt of not speaking out sooner, a guilt that crushed me at times. If only I had spoken up sooner, I might have been able to save Elly. But now here I was, learning that someone else *had* spoken up sooner, and yet nothing had been done. How many other girls could have been saved, if only someone had listened?

Mrs Bromberg informed the court that she had received another call ten or eleven days before Leifer fled Australia. This time, she was informed that the allegations against Mrs Leifer held some substance. She called another student to confirm the truth of the statement. When she confronted Mrs Leifer yet again, she was given the same answer: the rabbinical council was dealing with the issue, and all was in order. But this time, Mrs Bromberg wasn't satisfied.

Mrs Bromberg decided to contact the rabbinical council herself, and made an appointment with Rabbi Binyomin Wurtzburger. The overarching rabbi of the community, Rabbi Avraham Zvi Beck, led the rabbinical council, but Rabbi Wurtzburger was an esteemed rabbi in his own right, and Mrs Leifer had been known to seek advice from him as well.

Rabbi Wurtzburger's wife called Mrs Bromberg to cancel the appointment and said she had heard of these allegations the previous year, and while it made her feel sick to hear them, perhaps this was simply a girl's fantasy. After all, girls fantasise about people they are close with.

By the end of the phone call, Mrs Bromberg believed she had convinced the rabbi, who she could hear in the background, and his wife that this was no fantasy.

By then I was done with grief and had moved on to anger. They had all known, had heard the rumours and yet no one had acted. I had been carrying the guilt of not speaking up sooner, and yet someone else had, and still nothing had been done.

Mrs Bromberg told the court she had also contacted Rabbi Beck, who listened, but said little. She went into the Shabbat feeling she had acted appropriately and that the issue was in the right hands.

After the weekend, Mrs Bromberg was asked to attend the rabbinical council and tell them why she believed the allegations to be true.

Continuing her evidence, Mrs Bromberg said she attended that meeting the following Tuesday and informed the group of two further allegations that had come to light, then left the room.

The group reconvened the following evening – Wednesday, 5 March.

A week had passed since the school were aware of my disclosure and not only did Leifer still stand as principal, she had also been to a school camp with the girls.

At 1.20 a.m. on Thursday, 6 March, Leifer left Australia with four of her children. Her husband stayed behind with three boys; their son's bar mitzvah was to be celebrated that weekend. Less than forty-eight hours after being confronted, before the police had even been notified, Leifer was ushered out of the country.

On day seven of the trial, Mr Benjamin Koppel, former president of the Adass synagogue, took the stand and spoke of how Mrs Leifer had arrived in Australia. I had always wondered if another school had chosen to rid themselves of their problem by sending Mrs Leifer to the other side of the world. Reports in Israel would later back this up.

Mr Koppel told the court that Mrs Leifer had come with glowing recommendations from a school in Israel. A member of the Adass Israel School board belonged to the same Hasidic sect as Leifer, and was in contact with the sect in Israel. The board member was very keen for Leifer to take the position in Australia. My lawyers asked Mr Koppel if he was aware that Leifer and the school board could not agree on a salary, so the board member had agreed to fund part of Leifer's salary if she was given the role. Mr Koppel said he had heard rumours about this, but had no records of these discussions.

The trial wrapped on the eighth day. The judge spent the day clarifying issues with both sides, and then adjourned the case for judgement.

On 16 September 2015, the judge handed down his decision. I arrived at the court with my sisters and sat with my hands squeezed tight on my lap, quietly listening to the judge's words. In a landmark decision, Justice Rush found that my former school, Adass Israel, was directly and vicariously liable for the acts of Malka Leifer.

Justice Rush read parts of his judgement to the court.

> The power, control and authority of Leifer within the School was unrestrained and unrestricted. Leifer committed sexual abuse against the plaintiff both inside and outside the School, but at all times Leifer's appalling misconduct with the plaintiff was built on this position of unrestrained power, control and authority that had been bestowed upon her by the Board.

He found that Leifer held a pre-eminent position of power in a unique school where her authority involved religious beliefs, lifestyle and everyday behaviour. We were closed off from the world, naive concerning matters of sex, and Leifer's responsibilities and relationship with students centred around the core of our beliefs, values and living.

> In my opinion, 'the teacher-student relationship' between Leifer and the plaintiff 'was invested with a high degree of power and intimacy' and Leifer used 'that power and intimacy to commit sexual abuse'.

I felt a sense of sadness and grief at the pain and suffering I had endured throughout those years, but also a sense of justice knowing the court had acknowledged the profound impact of the abuse on my life.

Justice Rush continued:

> Overall, the evidence demonstrates the plaintiff, as a consequence of Leifer's sexual abuse, has suffered a major

psychiatric illness. The impact of that illness on her life has
been profound. The self-harm, lengthy in-patient admissions
at the Albert Road Clinic and the need for antidepressant
medication are markers of the significance of that injury. It
is difficult for one who has not experienced it to comprehend
the emptiness of depression: the inability to control the
nightmares, flashbacks, weeping and insomnia associated
with the degrading abuse suffered as a teenager; the inability
to breastfeed her baby; contested Family Court proceedings
concerning the ability of the plaintiff to be able to care for her
child; the inability to properly feel and express her emotions.

... The plaintiff's injury was aggravated by the fact that the
abuse occurred in circumstances of a massive breach of trust,
of the complete sexual innocence of the plaintiff and of the
fear that Leifer could disclose the plaintiff's family situation to
those within the Adass community.

... The injury will remain with the plaintiff, fluctuating in its
intensity for the remainder of her life. As noted, she is at risk
of major relapse depending on 'triggers' in her life.

The language Justice Rush used was incredibly important
in conveying the gravity of the situation, and in sending a
strong message of disapproval. The judge used powerful
words such as 'wantonly', 'destructive' and 'evil' to describe
Leifer's actions and their consequences. There was a certain
healing that came with the court's acknowledgement of the
harm Leifer had done.

The evidence overwhelmingly demonstrates that Leifer had
a contumelious disregard for the plaintiff's rights. I have
described Leifer's conduct previously as a massive breach
of trust, yet this description does not adequately set out
the destructive and evil nature of her sexual abuse of the

plaintiff over a period of years. The evidence discloses
the sole motivation of Leifer in her dealings with the
plaintiff was for her own sexual gratification. Leifer used
her position of control, power and authority within the
School to manipulate the plaintiff's sense of vulnerability
concerning her family situation so as to create the
opportunity for further abuse. The conduct of Leifer can be
described as wanton, carried out in complete disregard of
the plaintiff's rights and welfare.

It is conduct deserving of this Court's disapprobation; it
is conduct that is deserving of damages to punish Leifer and
deter others from similar conduct.

The judge awarded me $1 274 428 in damages. This comprised $300 000 for non-economic loss, $551 780 for past and future economic loss, and $172 648 for past and future medical expenses, most of which was paid back to my health insurance for my admissions at the Albert Road psychiatric clinic. I also paid back Victims of Crime Assistance for the pay-out I had received in 2012.

Included in that sum, the court also granted an award of exemplary damages from both Leifer and the school. These were not intended to compensate me, but to serve as a punishment to the respondents and a warning to others not to act similarly. The board's actions were labelled 'disgraceful', showing a total disregard for due process, and so the court imposed exemplary damages of $100 000 on the school.

Finally, the court ordered Leifer to pay me $150 000 of exemplary damages. She never paid.

CHAPTER 21

Rebuilding

The civil court judge's ruling carried a powerful message and with newfound financial stability, I embraced life, striking a balance between work, taking care of Lily and navigating the ongoing legal process in Israel where the criminal case against Leifer was still ensnared in extradition proceedings. Just as my life was settling into a rhythm, one morning in September 2015 a fateful knock on my door changed everything. As I hesitantly opened the door, half-dressed and wrapped in a towel, I had no idea that moment would ripple through the next few years, transforming my future entirely. That morning though, I responded with a firm no and closed the door in the face of the male reporter who had turned up at my home unannounced and uninvited.

I was astonished that he had managed to find me at the end of a nondescript street in Glen Iris; I hadn't realised my address could be sourced from court records. I managed to quickly message my sisters, telling them a journalist named Cameron Stewart from *The Weekend Australian* had turned up at my house and asked if I was willing to be identified in a feature piece he was writing about my story.

A few weeks later, in October, I set aside everything court-related, including the unsettling visit from Cameron Stewart, and set off into the wild with my friend Dassi by my side. Not long after I had arrived back from England after my sister's death, overwhelmed by the reality of the world, Dassi had taken me camping, and I had fallen in love with the solace of nature. We packed a tent, Dassi, Lily, me and a niece, and headed off to the Mornington Peninsula.

We spent time on the beach and exploring the bushland. It was a comfort to watch Lily and my niece in their element, running on the sand, their cheeks warmed by childhood exuberance. The beach at Shoreham was deserted; we couldn't see another soul, not even a footprint to prove that this mile-long piece of perfection had ever been discovered by humans before. It was easy to believe we were all alone in the world – just us, the sand, the surf and the seagulls.

On the second day, it rained, and when the rain abated, we set up a fire in our little corner of paradise and it felt like my soul was being warmed along with our dinner. I felt so in the moment there, it was hard to believe there was a whole other world back home – a world I was eager to forget. There was no better feeling than collapsing into the tent after our race against the edge of a storm, snuggling in beside Lily and reading a book aloud. All I could hear was the chirping of birds, the crash of waves, the crackling of the fire and the kettle singing its way to a warm cup of tea. *I'm appreciative of the time we have had, the memories of nature's dance between stillness and movement that I will hold forever in my heart*, I wrote in my diary.

I found camping life tranquil and slow. My mind was quiet, and yet somehow more alive. There was no schedule – we ate when we were hungry, slept when we were tired, bundled up when we were cold, and there was always a cup of tea if we were thirsty. On the last day I lay with my limbs stretched out to the sun, inviting the magical peace to make its home in my body. I closed my eyes and saw sand skipping over a beach that had no end, moved only by the wind and the waves. I took my last walk with bare feet across the wet ground, letting the magic fold itself inside me so I could carry it back to the city. The sun graced us all morning and just as we left, the rain waved us goodbye.

My small sojourn into nature over, I returned back to work in aged care. I had never fully finished my nursing degree; the stress of litigation had taken over. While I had completed the units and the four required placements, I had failed to hand in seven assignments. It had been four years since I had begun, and the university informed me that if I did not complete the degree before the end of 2016 my study would have all been for naught. I would have to redo four units, so I signed up to do them part-time the following year. Talking about Leifer's abuse repeatedly had felt like a black cloud hanging over my life; it had seeped into everything and coloured the way I saw the world. With the stress of the civil case behind me, I hoped I would have the concentration to complete my studies.

By the end of 2015, the Leifer case had been going through the Israeli court system for eighteen months. After she was arrested in August 2014, the court had ruled that she would remain in custody until the end of the extradition proceedings. But two months later, Judge Vinograd released Leifer from custody, placing her under house arrest. According to Israeli law, if a defendant does not physically attend a court hearing, the case cannot proceed. By October 2015 there had been nine further hearings and Leifer had not turned up for a single one. Her lawyers had faced the media and informed everyone watching that Leifer was never coming back to Australia.

We had met with the state prosecution team while we were in Israel for the first anniversary of Dalia's death. The state informed us that Leifer had been claiming mental illness and checking herself into a psych hospital before every court hearing, only to leave immediately after the court adjourned. Having experienced Leifer's manipulation, none of us were surprised.

Back in Australia, Nicole was kept updated on the case by Elizabeth Levy, a director of international relations at Israel's National Council for the Child. At times I felt guilty for not sharing this burden with her, but with the civil case behind me, I needed to create distance from Leifer's false claim of mental illness, for the sake of my own mental health.

Summer arrived, and with it came a sense of excitement. For the first time in a long time, my future felt open. I found myself clubbing and partying – reliving my teenage years, as my therapist put it, before I reminded her that I'd never had any. As I approached the end of my twenties, I was determined to make up for lost time and experience all the things I'd missed out on growing up.

Shua and I divided the school holidays between us, each spending three weeks with Lily. The weeks without her were filled with longing, but they also offered respite from the responsibilities of parenthood. And so, I welcomed in the new year with a friend in Thailand. While there, I walked the same streets in Phuket that Dalia had strolled with her family years before. She was never far from my thoughts, and seeing the things she had described brought me closer to her memory.

Upon returning home after two weeks of vibrant culture, landscapes and food, I set off on a road trip with Dassi and Lily, travelling through Victoria and South Australia. I had fallen in love with camping, and now I fell in love with the spontaneity of a road trip. It felt like I was answering the call of my curious spirit, which had been singing to no avail through all those years of rigidity. The idea of setting out with no destination, of taking the path as it unfolds, and finding beauty in the unexpected was liberating. It was the perfect start to the year.

I like to think of 2016 as the quiet year in between, but in many ways it was actually very loud. I don't believe I was single for a moment of that year, but I also wasn't in anything that could be considered a traditional relationship. It was a year of trial and error. I tested the waters, dabbled in the unknown, and in the process, I found myself. I experimented with my sexuality, unafraid and unashamed. I had discovered the power of self-worth and that allowed me to embrace the fluidity of love. Through all that, I worked to ensure Lily had a calm, stable home with a mother who was fully present.

February marked the start of prep for Lily. Nicole and I savoured the sight of our daughters in their matching school uniforms, heading off to their first day of school together. Nicole's daughter had been born three weeks after Lily, the only daughter among four siblings. Tamar too had four children, and when we gathered as a family, we enjoyed the love and closeness I had yearned for as a child. We had sisters' nights, sibling game nights and big family birthday parties. My siblings all carry the scars of our childhood but each of them has found a way through, and I delight in seeing my daughter surrounded by cousins, aunts and uncles.

I returned to university in March, the trudge into the city a familiar echo of years past. My former classmates had graduated, but now, with a better sense of who I was, I found new friends to share my days with. Without the weight of legal proceedings, I could focus on my studies, delve into the work and complete my assigned tasks.

But Leifer's case was never far away. Each adjournment of her court appearance was a blow, and my sisters and I were frustrated by the lack of progress. We gave opinions to the media when we felt able, commenting anonymously; Nicole even appeared on the ABC with her voice distorted and her image a silhouette. Following my refusal to speak on record with Cameron Stewart, we had stayed in touch, and he would always alert me before a story was published. It was a small kindness that made all the difference, allowing me to be prepared, rather than scrolling through social media and being unexpectedly confronted with Leifer's picture, the one picture the news used over and over that year. For several reasons, I decided not to identify myself for a feature story at that time.

I learnt to accept that each time Leifer appeared in court, and then subsequently in the media, the equilibrium in my life would be disrupted. The nights would stretch, growing longer and darker, and the nightmares became more intense. 'I think money is changing hands somewhere,' I said to my sisters in April. The reasons for the delays were ridiculous, they made no sense.

By the end of April, the funds from the civil case had been deposited into my account, a sum greater than I had ever possessed before. While I didn't receive the full amount awarded by the judge, due to expenses such as medical bills and legal costs, it was still a substantial sum. I was able to pay back the debt I had accrued from my travels, buy a better car and still have enough left over to establish financial security for the near future.

With the financial stability I had gained, I was able to embrace cultural experiences that were previously beyond my reach. I attended the ballet with friends, took Lily to the theatre, and explored art galleries together. It was great fun to be spontaneous. During one weekend escape, I surprised Lily with a helicopter ride over the Geelong waterfront.

In small interludes of my everyday life, I often found my mind drifting to the life I once led – whether soaring above the clouds, curled up beside a stranger, or indulging in a burger at a roadside cafe, for just a moment I would pause, step back into my former self and see the beautiful unpredictability of the life I now lived, so different from the one pre-ordained for me.

In May, the Office of Public Prosecutions in Victoria invited Nicole, Elly and myself to their office. It was an invitation we had never received before, and we knew the news wouldn't be good. Our premonition proved true: the OPP informed us that Israel was likely to drop the case. The following week, the judge halted the extradition proceedings based on a psychiatrist's report, with the final decision to be handed down the following month.

And so it was: in June, Leifer was released from house arrest and had her bail money returned to her. Her only requirement was to appear before a psychiatric panel for review every six months for the next ten years.

In the same moment I was dousing Lily's hair in a lice treatment and the power in the building flickered and failed, Nicole called to tell me the news. My voice, when I finally spoke, was a cry of 'What?', 'How could they?' and 'Why?'. Nicole, on the other end, had no answers. Tamar and Elly joined the call while we posted the news articles into our WhatsApp group, along with many expletives and exclamation marks.

I lay in bed that night, the sheets twisting and tangling as I tossed and turned, unable to find a comfortable position.

I forced my eyes to close, but sleep refused to come. All night I kept checking the clock, watching the minutes and hours ticking by. I listened to my tried-and-true meditation; it didn't help – my body had too much tension. Just before 6 a.m. I finally fell into a troubled sleep, only to be woken half an hour later by my excited six-year-old, eager to get ready for school.

Between parenting and an upcoming university assignment, I had to set aside this devastating news. Exhaustion and a lack of time left me unable to dwell on my frustration and disillusionment.

Michelle Meyer, CEO of Tzedek, a child sex-abuse victims group, had started an online petition to the Israeli Minister of Justice, Ayelet Shaked, pleading for Leifer's extradition. Fiona Sweet-Formiatti, an advocate in Canberra, had also launched another petition, and together they had been signed by thousands of people, all aghast at the ruling.

Days later, the *Herald Sun* released an article revealing that a bank account belonging to Malka Leifer was being topped up by people in Melbourne. I sat alone in my apartment, staring blankly at the article on the screen before me. The tightness in my chest and the ache in my stomach were palpable as I thought about the individuals who had aided Malka Leifer in evading justice. I wondered why this person, who had taken so much from me, was still being sheltered and sustained. 'How could they?' I asked my sisters.

It took me longer this time to quell my frustration and return to normal life. I had an exam requiring a hundred per cent in order to pass, and I put it off until I was in the headspace to study. A week later, when I passed the calculations test with a score of a hundred per cent, I skipped home, picked Lily up from school and took her out for dinner. Despite everything, I was finding a way through.

A couple of weeks later, we headed out for our first experience of winter camping. I'd thought I was prepared – I was not. It was a cold and bracing week, but definitely a great learning experience, and winter camping soon became our favourite type.

In July, Elly and I made the decision to get tattoos together. We chose the image of a dahlia flower. According to the Torah, tattoos were forbidden, and having one would mean I was no longer eligible for burial in a Jewish cemetery. This had always been a point of hesitation for me, but now, Elly and I both felt there was valid reason to move forward. The dahlia flower is on my left shoulder. It was painful, but worthwhile. It was a way to carry a memory of my sister Dalia on my body and I love catching glimpses of it in the mirror.

I was starting to find joy as well as hardship. On 18 August, there was cause for celebration in the family. Henry and Marilyn, my former father-in-law and his wife, welcomed a grandchild into the world. Marilyn's daughter Romy had given birth to a little boy. At the time, I didn't know Romy too well, but being a new mother, she was always eager for advice and companionship from another mum, and so we established a tradition of Wednesday morning coffee dates, Wednesdays being the one morning I wasn't at work or university.

As the year progressed, I seized every opportunity to broaden my horizons. I read extensively and attempted to learn a new language. At times, I felt as if I were a toddler, eager to undergo all my growth in a single bound. The unknown held a certain allure; there was such satisfaction exploring what lay beyond my comfort zone. My social circle grew, and I travelled for the second time that year, to Bali, where not even a bout of Bali belly stopped me from enjoying everything the country had to offer. And finally, on the 4 November 2016, after a hectic month at a hospital in Sale for my last nursing placement, I handed in my final university assignment.

The day I finally held my nursing degree in my hand was nothing short of thrilling.

It had taken me five years, a relentless dedication and many moments that put my resolve to test, and I celebrated the achievement by going out for drinks with my uni mates.

After a year of growth and learning, I finally felt prepared to publicly link my name with the Malka Leifer saga. I had come to recognise that I was more than just a victim of my past. I could proudly accept my identity without the burden of shame that had been draped over me for so long. I messaged Cameron Stewart and said I was ready to talk. In November, we sat down in a little cafe on Carlisle Street, not far from where I grew up, for an interview.

Over my road trip to Sydney that summer holiday, Cameron and I messaged back and forth, and when the story was near completion, a photographer was booked to visit my apartment in February.

I had packed up and left Glen Iris, which felt too far away from family, and moved closer to where my sisters lived. I had yet to have most of my furniture delivered, but I remember the photographer's excitement at the blank canvas of my living space. I was shy in front of the camera, and I had to stop myself from fidgeting with the buttons on my dress or jiggling my knee up and down. The photographer managed to put me at ease, but I still couldn't shake off my apprehension about the reaction from the community. I agonised over whether I was making the right decision.

In an effort to distract myself while waiting for the article to be published, I hosted housewarming parties in my bean bag–filled living room, as my couch was still several months from arrival. I also attended a nursing interview that February after registering as a nurse, and contemplated adjusting my parenting schedule, as the hours required for nursing did not align with Lily's school hours.

Despite this, every week I waited, a mixture of nerves and anticipation, for Cameron to tell me when the article would be published. Finally, the message I'd been waiting for came.

On Saturday, 18 March 2017, *The Weekend Australian* published an article titled 'Private Lessons', publicly identifying me as a victim of Malka Leifer.

CHAPTER 22

Campaign

At 10 p.m. that Saturday night, twenty minutes after Shabbat had ended and the usage of technology was once again permitted, my phone rang.

'You've exposed the community's dirty laundry,' said the indignant voice of a community leader. 'The synagogues are abuzz with what you've done.' I walked through my house with a smile on my face as I shared the outpouring of support I had received throughout the day. 'Perhaps,' I challenged the man, 'the problem isn't me. Perhaps the problem lies with the community.' The call abruptly ended, but my smile lingered.

Nothing was going to stand in the way of the truth.

A few days later, I embarked on my first venture into the realm of social media. I established a Facebook page, naming it 'Dassi Erlich: Beyond a Survivor', with the hashtag #bringleiferback as its backdrop. This platform would serve as a place to share updates on the case and to raise awareness about Mrs Leifer, who was still in Israel and claiming to have an incapacitating sickness that exempted her from attending court.

The page started with an active hundred or so followers. Within a few weeks, an individual affiliated with the Adass community began trolling my page, accusing me of exaggeration. This attack, which would once have silenced me, instead ignited a sense of empowerment within me. I no longer felt shackled by embarrassment; instead, I was eager to shed light on the multifaceted issues stemming from our community's insistence on harbouring secrets.

Gradually, the page garnered more followers. I shared the results of the mandated six-month reviews that Mrs Leifer was expected to attend after the Israeli judicial system had discontinued the case. Her own family referred to her as a 'sack of potatoes', completely debilitated, unable to perform even the most basic of daily tasks. It felt like the case would never see court again. Justice didn't seem possible.

I joined forces with Alex Fein, a community activist and remarkable woman determined to make a difference. Our mission was clear: reach out to every stakeholder in the Jewish community and beyond. Creating a comprehensive list, we initiated a Twitter thread, uniting them under the hashtag #bringleiferback. The response was overwhelming; the hashtag quickly gained traction and became the powerful tagline to the rest of our campaign.

The support I received from my social media followers, as well as my friends and family, in response to these revelations stirred a realisation deep within me. Something was egregiously amiss. I questioned why, as a society, we permitted a master manipulator like Leifer to continue her manipulations in order to evade justice. What did this say to others who sought the courage to report abuse?

During sleepless nights, I would lie in bed, haunted by the vivid imagery of the life Leifer was leading. In my imagination, she revelled in her audacity to defy the system, secure in the knowledge that she could forever evade the consequences of her actions. Did this confidence mean she continued to prey on young and vulnerable girls, all while pretending to be caring and concerned?

I wondered if she had ever truly cared about me at all. The care under which her abuse came was an enigma that still perplexed me. The younger parts of me, so desperate for Mrs Leifer's affection, found it difficult to accept that her love and care was nothing more than a deceptive facade. What did this say about my own worth? Was I truly unlovable, destined to be seen only as an object? Was love merely a game, used solely as a means of control?

I spent a lot of time in therapy unravelling this web of confusion. I learnt to challenge these distorted beliefs – Mrs Leifer's manipulation did not mean I was incapable of being loved.

The idea of other young women having to untangle this same confusion motivated me to work harder. I met with a series of Jewish organisations in Melbourne and Sydney, imploring them to support our cause on a grander scale. But the organisations I approached were apprehensive, concerned about the potential repercussions of criticising Israel within a broader context. They were eager to be a part of the narrative, so long as they retained control over its trajectory.

I, on the other hand, had no interest in relinquishing control of my own story. I had shown my face to the world, and I refused to be intimidated. Frustrated with the community's initial tepid response, my friend Dassi Herszberg introduced me to the former premier of Victoria, Ted Baillieu. One May afternoon, I sat in his office in the Old Treasury Building in central Melbourne. He was welcoming and attentive. I spoke of the hesitance within the community and he assured me that one day, the magnitude of this story would become so overwhelming that anyone not offering support for justice would be viewed unfavourably. I was sceptical. At the conclusion of our meeting, he promised to stand by my side wherever and whenever his presence was needed. True to his word, he never faltered. Through Ted's steadfast support, I came to understand the profound significance of actions outweighing words, which often rang hollow.

Shortly after that initial meeting, I approached Ted and requested his presence at a meeting with the Adass Israel School board. The meeting was to discuss the possibility of the school issuing a public apology for its actions following my disclosure of Malka Leifer's abuse. The meeting took place at the house of the board president. While the words spoken seemed promising, the subsequent actions revealed those words held no meaning.

Despite numerous discussions held over the course of the following year, which even involved bringing in a mediator after the school suggested that I write the apology myself, the promised public apology never materialised. The mounting frustration of an entire year's futile efforts ultimately led me to walk away from the project. It became clear that their actions did not align with their words, and I made the difficult decision to abandon any hope of the school genuinely supporting those who had been affected. I stayed in regular contact with Ted through this process, and he maintained that as long as the school prioritised their insurance over the wellbeing of their students, a genuine apology would never be forthcoming.

The #bringleiferback campaign really took off when in May 2017, Nicole received a photograph via WhatsApp from a former Adass student. It was of Malka Leifer, seemingly brimming with vitality as she attended the Lag Ba'omer religious festival in Meron, a city in northern Israel, teeming with thousands of individuals from around the globe. This was the very same woman whose family had claimed she was incapable of tending to her most basic needs, confined to her bed, gazing emptily at the walls for hours on end. I stared at the image for what felt like ages, seized by the chilling reminder of her cunning. Then I shared the photo on my Facebook page, accompanied by a message addressing her directly. 'Dear Mrs Leifer,' I wrote. 'Do you ever lie in bed, contemplating my existence in the same manner that I lie in bed, ruminating over yours?' The photo quickly went viral, attracting thousands of visitors to my page, and soon caught the attention of the media.

For the first time, I began dealing with multiple media outlets, and the surge of interest instilled a renewed sense of passion for justice within me. Finally, the story was getting attention. Ted Baillieu facilitated a series of radio interviews, during which I spoke out as Dassi Erlich, victim of Malka Leifer, demanding Leifer's return to Australia. The media's interest resulted in widespread community engagement with the case. My social media transformed into a bustling hub of activity, as people expressed their outrage at the apparent ease with which Leifer was able to exploit the system. In June, I addressed a packed Glen Eira Town Hall, tracing my transformation from a timid and abused child to an adult woman demanding justice.

The police commissioner himself, Graham Ashton, gave a follow-up interview on the radio. Meanwhile, Dave Sharma, Australian ambassador to Israel, contacted me personally to assure me of his efforts to raise the issue with Israeli authorities. The case was gaining momentum. I reached out to government officials in both Israel and Australia, pleading for support and an opportunity to present our case.

To amplify our cause, Victorian MP David Southwick organised a petition to gather signatures. The plan was for David to present the petitions, which when combined with those collected in 2016 totalled 17 000 signatures, to the Israeli justice minister, Ayelet Shaked, during his visit to Israel. The pressure was mounting, and other members of parliament, including Mark Dreyfus and Michael Danby, stepped in to assemble a delegation of Australian politicians to join the plea to the justice minister.

I recall walking down Carlisle Street in St Kilda one afternoon, accompanied by Dassi Herszberg, when the ABC's *7.30* called requesting an interview. I had been filling Dassi in about our plans to take the campaign to Israel, and the media in both countries was eager to film our efforts. Dassi remarked on how the case had consumed my life entirely, from meeting with visiting Israeli politicians to engaging in interviews with various media outlets. But it was garnering widespread attention, and I seized every opportunity to raise awareness.

'I will give this campaign six more months of my life,' I told Dassi. 'Six months dedicated to pursuing justice. If in that time we have made no significant progress, I will step away, knowing in my heart that I have done everything within my power.' It was a conversation Dassi never let me forget, and one that I revisited countless times in the ensuing years as the case gained global prominence, permeating my life in ways I could never have fathomed.

Our first exposure on Israeli TV began with a chance encounter on a plane, when Harriet Warlow-Shill, a Melbourne lawyer, sat next to Member of the Knesset (the Israeli parliament) Michal Biran, who was visiting

Australia. Their conversation delved into the danger and injustice of Malka Leifer living freely in Israel. Michal had been unaware.

Michal Biran then continued the conversation with Victorian MP Philip Dalidakis. Dean Sherr, a staffer for Mr Dalidakis, suggested that Michal speak with me. Michal followed up and connected me with Channel Arutz 10 in Israel. The National Council of Jewish Women of Victoria found us a cameraman to film in Australia. And just like that, in a series of coincidences and connections, our first major story in Israel took flight, putting a spotlight on the injustice we were battling.

Nicole, Elly and I filmed this news segment for Israel at the same time as I filmed for 7.30 in Australia, and the experience exposed us to the intricacies of the media world.

Half-day interviews condensed to one-line grabs for final broadcast. The simple walking into a house portrayed at the start of a news story could require six takes, each filmed from a different angle. We learnt about 'b roll' – extra footage, like coffee making or staring awkwardly through a window, used to enhance the main content – and how to appear natural as the cameras followed us. It felt strange and surreal, almost unbelievably so. We had grown up in a world where TVs were strictly forbidden and now, here we were, appearing on those very screens. The occasionally ridiculous instructions from film crews had my sisters and I apologising to producers for our fits of giggles. Going through this new reality together made it somewhat more manageable.

Shortly before Nicole, Elly and I were due to leave for our first lobbying trip to Israel, my parents called for a family meeting. It was a difficult moment, given my father had recently been diagnosed with ALS, also known as Lou

Gehrig's Disease, a degenerative and fatal disease of the nervous system. My parents expressed a desire to rebuild a relationship with us, with one condition – that we apologise for the disrespect we had shown by distancing ourselves since they had decided we were no longer their children. I contemplated the impact on re-establishing contact – the guilt, the misplaced expectations of servitude, the unresolved abuse, and the distressing flashbacks it would trigger. It wasn't a relationship I desired, especially when my parents had shown no remorse for their past maltreatment. I made the decision not to offer an apology. Neither did any of my siblings.

While the Australian media had shown an interest in our cause, gaining traction in Israel proved more challenging. Mark Leibler, a highly regarded lawyer in Melbourne, reached out to me to offer assistance. Mark and his son Jeremy, also a respected lawyer, readily joined our cause, connecting me with individuals in Israel who could help us secure meetings with members of parliament. Once Mark Leibler, a respected figure in the community and a staunch Zionist, pledged his support, others began to follow suit. I wondered if his backing showed that one could support Israel while still criticising its flaws.

The president of the Executive Council of Australian Jewry, Peter Wertheim, and I drafted a letter to the Prime Minister of Australia, Malcolm Turnbull. Through the ECAJ's support, we were able to secure an audience with Mr Turnbull. The meeting took place on the morning of the grand final footy parade in Melbourne, and Elly, myself and Ted Baillieu convened outside the Victorian Parliament at the top end of Bourke Street. The streets were cordoned off in preparation for the parade, which was scheduled for later that morning.

During our meeting, Mr Turnbull was attentive, and expressed his commitment to addressing the issue. He assured us he would raise the matter with the Israeli Prime Minister Benjamin Netanyahu when he visited Israel later that year. The promising exchange left us feeling hopeful that our cause would receive attention and consideration at the highest levels of government.

As we prepared to fly out to Israel in September 2017, both Nicole and Elly, who had provided support behind the scenes without publicly identifying themselves, were ready to step into the spotlight. On my Facebook page, I shared a picture of the three of us at the Australian airport, declaring their status as victims of Leifer. The journey ahead was daunting, but we were united in our resolve to seek justice.

Our trip to Israel coincided with the centenary of the battle of Beersheba, an important Australian World War I milestone. We were meeting in a Jerusalem hotel with Cameron Stewart, who was in Israel covering the Beersheba centenary, when the lobby suddenly became a hub of activity and in walked none other than Prime Minister Turnbull. The media reported later that week that the Prime Minister had raised the issue with his Israeli counterpart.

News of our journey had caught the attention of the producers working for *Australian Story*, an ABC documentary series, and their camera crews followed us, capturing our experiences to produce a two-part saga set to air in early 2018. From dawn till dusk, our schedules were packed with back-to-back meetings, often accompanied by an entourage of media personnel. We had an Israeli team and an Australian team – an amalgamation of sound technicians, videographers and producers – trailing in our wake, creating quite a stir wherever we went. The amusing clashes between the Israeli and Australian journalists became anecdotes we continue to chuckle about to this day.

We swiftly acquired the skill of fixing a microphone beneath our clothing while in public. We also soon discovered that even in moments when the cameras ceased to roll, the ever-attentive microphones still captured our whispers and musings – travel toilet habits included.

As our faces were aired on TVs across Israel, our anonymity was lost. Soon, we were being greeted by people as we walked the streets, and in the taxis we took from one meeting to the next. One afternoon while sitting in a cafe in the middle of Jerusalem, enjoying the peace of a moment between meetings, a young girl approached our table with timid steps. In broken English, she uttered words that left an imprint upon our souls. 'My principal, also a woman, is sexually abusing me, but I saw you on TV, I understand what she is doing now. Not anymore,' she told us. 'Now it is time to look after myself.' As we dragged ourselves out of the cafe for the next meeting, we knew with certainty that those days, consumed by a whirlwind of chatter, promises and the gaze of the media, had undeniably made a difference. In the eyes of that brave young girl, we glimpsed the power of our shared stories.

Our meeting with the prosecution team in Israel proved frustrating. As the case gained more attention, we heard from many sources, both Australian and Israeli, of interference surrounding the falsified medical reports regarding Leifer's mental illness. Disturbingly, these allegations even implicated the Israeli health minister, Yaakov Litzman.

When we raised these concerns with the prosecution team, their response was dismissive and incredulous. The head prosecutor, Aviad, declared, 'If this is true, I'll eat my hat!' Unfortunately, he failed to make good on his promise when these claims were later substantiated. The realisation that improper influence had infiltrated even the highest levels of authority only deepened our sense of disillusionment and intensified our determination.

Before departing Israel, we had a rushed meeting with Shana Aaronson, a woman who would become an integral part of our story. Shana worked for Jewish Community Watch, an organisation in Israel and the US that supported victims of sexual abuse. Shana was a woman full of passion who dedicated herself wholeheartedly to the job. At the time, we had no idea of the significant role she would come to play. She hurriedly greeted us after leaving court, where she had been supporting another woman. We shared our concerns about Leifer and pondered how to gather more evidence of her feigned illness. 'Leave it with me,' she assured us. 'We may have a way.'

On the way to the airport, we made a pitstop to meet with attorney Rivka Schwartz, a religious woman leading the charge against sexual abuse within the ultra-Orthodox communities. Our live interview was streamed on her Facebook page, with thousands of followers tuning in, allowing our voices to reach deep into the religious community. The comments that flooded in during the live session were both heartbreaking and revealing. Women who had once been students under Leifer before she came to Australia opened up about disturbing behaviours they had witnessed. Some courageously disclosed their own experiences of being groomed by Leifer. The significance of this moment was profound, as it underscored the urgency and necessity of our fight. We were determined to ensure that Malka Leifer would never have the chance to harm another vulnerable girl.

Back in Australia we went back to campaigning, which by then had become a full-time job. The Premier of Victoria,

Daniel Andrews, got behind us and wrote a public letter of support. The political support from both sides generated increased media interest, and the papers began running regular stories about our efforts for justice.

In between meetings, we spent hours with *Australian Story* producer Belinda Hawkins, a woman with a wicked sense of humour, filming segments for the two-part documentary. The cameras were our constant companions, capturing glimpses of our daily lives – from family dinners to camping trips and exercising at the 1000 steps in Dandenong. Each day of filming would translate to roughly thirty seconds on the screen.

While we continued our campaign, making trips to Canberra, visiting Parliament House and providing regular updates on social media, there was a significant development we couldn't share with the public.

Shana Aaronson and Meyer Seewald from Jewish Community Watch had engaged a spy firm in Israel to investigate Leifer's alleged illness.

We wondered how they had access to the closed and exclusive community Leifer resided in. This remained a mystery until the *Australian Story* documentary aired the following year, revealing the covert tactics employed by the firm, including hidden cameras concealed within water bottles carried by fake repairmen positioned across from Leifer's building in Emmanuel.

It was in a grainy picture Shana sent us that we finally caught a glimpse of Leifer – our first since the picture that had been sent to Nicole back in May 2017. 'Is this Leifer?' Shana asked. We scrutinised the images of a woman on a balcony, her head covered with a scarf, smiling and engaged in conversation with someone below, and confirmed that it was indeed her.

Several more pictures followed. Leifer socialising with guests she hosted. Leifer strolling back from the shops. *'It makes me so angry; why does she feel so safe? They are all with her, supporting her lies,'* I wrote back to Shana.

Nicole, Elly and I pondered the implications of these findings. Would the photos be enough to debunk her feigned claims of incapacitation?

Three weeks prior to Leifer's next biannual review, Shana called us, all excited. They had handed over their investigation to the Jerusalem police, and Interpol had initiated their own inquiry. Interpol, with access to extensive surveillance resources, used audio and camera footage to track over 200 hours of Leifer in the days leading up to her review.

During the biannual review, which would assess Leifer's health and determine whether extradition proceedings could resume, Leifer once again appeared hunched over and unresponsive. Her family spoke on her behalf, painting a picture of a life confined to a bed, staring at a wall, unable to tend to her basic needs. It was a narrative we had heard many times before, but this time, we knew the truth.

Two weeks passed. During this time, we barely slept, as we waited, worried and wondered. Concrete evidence existed of Leifer's deceit; when would the police take action?

Several days later that action finally came. In the late hours of a February afternoon a door was forcefully kicked in, and an unwilling Leifer, who had barricaded herself in her house all day, was handcuffed and led down the stairs. She was arrested and charged with fraud and obstruction of justice.

The news of her arrest reached us in an instant and pushed us into our first experience with the relentless twenty-four-hour news cycle. It was our first encounter and it would take us a year to learn the concept of media pooling – the practice of conducting one interview and having multiple channels share the footage. This would have saved us from enduring days of interviews across Australia. Unfortunately, Israel never adopted this approach, and we spent hours repeating our story over and over to the Israeli media outlets.

The first image of Leifer that circulated in the media had a profound impact on us. Committed to her charade of mental illness, she kept her head down, and shielded her face with her hands as the barrage of cameras confronted her. After the final round of interviews, with my voice nearly gone, Nicole, Elly and I sat on my grey couch, reflecting on our emotions upon seeing Leifer's face. The rush of adrenaline from the media exposure seemed to numb my feelings. Nicole and Elly felt similar.

However, after Nicole and Elly left, I began to experience uncontrollable shaking. I reached out to Hatzolah, an emergency medical service within the Jewish community. While my vital signs appeared normal, the trembling persisted, and I began experiencing chest pains. Unsettled, I ended up at the Alfred Hospital, where I would make several subsequent trips over the next six months. When the shaking eventually subsided, my blood pressure plummeted, and my heart rate accelerated to compensate. Departing the hospital feeling light-headed and faint, I still had no idea of the cause of my symptoms.

In Jerusalem, a pattern began to emerge. Leifer, ever the master of deception, persisted in feigning her illness. And the judge, overwhelmed with the complexities of the situation, frustratingly ruled for one psychological evaluation after another.

As the slow wheels of Israeli justice turned, court hearings seemed to be multiplying with each passing day.

Around the time of the twenty-fifth court hearing, I decided to keep a count of the hearings and briefly summarise what had happened at each one. Twenty, thirty, forty, fifty ... The number steadily climbed, a procession of court dates that tested the limits of our endurance as we tried to follow along in Melbourne.

The twenty-four hours around a court hearing were always set in a bubble of adrenaline. The day leading up to a hearing was spent speaking to the Israeli prosecution to ensure the court was going ahead, arranging at which home Elly, Nicole and I would gather that evening, fielding calls from reporters, informing the documentary team about where they would film us watching the hearing, preparing statements for social media, and, of course, striving to be present parents for our children. During a long hearing that night, we would order Uber Eats if the adrenaline allowed us to eat. Many times it didn't.

Over the years, our WhatsApp group of Israeli supporters became filled with many reporters and would ping constantly with updates and pictures of the courtroom. Once court was over, we would quickly update social media, answer journalists with requested comments, and conduct multiple interviews over Skype. When the media frenzy calmed, we would speak with the Israeli Ministry of Justice to discuss potential next steps. Sleep those nights was often elusive, and if it did happen was filled with nightmares.

The following morning, we would spend hours interacting with the Australian media, either with a producer in front of a camera or staring at a random spot on the wall and listening to the questions through an earpiece. When I would pick up Lily at the end of the day, and she asked me what had happened, I would tell her only the basics. In the evening, if she was occupied, I would watch our

#bringleiferback campaign on the news, but usually I waited until she was asleep to view online clips.

I recall one harrowing twenty-four-hour news cycle that repeated itself, like a never-ending loop, for five consecutive days. The news broke that Litzman, the health minister in Israel, had been shamelessly tampering with justice, exerting undue pressure on psychiatrists to declare Malka Leifer mentally unfit. The chief psychiatrist of Jerusalem, who was responsible for signing off all Leifer's medical reports, was found to have been unduly influenced. We weren't surprised. We knew all too well that Leifer's supporters would stop at nothing to shield her from facing the consequences of her actions. Cultural mechanisms remained that provided a haven for predators to perpetuate their abuse.

During our second trip to Israel in 2018, we unexpectedly crossed paths with Litzman himself as we walked the corridors of the Knesset in Jerusalem. 'I've already heard the other side of the story. I want nothing to do with this,' he told us. 'I will not support extradition, but I will also not interfere against it.' It was an outright lie, delivered straight to our faces.

The moment Prime Minister Netanyahu learnt of Litzman's interference was splashed across the television channels. He received the call as he was walking through the airport, and he slumped down over his suitcase with a worried look on his face. Netanyahu relied on Litzman to remain in power, and Litzman's ultra-Orthodox party was a key member of Netanyahu's coalition government. When we watched the footage, we didn't see concern for the victims; only concern for Netanyahu's own political future.

Meanwhile in Melbourne, it took an entire year of visits to doctors and specialists to identify the cause of the debilitating symptoms that plagued me after each court hearing. The tremors that coursed through my body were a manifestation of adrenaline surges, while the fainting was the result of my blood pressure plummeting in response to the stress.

One particular evening I was scheduled to speak at a gathering of sixty or seventy women belonging to a Jewish community group. I attended the evening having come straight from the Epworth Hospital, where I had spent the week and been diagnosed with a condition known as POTS.

Postural orthostatic tachycardia syndrome (POTS) is a medical condition involving a dysfunction in the autonomic nervous system. In my case, my body struggles to adequately control blood flow and heart rate, leading to symptoms such as light-headedness, dizziness, rapid heartbeat and fainting.

Adrenaline, often referred to as the 'fight-or-flight' hormone, plays a pivotal role in our body's response to perceived threats. However, for individuals with POTS, the adrenaline surges exacerbate the already impaired regulation of blood flow, causing blood vessels to constrict. This, in turn, intensifies the abnormality in blood flow regulation, magnifying the severity of symptoms. I was informed that managing and regulating my body's response to stress was a crucial aspect of my treatment. I had no clue how I was going to manage that.

That night, as I confronted my diagnosis, I found myself sprawled on the cool tiles of the bathroom floor, feet raised on the toilet seat ten minutes before I was due to address a packed room. The weight of my speech hung heavy in the air as I contemplated the profound impact of our campaign, and the toll it was exacting on my physical wellbeing.

In moments of triumph, I revelled in the power I wielded, the capacity to ignite change in a community yearning for transformation. But beneath the surface, an overwhelming sense of responsibility gnawed at me as I recognised the magnitude of the change still needed. The campaign had become an all-consuming force, at times leaving me depleted and vulnerable.

Lying there on that bathroom floor, I questioned my capacity to persevere. It wasn't merely strength that propelled me forward, but a profound ability to sacrifice myself for the greater good – a lesson learnt in my childhood. My therapist once remarked on the remarkable self-sacrifice children possess, their unwavering determination to connect and survive amid adversity.

I bore the weight of this sacrifice, willingly subjecting my wellbeing, and at times the needs of my daughter, to the demands of this mission. I cloaked my fragility with dissociation, projecting strength even when there was none to be had. Applying make-up, straightening my hair, assuming the persona that appeared before the camera – I had somehow mastered the art of exuding a confidence that at times wasn't there. Once the fervour of the media dissipated, I would curl up at home and seek refuge under a blanket. There, I would allow the deluge of emotions to subside, the memories of the abuse to fade enough that I could remind myself I still had a life to live in the present. Sometimes, this respite could last days.

In the year that followed, the unrelenting stress triggered the emergence of several chronic illnesses, hidden beneath the surface. The doctor explained that these autoimmune afflictions may have always been within me, awaiting the perfect storm of stress and adrenaline to reveal themselves.

The campaign wasn't all stress; we also bore witness to moments of extraordinary unity. Passionate individuals, people who cared deeply about supporting survivors and dismantling the mechanisms that enabled abusers to perpetrate harm, rallied together.

It struck me how unjust a burden it was for those who had already endured abuse to then have to fight so hard for justice. Often it seemed that the victims themselves were the only ones willing to raise their voices, aware that silence would only perpetuate the heinous crime. We, the survivors, drew strength from the depths of our trauma, pushing forward when others might falter. At times, I perceived it as post-traumatic growth, an unwavering resilience to persist against all odds. At other times, I did not.

I climbed off that bathroom floor and delivered the speech. The fight had to go on.

CHAPTER 23

The wheels of justice

Rabbi Grossman's dramatic courtroom entrance in March 2018 marked a pivotal point in our battle for justice. Nicole, Elly and I were in Australia, eyes glued to WhatsApp, receiving real time updates of the thirtieth extradition hearing from three ABC reporters – Fouad Abu Gosh, Sophie McNeill and Eric Tlozek – along with Shana Aaronson.

The 2004 Israel Prize laureate, Grossman arrived at the district court leading an entourage in support of Leifer. Judge Vinograd, apparently in awe of the esteemed rabbi, granted him the floor. 'It is humiliating for Leifer to be in custody; she should be released under my supervision,' Grossman declared. My cheeks felt flushed; I looked at Nicole and Elly and saw the same look of betrayal on both their faces. We were agitated – this was the same judge who had released Leifer to house detention after her first arrest in 2014. 'Why can these random people speak in court? Where is our voice?' I furiously typed into our chat.

After an agonising twenty minutes, during which even Grossman's two assistants addressed the court, a shocking decision was reached. Judge Vinograd approved Leifer's release under the supervision of Grossman's assistant, with the release scheduled to occur two days later. Prosecutor Matan Akiva swiftly vowed to appeal the ruling in the Supreme Court. It felt like the ground was shifting beneath us. 'That's it, she's going to leave the country,' we all exclaimed, speaking over each other.

Following the courtroom commotion, Shana immediately began planning how to distribute Leifer's image to all the airports and seaports in Israel. Rabbi Grossman was the founder of Migdal Ohr, an organisation dedicated to child protection which relied on funding from the Israeli government, foreign governments and private donors worldwide.

In the US, Meyer Seewald informed us that Migdal Ohr's American donors were considering withdrawing their millions in donations. Apparently, Grossman's court appearance in support of an abuser was poorly received, resulting in an overwhelming flood of furious phone calls from its board members, funders and the public to the extent they had to disconnect the phones.

We later learnt that this was not the first instance of Rabbi Grossman using his influence for an ultra-Orthodox predator. Two years prior he had flown to a South African court to help Rabbi Berland, who was evading extradition to Israel and subsequently confessed to charges of rape and assault.

The next day, the Supreme Court ordered that Leifer would remain in jail until a final ruling on bail was delivered. In the week that followed, there were moments we were too distraught to engage with the media. Our supporters, including Ted Baillieu, stepped up, spoke to the media, and mobilised people worldwide to rectify this miscarriage of justice. The sight of a rabbi standing in solidarity with a predator was a disturbing development. Our supporters' efforts were highly effective. Within a few days, Rabbi Grossman withdrew his support. By the time the appeal decision arrived, Leifer had no backing for bail. A testament to the power of caring individuals who recognised vulnerability and sought not to exploit it, but to uplift and support those in need.

Leifer would remain in custody until the end of the extradition process.

That evening, I sat on the couch and sank deep into my thoughts, envisioning Malka Leifer's frustration as her brief taste of freedom was snatched away. I thought about all the people who had rallied together to ensure my abuser would not go free, and the media that had shone a light on the darkness only she and I had once shared. How I longed to confront her and whisper, 'Look at all these people I have welcomed into your twisted realm.'

I scrolled through all the messages I had received that day and saw the collective anger at the idea of an abuser being freed. The people we had invited into the world she created now shouted their anger, too; we were no longer screaming alone. This burden was no longer solely ours to bear.

In November 2018, Nicole, Elly and I journeyed back to Israel for the second time that year, accompanied by the ever-present and supportive Australian media. Having cameras follow us had become our new normal. Throughout the entire eighteen-hour flight, our conversations revolved around the anticipation of facing Leifer in the courtroom for the first time. I wondered how her presence would impact me, and if I would regress to the submissive young person I had been in her presence all those years ago. I hoped that I had transcended that phase, but trauma had a way of wresting control over my reactions when triggered. I hoped the confidence I had gained from repeatedly stepping in front of the cameras would keep the fear from overpowering my resolve.

We were walking the halls of the Knesset, alongside Jodi Lee, a Channel Seven reporter from Melbourne who had flown with us to Israel to document our journey, when we learnt that Leifer, having heard of our impending presence in Israel, had applied to be exempted from appearing at the upcoming court hearings. The judge granted her request. We were shattered. We had hoped to gain a sense of empowerment facing our abuser. We didn't want our first encounter with her to be during a trial, as we shared our testimonies.

When we turned up to the closed court hearings, Leifer's family attempted to force us out of the courtroom, asserting that we were not parties to the case and therefore should not be granted entry. After a morning of arguments, the judge permitted us to enter along with Ayelet Razin, our support person from the Rape Crisis Centre. We took our seats on the opposite side of the small room as Leifer's family glared at us, clutching pictures of revered rabbis and reciting prayers from their miniature prayer books. At that moment, one question reverberated through my mind: *Which God endorses such behaviour?*

The court hearing was adjourned. The cross-examination of the psychiatrists would continue the following year, in January 2019.

Determined to uncover more about Leifer's surroundings and the community she resided in, we embarked on a visit to Emmanuel, a gated community nestled within the stone-stepped mountains of the Israeli-occupied West Bank, known for its ultra-Orthodox residents. Eager to gather information, we went from door to door, seeking insights from Leifer's neighbours. To our surprise, everyone we spoke to had only 'recently moved in' and knew nothing of what we were referencing. As we descended the stairs, one of Leifer's teenage sons appeared, brandishing a camera in our faces and filming our every step. The situation escalated as we made our way out of the building – open windows framed our departure, revealing dozens of cameras capturing our every move. Word had spread throughout the community to isolate us, and the security guards, who had swiftly approached us upon our arrival, pressured us to leave. The scene unfolding before our eyes illuminated how easily Leifer had managed to blend into the fabric of the community, evading detection for numerous years.

The court hearings stretched on and on, seemingly with no end in sight. Meanwhile, back in Australia, our cause continued to gain momentum. Premier Daniel Andrews slammed Leifer as a fraud to the media, and we took heart in knowing her manipulation wasn't going unnoticed. Josh Burns, a Labor member of the Federal Parliament, and former ambassador Dave Sharma, who had been elected a Liberal Party Member of Parliament, extended an invitation for us to visit Canberra, where we had the opportunity to meet with politicians from all sides of the political spectrum, including the new Prime Minister, Scott Morrison. It was a crucial moment – we finally felt our voices were being heard. In particular, the then-Opposition Leader, Anthony Albanese, demonstrated a genuine understanding of our plight and stood in solidarity with us. Both sides of parliament were united in condemning the gross injustice being perpetrated by these prolonged delays.

Mr Albanese, along with Mr Burns and Mr Sharma, put together a motion to be presented in the House of Representatives. The motion read as follows:

(1) notes that Malka Leifer, the former Principal of the Adass Israel Girls School in Melbourne, fled Australia in 2008 as child sexual abuse allegations against her surfaced;

(2) reaffirms the formal extradition request that was filed by Australia in 2014 requesting she be returned to Victoria to face 74 charges of child sexual abuse;

(3) acknowledges the bravery of Ms Leifer's alleged victims – especially Dassi Erlich, Nicole Meyer and Elly Sapper for their tireless pursuit of justice;

(4) further notes that over 5 years have elapsed, and over 60 court hearings have been held in Israel, since this extradition request was first lodged, without any significant progress having been made;

(5) expresses regret and concern at the numerous attempts to prevent and delay Malka Leifer facing justice in Australia; and

(6) calls for the immediate extradition of Malka Leifer to Australia to face 74 charges of child sexual abuse.

Australia stood firmly behind us. The unity displayed by both sides of parliament was truly a unique and powerful sight to behold. The federal and state governments voiced their unwavering support, calling for a swift extradition and an end to the charade of Malka Leifer's supposed mental incapacitation.

Meanwhile in Israel, efforts were mobilised on a mammoth scale to ensure that Leifer would never face justice on Australian soil. Leifer's legal team, in a desperate attempt to sway public opinion, took to the media and boldly proclaimed that she would never be extradited to Australia. Her family hired a PR firm to launch a smear campaign against Justice Minister Ayelet Shaked, who held the authority to sign off on the extradition. Their plan was to paint Shaked as biased against Leifer, alleging that she had close ties with Australian authorities. However, their campaign was foiled when the details were leaked to the Israeli media before it could even be set in motion.

The leak of the proposed PR campaign was a significant triumph for our cause. It showcased the resounding public support we had garnered, and exposed the lengths Leifer's family would go to in order to obstruct justice.

Our public campaign felt like an active force. Each day, I would receive an overwhelming influx of messages from survivors, expressing their solidarity and sharing their own stories. Starting in America, the hashtag #whyididntreport had begun trending on Twitter at this time, as millions of women bravely shared the reasons they had been unable to report their abusers. It felt as though we were living in a time of reckoning. Long-suppressed voices were finally being heard.

In Australia, Prime Minister Morrison extended an invitation for survivors of institutional abuse to come to Canberra, where a public apology from the nation awaited us. I joined Dassi Herszberg, also a survivor, and we travelled to the capital and met a remarkable group of individuals who had escaped the closed Jehovah's Witness community. We stood together, united, advocating for change and education regarding sexual abuse within these exclusive communities. While the apology was a powerful moment, Morrison's approach to addressing sexual abuse and women's rights was subsequently discovered to be grossly inadequate.

Several months later, I had the privilege of sitting down with the police in Melbourne, sharing insights and guidance on how to sensitively approach and communicate with young sexual abuse victims within the Adass community.

It was crucial to address the cultural aspects delicately, fostering an environment of safety and support for these vulnerable young individuals.

Our journey was far from over, but with each step, we moved closer to a society that would no longer tolerate the atrocities of sexual abuse and would instead champion the cause of protecting and empowering survivors.

The news from Israel infiltrated our daily lives. The impact of the ongoing court hearings extended to our entire family. Isaac, Ben, Tamar and the partners and children of my siblings all felt the weight of the proceedings. My friends did, too. Tamar's husband would receive urgent phone calls from us, requesting his expertise editing social media posts – particularly in the immediate aftermath of court hearings, when our minds were overwhelmed. Meanwhile, Isaac and Ben supported us in their own unique ways. They became the dependable couriers of sustenance, medication or forgotten phone cords during those long, exhausting evenings spent on my grey couch. We were a network of love and shared determination, committed to seeing this through.

Barely a week passed without a court hearing, a revelation of Leifer's continued manipulation, or news of efforts by grassroots organisations fighting alongside us for justice. We were a regular presence on the news in Australia and Israel and later, in other countries around the world.

Among the whirlwind of overwhelming publicity, there were significant moments that anchored me to reality.

It was through our mutual friend, Helen Tachos, that I had the privilege of meeting Tessa Sullivan. She was an extraordinary woman, unyielding in her refusal to remain silent about the sexual harassment perpetrated by her former boss, the former Lord Mayor of Melbourne, Robert

Doyle. The media frenzy surrounding her was relentless, with reporters camping outside her home, eroding her sense of safety. At our very first meeting, everything poured out – her fears, her overwhelming emotions, her longing to retreat from the spotlight. It was the start of a profound and beautiful friendship with one of the strongest women I've ever known.

Another source of solace came in the form of my weekly coffee ritual with my dear friend Romy and her precious toddler. Every Wednesday morning, we would meet at her favourite coffee spot in Elwood. The sheer delight on her son's face as he experienced his first babychino, and the sight of chocolate foam adorning his tiny mouth – these simple moments brought a sense of normality amid the chaos. Babies have this incredible ability to ground you, and Romy always exuded an aura of serenity that instantly calmed me.

Tragically, towards the end of 2017, our world shattered when Romy, a non-smoker, received the devastating diagnosis of stage 4 lung cancer. The prognosis was grim, but regardless of whether we were in the coffee shop, at her home, in the park or even in the hospital, we kept our Wednesday meetings going. Romy would insist that I share all the intricacies of my tumultuous week. When I hesitated, fearing that my burdens might weigh her down further, she would hush my concerns, insisting that it helped to occupy her thoughts. Wise and intelligent, Romy would offer guidance on how to navigate difficult situations and handle challenging individuals. Those sacred hours of the week became my sanctuary, and they were moments I treasured. Over the course of the campaign, I witnessed the magnitude of Romy's love as she poured every ounce of it into her small son. Despite the gruelling treatments she silently endured, which gave her more time than initially anticipated, the cruel reality remained: she would not be there to see her son grow up. I promised to be there for him when she could not.

Early in 2019, Nicole and I travelled to New York. I had speaking engagements with several organisations, and we were filming for a follow-up third episode of *Australian Story*. Our plan was to meet Elly in Israel a week later to continue our campaign. While in New York we heard that activists had placed dozens of baby dolls in front of the Health Ministry in Jerusalem to protest Litzman's efforts to help Malka Leifer avoid facing trial. I felt a deep sense of validation, and of gratitude to the grassroots organisations rallying against those who were complicit in covering up abuse. *Survivors will not be silenced*, I thought, *no matter the powers against them.*

While en route to Israel, news broke that some of Leifer's previous victims in Israel had come forward anonymously to the media, exposing the sexual abuse they endured under her leadership. Messages of congratulations flooded my phone; these new allegations lent credence to our claims, shattering the notion that we were the sole accusers, as Leifer's defenders claimed. Three women from a broken home, who had left religion, clearly seeking fame and money. What money, I wondered? Who would desire this fame? That Nicole still remained religious was also a fact they ignored.

It was a confusing time. I took no satisfaction from the messages of congratulations. Instead, I was angry. Angry at the community in Israel, who most likely knew of Leifer's abuse yet chose to send her away to Australia. Instead of reporting her to the police, they allowed her to roam free. My sisters and I experienced heinous abuse because they had all refused to confront her. I couldn't help but think how different my life would have been if they had addressed the issue earlier. I was furious that community expectations had silenced those girls for so long; it was only by raising our voices and making Leifer a household name in Israel that their stories finally emerged. Would fundamentalist closed communities learn from our experience? Would misplaced shame finally be redirected to the right people?

As well as the emotional toll, the campaign proved a heavy financial burden. Our trips to Israel, including accommodation, had cost us thousands. Adam Segal, a Melbourne man living in Israel, emerged as an invaluable ally in our campaign for justice, and by our third trip he had found us generous donors who pitched in to cover our flights. The Windows of Jerusalem hotel, having heard of our story, invited us to stay with them at a discounted price.

Sitting on the plane with Nicole, we reflected on our journey. We thought about the submissive young girls we once were, believing ourselves to be without value. Yet here we were, fearless women, speaking our truth to the highest echelons of government and facing the scrutiny of the media. As we walked up and down the dimly lit rows of sleeping passengers, a profound sense of awe came over me. I was ready to face the chaos that awaited us in Israel.

CHAPTER 24

Extradition

And chaos it was. In March 2019, we found ourselves in yet another extradition hearing in Israel, but this time it felt different. When the judge entered, Leifer's family demanded our removal and as the argument escalated a horde of cameras swarmed over the court benches to capture our anxious faces. Eventually, the judge ruled in our favour, closed the courtroom to the public, and Dr Brian Trappler took the stand.

Elly, Nicole and I exchanged astonished glances when we realised that the New York psychiatrist was being granted permission to testify. The previous evening, prosecutor Matan Akiva had told us about Dr Trappler's involvement on behalf of Leifer but had no further information to give us. What followed was an hour of digging where we discovered Dr Trappler's Facebook posts expressing his unvarnished views on the case. That morning we had provided the prosecutor with printed copies.

All through the morning, as the psychiatrist presented his report declaring Leifer unfit for trial, we stared at him from where we sat. It was a small courtroom – empty white walls, a judge's bench, two tables and three rows of unforgiving wooden pews. It seemed that Dr Trappler was making every effort not to meet our gaze.

When Matan finally began the cross-examination, he delved right into Dr Trappler's Facebook comments, where the psychiatrist had declared Leifer's innocence and accused us of being liars simply because he had seen our pictures and saw we did not look religious. I *suggest that before the lynch-mob commits the ultimate crime of Mesira, they pause to realise that this case is not what you've been told*, he had written, referring to the religious prohibition against reporting a fellow Jew to non-rabbinic authorities.

I had to bite my tongue to keep me from speaking out. Did he truly believe that her religion exempted her from inflicting harm upon me? How did his twisted reasoning reconcile with the fact I had been religious when she subjected me to abuse? It was an oft-repeated sentiment among religious community members who wanted to dismiss us.

The day proved to be long and exasperating, but as we emerged from the courtroom, we were heartened by the sight of a group of individuals from Israel and Australia gathering in protest outside the District Court. Their voices resonated with our own, echoing our shared discontent and frustration with the protracted delays in the case. The atmosphere was charged as we collectively demanded a swift and equitable resolution to this ordeal.

But we couldn't stay for the next hearing and back in Melbourne, we found ourselves entangled in the ongoing courtroom drama as the hearings unfolded half a world away. It felt like a never-ending circus as psychiatrists from both sides presented multiple conflicting reports. Jerusalem's head psychiatrist, Jacob Charnes, who had been implicated in ceding to pressure from Litzman to change his reports, was removed from the case.

An Israeli-Australian abuse survivor, Manny Waks, attended the court hearings and would publicly share the details of each proceeding on his social media platforms. We relied on his posts to keep us informed, while a small group of unwavering supporters, including Shana Aaronson, Ayelet Razin, Rachael Risby Raz, a former Diaspora Affairs Advisor to the Prime Minister of Israel, our supporter Adam Segal, and occasionally Fleur Hassan, the Deputy Mayor of Jerusalem, sat in the courtroom, providing us with blow-by-blow accounts. The use of the popcorn emoji became common, as events in the courtroom appeared more like scenes from a work of fiction than the reality we faced. At times, the humour of our WhatsApp group – the 'Base Leifer Gang', as we called it – had us rolling off the couch, providing welcome moments of lightness amid the chaos and uncertainty.

I recall the comments pouring in on our WhatsApp group as I was conducting an interview over Skype with an Israeli journalist. I glanced at my phone and started laughing so hard the reporter believed I was crying. I didn't correct him; I didn't think he'd understand our dark humour.

On 15 June 2019, I drove up to Sydney with Dassi Herszberg to give a speech about the costs and conflicts of the #bringleiferback campaign. After spending a clear but cold afternoon on the Hume Highway, we stopped to park our campervan in Holbrook overnight. Plagued by a migraine, I went to sleep early. When I woke up at 6 a.m. to finish my speech, I was met with a whirlwind of missed calls and WhatsApp messages. My father had passed away.

'My father is dead,' I told Dassi, 'my father is dead.' The words repeated like a broken record all day as she drove us back to Melbourne.

The news of my father's death unleashed a torrent of emotion that I struggled to comprehend. How does one really feel when a parent, who was also their abuser, passes away? I was engulfed by a mixture of grief, anger, relief and confusion, making it hard to process his death.

Memories, long repressed, flooded my mind. Memories I couldn't quite comprehend – memories that could only emerge now that he was gone, my therapist would later explain. I felt like I was being transported back to my childhood, to a time when I couldn't fully grasp the concept of death.

I didn't get to decide whether to attend the funeral, as it had already taken place when I returned to Melbourne. I never heard from my mother. My siblings each coped with our father's death in their own way. Together, we decided to spend a week in the country, opting not to partake in the traditional Shiva rituals, instead finding comfort with each other during this disorienting time.

My survival system kicked in, compartmentalising these confusing memories and allowing me to focus on the campaign. The last thing I wanted was to be entangled in the web of my unhappy childhood. My father was gone, I needed to look to the future.

By early 2020, it felt like the case had reached a critical juncture and was straining diplomatic relations between Australia and Israel. The mounting pressure on Israel became undeniable. Suddenly, after months of silence, the Israeli Ministry of Justice released a press statement on 13 January 2020, acknowledging the State Attorney's request to expedite the case. It was a pivotal moment. Even Israel's Ambassador to Australia, Mark Sofer, dropped his diplomatic facade, and took to Twitter to condemn the prolonged pursuit of justice.

The repercussions extended beyond diplomatic circles. The Australian UN delegation in Geneva took a firm stance, refusing to cooperate with an Israeli initiative against the sexual exploitation of children due to the perceived foot-dragging over Leifer's extradition. Prime Minister Morrison issued a statement emphasising the importance of resolving the case. Prime Minister Netanyahu offered assurance that once the extradition announcement was made by the court, Israel would swiftly sign off on it. The then-Australian Attorney-General, Christian Porter, was also present in Israel, engaging in talks on the matter.

As the case garnered international attention, the world began to closely monitor its progress. Requests for information and interviews flooded in, ranging from outlets like *The New York Times* to Chinese international media. The global spotlight was firmly fixed on this pivotal fight for justice.

Despite the mounting pressure, Malka Leifer's supporters remained steadfast. Religious communities in Israel came together to raise money for her legal costs, proclaiming 'Pidyon Shvuyim' – the religious duty to bring about the release of a Jewish person who has been unjustly imprisoned by secular authorities. I recall one heated phone call from a globally renowned rabbi fundraising for Leifer. For a full hour, he attempted to convince me I was lying and had spearheaded a worldwide campaign solely driven by the pursuit of financial gain and fame.

The stakes were high, but we continued to navigate this challenging terrain, driven by the conviction that the truth must prevail.

In March 2020, as whispers of a strange and dangerous new virus began to spread, Nicole embarked on a solitary journey to Israel, to lobby the Israeli government and have her presence marked within the courtroom. Just as she returned to Australia, the government mandated a two-week quarantine for all incoming travellers. It was a tumultuous time. On 11 March, the World Health Organization declared COVID-19 a worldwide pandemic.

Amid this early uncertainty, we held a rally outside Adass Israel School together with LOUD Fence, an organisation that tied ribbons around institutions where sexual abuse had occurred, conveying messages of support to victims, their loved ones and the community. Red ribbons draped the Adass Israel School gate, and remained there throughout Melbourne's first lockdown, while the school was closed. They were subsequently removed upon the students' return several months later.

As the pandemic began to sweep the globe, it felt as if the world was grinding to a halt. On 18 March, the judge in Israel made the decision to adjourn the sixty-sixth court hearing, urging both parties to submit their final arguments in written form.

On 26 March, Nicole, Elly and I took up our usual positions on my grey couch, readying ourselves for court date sixty-seven – Judge Lomp's final ruling on Malka Leifer's fitness to stand trial. It was a hearing that Leifer's lawyers had claimed we would never witness. Through a video call with Plus 61J reporter Ittay Flescher, we watched as everyone arrived at court. Yehuda Fried, Leifer's attorney, ignored the questions thrown at him as he climbed the court's steps, while his partner Tal Gabay paused to face the press and share his thoughts.

'Where's the #bringleiferback hashtag on your masks?' I asked our support group on WhatsApp as they took pictures of the media circus. There was no sign of social distancing.

Six minutes after 9 a.m., the verdict was in. 'Fit!' our supporter Ayelet messaged our group from the court in Israel. One word that captured a decade of waiting and fighting for justice.

Parts of the forty-page judgement were read as the press pushed into the courtroom. Leifer had been found to be 'impersonating someone with mental illness'. In a state of shock, Nicole, Elly and I slid off the couch and onto the floor, silently staring at each other. The truth transcended any words we could speak. 'We are dead quiet,' we wrote to the reporters requesting our response.

That night was surreal. Heated discussions in the courtroom finally led to a commencement date for extradition proceedings: 20 July. We were bombarded by the Israeli media for hours – even as Tamar, Isaac, Ben and Dassi came and went to offer their congratulations, we squeezed ourselves into the computer frame and fielded the same inquiries over and over. We barely slept that night, and the next morning, as I stood before the bathroom mirror, mascara brush in hand, the shock lingered, but I knew the press wanted to see emotion.

Together with Ted Baillieu, Josh Burns and David Southwick, we gathered at a press conference outside Glen Eira Town Hall. The air was abuzz with excitement. Social media had exploded; Mark Sofer, Israel's ambassador to Australia, took to Twitter again and said the decision was truly wonderful. I shared my thoughts with the press, followed by Nicole and a visibly pregnant Elly. The media, family, friends and well-wishers all shared our elation.

The photos captured that day marked our final public appearance together for the next three years. The following two years were shaped by lockdowns, and our world became virtual. The media used these pictures in numerous reports on the case, and long after Elly's daughter was born in June 2020, the images of her pregnancy persisted. Elly didn't appreciate appearing to be pregnant for three years.

Only days after Elly's daughter was born, I learnt that Romy had been readmitted to the hospital with breathing troubles. We exchanged messages, and I planned to visit on Wednesday, which was also my thirty-second birthday. However, that morning Henry and Marilyn informed me that Romy's condition had worsened significantly. She was in the ICU, and to visit, I would need a negative Covid PCR test, which I would never get in time, due to lengthy delays in Victoria's testing laboratories.

In the shadow of looming grief, I spent the morning with Freda, her partner Peter and Romy's young son, hiding my tears as we played in the park, clinging to the hope that the doctors were mistaken. Devastatingly, Romy passed away later that day. The sorrow was overwhelming, a beautiful woman taken far too soon, and even now, I find myself reaching for my phone to call her, aching to share all the news she's missed, moments she was once such an integral part of.

Amid the anguish of Romy's passing, life's complexities and challenges marched on. I was mourning the loss of my friend and it was hard to stay focused, but the games in Israel didn't stop. Leifer's lawyers filed a lawsuit against the prison for negligence in administering antipsychotic medication for a mentally fit woman. In response, the prison had issued a letter declaring Leifer mentally unfit, which her defence team then sought to exploit as 'new evidence' for an appeal. The appeal judge acknowledged that some of the events in this case were unprecedented, and her appeal was denied.

In the new reality of homeschooling and while grappling with my grief, I continued to engage with journalists, striving to convey the complexities of these convoluted manoeuvres while I stood pressed against my bedroom wall, hoping the sound of my daughter's teacher beaming in online couldn't be heard. It appeared that Malka Leifer's legal team, led by the newly appointed extradition lawyer Nick Kaufman, an expert in international criminal law, was tirelessly pulling at every available string.

Finally, the extradition proceedings began. There was no way to brace ourselves for details of our abuse being laid bare in the public arena, or for Leifer's lawyers' claim that the abuse we endured was consensual. Overwhelmed, we sought solace in the support of the wider community. Around this time, Premier Daniel Andrews acknowledged our struggle in his daily Covid press conference, offering us well wishes for the Jewish New Year. It was in this community support that we found the source of our resilience.

But the confidence we drew from that support was obliterated when on 26 August we discovered that new laws in Victoria had quietly been passed in February, criminalising the public dissemination of information that could lead to the identification of a sexual assault victim. Shockingly, the law offered no exceptions for victims identifying themselves, threatening potential jail time simply for sharing their stories.

It was through Nina Funnell, a journalist and survivor advocate, that I became aware of these laws. Her success in founding the #letusspeak/#letherspeak campaign in Tasmania and the Northern Territory, addressing similar laws, inspired her to take action once more in Victoria.

I reached out to Nick Mazzeo, who had represented me in the civil case and had continued to provide me with legal advice during the campaign. Nick, along with Adrian Strauch, a barrister from the Victorian Bar, generously offered to represent us pro bono and immediately commenced an application to lift the gag. They patiently listened to my frustrations and anger. 'Doesn't this forced silence imply that the burden of shame is placed on survivors?' I asked Adrian as they worked tirelessly on preparing our affidavits.

It was the one time during our campaign that I felt conflicted with the widespread support we received. The personal calls from Daniel Andrews and State Attorney-General Jill Hennessy, promising to take immediate action to fix the law was very encouraging, as was the backing received from our local MPs Josh Burns and David Southwick. However, I grappled with the realisation that the high-profile nature of our case had played a role in garnering such attention and having a court hearing scheduled so quickly. While the support was heartening, I wondered about all the other survivors affected by the law who did not have the same level of visibility or assistance.

In the first application of its kind, Magistrate Johanna Metcalf heard our case in the Melbourne Magistrates' Court on 2 September, and our right to speak out using our own names was restored, making us, bizarrely, the only survivors in Victoria allowed to do so. We hoped this landmark decision would pave an easier way forward for other survivors.

Later that year, in response to the #letusspeak campaign, Attorney-General Hennessy reversed this error in the law, allowing survivors to identify themselves in public without requiring the court's permission.

The restoration of our voice couldn't have come at a better time. Only a matter of weeks later, the court ordered Malka Leifer to be extradited to Australia. I rewatched the news clips of that day, seeing us standing in the driveway of my apartment, our faces beaming with joy. The Premier proclaimed it as a victorious day for survivors, and indeed, it was.

We had fought against the system that Leifer had manipulated and, with the support of countless people around the world, we had emerged triumphant.

Malka Leifer would finally be brought back to Australia to face justice.

Two months later, on 3 December, in the seventy-fourth and final court hearing in Israel, Leifer's extradition appeal was denied.

All that was left before Leifer returned to Australia was a signature from the Israeli Minister of Justice.

'After many years and after a despicable attempt to pretend she was mentally ill, and in light of the Supreme Court ruling, it is our moral duty to allow Malka Leifer to stand trial,' said Avi Nissenkorn, the new justice minister, as he signed the extradition order the following day.

We were in contact with prosecutor Matan Akiva, who had become a trusted ally throughout this gruelling process. His calls before and after each court hearing, explaining the intricacies of law and what we could expect, had been a lifeline to us, giving us a sense of control amid all the uncertainty. However, there was one piece of information that he was strictly forbidden from sharing with us – the date of Malka Leifer's return to Australia. Until she touched down, we would have no idea it was happening.

All of a sudden, everything began to feel incredibly real. I received a call from police detective Danielle Newton, the very same officer I had given my first statement to in 2011. Danielle had left the Sexual Offences and Child Abuse Investigation Team (SOCIT), pursued a different area of policing in a different department, and after seven years, returned to SOCIT to take up the case once again. She would be one of the police officers responsible for picking up Leifer. The next time I heard from her would be with news of Leifer's return.

In a coordinated effort, authorities in both countries maintained ironclad secrecy surrounding Malka Leifer's flight details, worried that efforts would be made to derail their plans.

During that month, the anticipation consumed us, even taking over our dreams. Elly, Nicole and I spent countless hours on the phone together, imagining how it would all unfold.

By January, in an effort to distract myself, I headed out to the country on a road trip. News had reached Nicole, through the community grapevine, that kosher food had been ordered for the prison. We also heard that members of the school board responsible for Leifer's flight out of Australia in 2008 were selling their businesses and leaving the country. Her return had to be imminent. But we were worried – due to rising Covid cases, Israel announced it was entering into a full lockdown for two weeks from 8 January 2021, and was enacting a full travel ban in and out of the country.

It was a stormy day as I drove back into Melbourne on 25 January 2021, and even with the wipers on full speed, I struggled to see the car ahead of me. My phone, connected to Bluetooth, began to ring incessantly, but I didn't dare take my eyes off the road. As the calls continued without a break, I sensed that something significant was happening. I tried to get my phone to respond to a verbal command and call Nicole, but the flood of incoming calls was interfering. Finally, I spotted a petrol station ahead. I quickly pulled in, and after what felt like an eternity of declining calls, I finally managed to call my sister.

'Oh my God, she's coming back,' she managed to say. 'The picture, the picture.' I found myself planted on the wet footpath outside the petrol station, squinting at a photo of Leifer in handcuffs, her figure framed against the entrance of a plane on the tarmac at Ben Gurion Airport. Danielle stood beside her. Someone had managed to snap the picture, capturing a moment that was not meant to be seen, and promptly sold it to the media. Danielle later told us, in a mad rush of events, that they just managed to get on the last plane out before Israel closed their airspace.

'What do I feel?' I asked myself, but there were a million thoughts clamouring in my mind. I kept staring at the picture as though it would provide me the closure I was seeking. As I travelled down the highway I spoke to reporters from across the globe, their voices a cacophony of urgency. Caught unawares, we did not have a social media statement ready, and the reporters were each desperate for my immediate thoughts on this massive moment.

That night, after the phone had finally fallen silent, I set aside a moment for meditation. The overwhelming rush of sensations had left me numb, but I knew there were emotions lurking just beyond my reach. In therapy, I had made it a goal to reunite the fractured parts of myself and learn to connect and truly feel my emotions. However, I've learnt that when my emotions become too intense, my mind has an instinct to dissociate. So, with my noise-cancelling headphones on, cocooned under my favourite blanket, I invited those feelings to rise and welcomed them into what I liked to call my 'soul space'. I understood that sitting with and acknowledging the overwhelming emotions, offering them the love and attention they deserved, was a crucial part of my healing journey. I went to sleep feeling lighter.

Over the following days Nicole, Elly and I scanned the flights arriving into Australia, wondering which plane might be carrying our abuser. The journalists who had become not just observers but companions too during the years of struggle also kept in touch, messaging their calculations and assessments. One reporter claimed to know when Leifer would arrive via an inside source, and made us swear on our lives to keep the information confidential. The situation felt nothing short of insane, with emotions at fever pitch.

A film crew we were working with wanted to capture the moment we finally saw Leifer step onto Australian soil. When we concluded filming the third and final episode of *Australian Story* the previous year, we had been inundated with offers from multiple production companies, all eager to continue documenting our journey. After careful consideration and negotiations, we decided to collaborate with director Adam Kamien, whose vision and approach resonated deeply with us. We tried to ensure we would be together for this moment, but due to the uncertain timing of her return, along with our moving schedules during school holidays, getting us all together proved impossible.

The intensity of the situation reached a crescendo when a worker at Melbourne airport shared an image of several police cars with flashing lights on the tarmac, tipping off the news. Adam's film crew spent hours at Nicole's house, filming her, with us on the phone, while we gazed intently at the tarmac through the lens of Jodi Lee's phone. The airport was teeming with reporters, all camped out, awaiting Leifer's arrival.

At one point that night, we believed we had caught a glimpse of Leifer stepping off the plane, but the ever-mounting anxiety had taken its toll, and by 11 p.m. we were in a state of delirium. According to the news, Leifer was in Australia. Across my social media I changed the #bringleiferback hashtag to #leiferisback. It was a defining moment in our quest for truth and justice.

The next morning Leifer was arraigned in court and charged with a staggering seventy-four counts of sexual abuse, consisting of eleven counts of rape, forty-seven counts of indecent assault, three counts of sexual penetration of a child, and thirteen counts of committing an indecent act with a child. The charges related to three victims – me, Elly and Nicole. As I watched the court online, jumping around my living room, unable to sit still, I realised something: our journey was far from over. In fact, we had just taken the first steps on a much longer path. My therapist's words echoed in my mind: 'This is where most people begin their quest for justice, Dassi. The hardest part is still ahead.'

CHAPTER 25

Committal

With the case now firmly in the hands of the Australian courts, our first challenge in this new chapter was to sever ties with the publicity that surrounded us and get comfortable with silence. 'No comment,' I wrote in response to the flood of requests I received from reporters around the world following Leifer's arraignment. The option of engaging with the media was now barred. The legal process asked for our silence to prevent prejudicing the case. 'It's been the quietest week of the campaign,' Nicole wrote in our chat, and just in that moment, no longer having to respond to the media felt like a blissful respite.

A couple of days later, I received my first email from Ailsa McVean, the solicitor at the Office of Public Prosecutions responsible for handling the case. She was reaching out to establish contact, and suggested we arrange a time to speak. She also introduced us to Merryn Brown, a social worker at the victims and witness assistance service, who would guide Nicole, Elly and I through the complexities of the court process.

Victoria's zero-Covid suppression approach meant it was easier to organise our first conference over Zoom. It turned out to be a wise decision – by the time we met with the prosecution ten days later, Melbourne was on the brink of its third lockdown. In response to an outbreak of thirteen cases, the government issued a snap five-day stay at home order, allowing only four essential reasons to leave.

Ailsa informed us that Covid had caused a backlog in the courts, so it could take a considerable amount of time for the case to progress. There we were, back to the waiting game, but this time it was different: Malka Leifer was in Australia. We were closer to justice than ever before.

Weeks after the February lockdown lifted, I joined the March 4 Justice, alongside Nicole and Dassi Herszberg. Over 110 000 people, most of them women, stood together in forty cities across Australia, united in their demand for justice, equality and an end to gendered violence. The catalyst was the federal government's response – or lack thereof – to distressing reports of the alleged rape of a political staffer and historical rape allegations against a parliamentarian. I held my sign firmly, my face angry beneath my mask. It was disheartening that in 2021, we were still fighting for gender equality.

Ailsa sent us another email. Leifer had retained Tony Hargreaves as her lawyer, and the defence had made their intentions clear. They would not be seeking bail, which was a huge relief. And surprisingly, they would not be contesting Leifer's fitness to stand trial, which caught us completely off guard. However, the accused would be contesting all charges and pleading not guilty. The news hit me like a physical blow, and instinctively, I clutched my chest before rushing to call my sisters. Not guilty! It felt like a punch to the gut. How could she so easily deny the suffering she had caused us?

The not guilty plea meant the case would move forward to a committal hearing, where a magistrate would determine if there was enough evidence to proceed with a trial. It was a lot to process.

As Melbourne moved into yet another fourteen-day lockdown, I tried to set aside the looming court case and channel my energy into writing this book. Louise Adler from Hachette had approached me in 2020 about writing my autobiography, and my love for writing meant I embraced the opportunity. I naively imagined that writing would be a simple task. I had no idea of the emotional stamina it would demand, nor the way I would grapple with the complexity of my own history. I wrote the chapter about Dalia's death first; my grief surrounding her death demanded expression. Other chapters followed in no chronological order. I ignored the book for a year until I found the strength to confront my childhood, though not everything I wrote made it into the final copy – some experiences were just too raw and intense. There was only so much time I could dedicate to writing before I found myself needing to turn away from it. Homeschooling and virtual court hearings provided ample distractions.

Just days before a committal mention on 10 April, Ailsa informed me that Shua would be a witness in the case. Communication since our divorce had been focused solely on our daughter, and I'd had no inkling that he would be involved in the legal proceedings. Even after I had been told, it was not something I discussed with him.

During the committal, the defence questioned my knowledge of Shua's statement, and I told them that I had been unaware of it until Ailsa informed me. The barrister questioned me: 'And you did not ask why he was giving evidence? Were you not curious to ask what he might be saying?'

'Of course I was curious,' I replied, 'but I knew that was not a question she could answer.' Ailsa couldn't reveal the identities of the other witnesses, either.

The discrepancy in access to information was incredibly frustrating. While Leifer was privy to all the court details, we were not a party to the proceedings. It was the state versus Malka Leifer, and we were just the three main witnesses. We were barred from virtual court hearings because case strategy could be discussed, details we were not permitted to know. The media provided us with information that the prosecution couldn't disclose. According to their reports, Leifer's lawyers intended to probe into our home life. I felt incredibly disturbed reading how the defence intended to trivialise my trauma, as if my experiences were just pieces on a board they could use to advance their agenda.

Their games seemed to know no bounds. I remember rushing home to scream into my pillow when I heard the defence intended to subpoena my medical records. I was completely overwhelmed. I called my lawyers, Nick Mazzeo and Adrian Strauch, who once again agreed to fight the subpoena pro bono. The weight of it all, the mounting price of being a victim, consumed me. I barely slept, my thoughts circling endlessly. How dare they use my vulnerabilities as ammunition against me? Why were the wounds I had bared in confidential sessions now fair game in the court process? The therapy space I had once believed safe now felt tainted and ugly. I had been making progress, learning to trust again, but now I wondered if I had been naive to trust anyone.

In a deal negotiated by my lawyers, I agreed to relinquish the therapeutic reports used in my civil case and parenting matters, on the condition they retracted their request for my medical file. In a small win, the magistrate granted me a nationwide suppression order, recognising the high public interest in the case. The order covered only my medical records but would extend to the trial and any potential appeals. It wasn't much, but it gave me some comfort.

On the same day that the subpoena issue was in court, we received news from Israel that the former health minister, Litzman, had been indicted over his interference in Leifer's extradition case. My head was a complete whirlwind.

Litzman had remained in government despite the revelations that he had abused his position, pressuring psychiatrists to find Leifer unfit to stand trial. At an opening event for a new hospital in Ashkalon, Litzman had told the Israeli media that, 'It was all for the good of the public.' He had even gone on to be promoted to Minister of Housing. At last, Israel had acknowledged all was not well and charged Litzman with interfering in court proceedings. Police had obtained recordings of Litzman and officials in his office pressuring Health Ministry employees to act in favour of Leifer. Those in positions of power, especially, must be held accountable.

Meanwhile in Australia, just nine days after Victoria's fifth lockdown had been lifted, we found ourselves headed into lockdown number six. The Victorian government took the unprecedented step of implementing the lockdown from 8 p.m. on the day they announced it. My siblings and I managed to squeeze in a quick dinner together before hurrying to our homes. Little did we know that the committal hearing would come and go before we would be able to gather again.

Preparing for the committal hearing within the confines of lockdown was hard. Every night after putting Lily to bed, I would sit on the beanbag in my lounge and read my six police statements. It was the last thing I did before I closed my eyes, and the memories of Leifer's abuse would visit me in my sleep.

I spent my therapy sessions over Zoom creating a timeline of the abuse. My statements had been given as the memories surfaced, not in chronological order, but the court demanded I know which incident had happened first. My memory didn't work like that. To make sense of it all, I spent hours with the fifty-seven pages of my statements, cutting and pasting them onto a single document in the correct order. I felt overwhelmed, and as the committal hearing drew closer Lily spent more time with her father. I began to see Leifer everywhere, in every corner of my once-safe apartment.

My therapist provided me with a letter that allowed me to travel beyond the 5 kilometre radius stipulated by the lockdown, and to stay out past the 8 p.m. curfew, for the sake of my mental health. I needed the support of my sisters, and they were struggling too. We could not speak to each other about the abuse, but we could sit together and silently read our statements. We decided to stay together the weekend before the committal hearing.

Tensions ran high that Friday night, and we found ourselves bickering over trivial matters. In the morning, we apologised and resolved not to let our shared trauma come between us. While I vaguely remember doing some filming for the documentary during that time, my mind was overwhelmingly preoccupied with the presence of Leifer, haunting me whether my eyes were open or closed. It felt as though I was trapped in the bubble of my abuser once again, unable to escape her grip on my thoughts.

By the time I took the witness stand, I was desperate to get her out of my head. It was September, and Melbourne was still in strict lockdown. The court proceedings were conducted over Webex. As witnesses, we were required to be present at the Office of Public Prosecutions in the city, where we faced the magistrate, who sat in the court alone. And on a big screen in front of us, in separate panels, were Leifer and the defence.

Nicole testified first, enduring two days of cross-examination. On the third day, it was my turn. The city felt strangely quiet as I pulled up at the Office of Public Prosecutions. I was told to wear a mask until the moment I was asked to speak. I had to stay away from Nicole during the breaks. I wasn't allowed to see or speak to her, although we managed to share a brief wave across the hall as she left the witness room and I entered.

In the small, dimly lit room, I removed my mask and set it aside before positioning myself in front of the camera. Merryn sat beside me, her face just outside the camera frame. Tamar, my support person, waited outside.

The prosecution initiated the proceedings, asking me to affirm the truthfulness and accuracy of each of my six statements. That done, Merryn set my statements aside. From this point forward, I wouldn't be allowed to refer to them again. Then, it was the defence's turn to take the reins. The prosecution had explained that, unlike the trial proper, we would not be taken through our evidence.

Ian Hill, Malka Leifer's barrister, stood up and began his questioning, asking first about my childhood, and the bedrooms where each of my sisters slept. I clasped my hands tightly on my lap, my knuckles white with the pressure. Beneath the table, my leg bounced uncontrollably. On that first day, my voice quivered and I felt overwhelmed with the relentless barrage of questions. But as the days passed and the cross-examination intensified, adrenaline surged through me and it was an effort to avoid defensiveness that would undermine my credibility. I glanced once or twice at the on-screen image of Leifer, who was sitting in a room at the Dame Phyllis Frost Centre, a women's prison in Melbourne, then chose not to look at her again. Having her lawyer insist I was lying was hard enough.

My testimony lasted four gruelling days. Throughout it, I believe I upheld my commitment to unwaveringly speak my truth.

The one saving grace of that week was our new kitten, Stormi, whom Lily and I had welcomed into our home two months prior. Each day, after hours of sitting and immense focus in court, I found myself playing with Stormi for hours. His mischievous energy and the gentle purring as he slept on my chest offered a much-needed way to unwind from the emotional intensity of my days. Being new to the world of cats, I had no idea he would be exactly what I needed after giving evidence.

The committal, initially expected to last one week, extended to two, coinciding with the holiest day of the Jewish year, Yom Kippur. Leifer was excused from attending the hearing, while Danielle and a cleaner at the school, the only two non-Jewish witnesses, were questioned on that day. We were not allowed to listen to the other witnesses. Finally, on the last day, Magistrate Metcalf delivered her decision to send the matter to trial.

As the case began its journey in the County Court in Melbourne, I recognised that it would take time for the trial to begin. During the ensuing months, I deliberately tried to divert my thoughts from Leifer and concentrate on other facets of my life. It was exciting to envision a future beyond the trial, where I could pursue my dreams and aspirations without the burden of the case. We had monthly meetings with the prosecution to keep us informed about the progress of the case. These meetings offered us some sense of control amid the uncertainty, and we appreciated being kept in the loop.

By the end of 2021, I embraced a new opportunity and joined the board of Pathways Melbourne, a remarkable organisation founded by Leah Boulton. Pathways' goal is to support and empower people from the Orthodox and ultra-Orthodox communities who are questioning their lifestyle, practices and beliefs.

I couldn't help but think how valuable Pathways would have been during my own transition away from the Adass community. It was a time of great innocence and great danger, and I had nearly lost my life in the process. Since meeting Leah in 2018, she has become not just a colleague but a dear friend and being part of the Pathways board allows me to contribute to a cause that I am deeply passionate about. I feel a profound sense of pride in supporting others who might be going through the same challenges I once faced.

But no matter where I turned, I couldn't escape the looming presence of the court or the relentless attacks from Malka Leifer's supporters. There was constant trolling of our social media pages and hateful blogs labelled us monsters and accused us of selling our souls for revenge, asserting that we were no longer human beings but predators. I sought support from Shana Aaronson of Jewish Community Watch to deal with it. Shana was unwavering and helped uncover the identity of some of the most hateful. A court in Israel instructed that the defamatory posts be removed and at the time they were, but since then more posts have been made.

With lockdowns finally behind us, in 2022 life gradually started to open up again. Amid this newfound sense of normalcy, Lily began her final year of primary school.

Within a few weeks, we both contracted Covid, and then, exactly three months later, we found ourselves battling the virus again. Our case was routinely in the papers or the nightly news. Although Lily had a better understanding of the case by that time, I still shielded her as much as possible, wanting to protect her from the weight of it, and to preserve her innocence for as long as I could.

With Lily back in school, I immersed myself in writing this book, working closely with journalist Ellen Whinnett. This meant taking a deep, introspective journey into my past. I started by delving into my old diaries, which spanned my teenage years, and then the thousands of diary entries I had made since then. I sifted through boxes of childhood mementos and notes, searched through old emails and digital records, and met with each of my siblings to explore our childhood through their eyes.

I had to find, confront and sit with the innocence and vulnerabilities of my younger self. It was only after I had spent thousands of hours pouring the rush of memories onto paper, shared it with Ellen, received her suggestions, spent hours more reworking and rewriting it, and then sent it back, that I began to feel a sense of cathartic release. I organised and structured my narrative, then with Ellen's help created a chapter timeline that connected the dots of the events in my life. Finding the balance between sharing my trauma without overwhelming the reader was challenging.

I worked with Dr Deborah Rechter, a writing coach and curator who generously gave hours of her time to teach me about the writing process. She had a creative and intelligent perspective that allowed me to see my writing from a completely different angle. Deborah taught me the art of weaving reflection throughout my narrative and guided me to voice the tensions and complexities of my experiences, offering a deeper understanding of my journey.

There were many moments when I felt like giving up. Ellen was there to encourage me. Deborah spoke of her faith in my abilities. I discovered new facets of myself, and I realised that my story was not about the trauma I had endured, but rather, the choices I had made to navigate through it. There were times when I paused writing just to read back and marvel at the distance I had travelled, both in my writing journey and in my life.

Meanwhile, Elly, Nicole and I delved into negotiations with numerous production companies, all vying to bring a dramatised version of our story to the screen. After thoughtful consideration, we chose to entrust our story rights to Gal Greenspan from Sweetshop & Green, having full confidence in his ability to create a powerful dramatisation of our journey. Juggling writing sessions, production meetings and filming for the documentary, life was brimming with activity. Yet, amid it all, the looming presence of the court case remained.

We were still excluded from listening in to the court hearings, but the prosecution continued to keep us abreast of developments. They explained that they could not take seventy-four charges to trial as this would overwhelm a jury, so they had selected twenty-nine charges for the indictment – fourteen for me, ten for Elly and five for Nicole. Despite this development, Ian Hill, Leifer's lawyer, continued to argue for further reduction in charges. It was a significant breakthrough when the prosecution successfully argued for the consolidation of charges from the three of us into one trial, avoiding the burden of multiple separate trials. In April, we were asked to confirm our availability for the upcoming trial set for August.

Judge Mark Gamble had been appointed to preside over the proceedings.

Again, Nicole, Elly and I faced the weight of reading and re-reading our statements leading up to the trial. Knowing the profound impact this had on us before the committal, we knew that our emotional wellbeing would be better preserved if we faced this journey together. A week prior to the expected trial date in August, Nicole, Elly and I packed up our lives and moved into an apartment in the city. During that crucial week, we dedicated ourselves to trial preparations. We stayed in close contact with the prosecution, doing everything in our power to ensure we were ready for the chance to bring Malka Leifer to justice.

Initially, Ian Hill had estimated two days for pre-trial arguments, but as the hearing extended to a week, it became evident that there was still much left to argue. Sadly, the judge declared that due to unresolved legal issues, the trial would not proceed as scheduled, dealing a devastating blow to our emotional and mental health. The trial was adjourned to the following year, set down for February 2023, prolonging our already lengthy journey towards justice.

Only several days later there was another blow; the court had accepted the plea bargain for Litzman, the former Health Minister and Chair of the United Torah Judaism Party. Litzman took a deal which dismissed the 'obstruction of justice' charge for a guilty plea on the 'fraud and breach of trust' charge in relation to the Malka Leifer case. The deal was criticised heavily by the public, as it spared him serving prison time, imposed only a fine of NIS 2800 ($1141) and did not carry the designation of moral turpitude, which would have barred Litzman from holding a Knesset office for seven years. During the final speech he gave in the Knesset before resigning in June he vowed to return to politics.

Nicole, Elly and I were shocked, blindsided and let down. A man who had reportedly leveraged his position – one of the highest in Israel – to aid an abuser, had gotten away with nothing more than a mere slap on the wrist. He had intensified the depth of our trauma and compelled us to wage a gruelling battle against the most formidable forces. In our view, this was trivialisation of an egregious betrayal. What message did this send to the most vulnerable in Israel – those who dared to face the system, only to encounter corruption and be told it was irrelevant, their cumulative trauma not a concern?

The Israeli media urged us to rally against this injustice and implore the courts not to accept this plea, but our voices were muted with the legal process for Malka Leifer before the courts in Australia.

I had turned thirty the year I shared my story with the world, never anticipating that at the age of thirty-five I'd still be entangled in the never-ending saga of Malka Leifer.

CHAPTER 26

Leifer trial

It was my second day on the stand. After the jury filed out of the closed court, I could still count fifteen pairs of eyes following my every move. Sexual assault victims give evidence in a closed court, so there were no media or onlookers present, but the court still felt crowded. The judge, his two staff, four members of the prosecution, three members of the defence, Leifer, her police escort, Tamar, Merryn and a security guard at the door.

Judge Gamble turned his attention towards the witness box where I sat, just beneath his elevated platform. 'Ms Erlich, please remain seated. The defence will be questioning you without the jury present. Do you understand?' Normally, this would be the moment I would be excused for a break. I nodded, and then quickly remembered to verbalise my understanding. 'Yes, your Honour.'

With a nod from the judge, Ian Hill KC, the barrister for the defence, rose from his seat and positioned himself at the lectern in the centre of the bar table. I turned to face him, but avoided eye contact. Each time I'd inadvertently caught his eye, I had been met with a look that felt contemptuous and disdainful. Instead, I gazed past him towards my support people, seated behind the jury box, on the other side of the court.

I took a deep breath and straightened my back. *I wonder if he ever has trouble sleeping at night*, I thought, although I understood that Ian Hill's job was to question the truth of victims.

I tugged at the hair tie in my hands until it nearly broke. I knew the questions that followed would be about my father.

Just days before the trial, Danielle had informed me that the defence wanted a copy of the manuscript I was working on. I was distraught. This book was my story in my very own words. How could I surrender those words to be exploited, used as weapons against me? I met with the prosecution team and asked them to contest the subpoena, but they were not certain I would win, and warned me that an objection could delay the trial. I made the difficult decision not to fight and handed over my book.

At the time of the trial, I had only written about the events up to 2016. I also had eight pages of dot point notes for what I called the 'campaign chapters'. All this was given to them. I suspected they only learnt of the existence of my book through messages that had been subpoenaed in a completely different criminal case involving another survivor.

In May 2020, 'Joan', an abuse survivor residing in Melbourne, reached out to me through my Facebook page. Her first message thanked me for sharing our journey publicly, as our story had given her the strength to report her abuser that very week. Her abuser, too, was a teacher, and a female. 'If I didn't see the freedom in yours and your sister's faces, I don't know I would have had the courage to follow in your steps,' she had written.

What followed was a mentorship turned friendship, as Joan embarked on her own journey through the criminal justice system. I was transparent with her about the challenges, the way the system was legally allowed to retraumatise you. Joan and I discussed our therapies, and the coping mechanisms we used to find pockets of peace throughout the process.

During the committal hearing against her abuser, Joan mentioned being inspired by Dassi Erlich. The defence in her case promptly subpoenaed all the messages we had exchanged. In those messages, I had discussed writing a book. Ian Hill was now in possession of those messages. Nothing was sacred or beyond their reach, it seemed.

I spoke to Ailsa, the solicitor responsible for our case. I was struggling to come to terms with the thought of them tearing me apart with my own words. Ailsa assured me that they would redact anything not relevant to Leifer or my childhood, but as I went through the book, I could not find a single chapter since Leifer had entered my life where she wasn't somehow involved. It took several sleepless nights and a frenzy of diary writing to realise Leifer had impacted every period of my life since she chose to abuse me. In my diary that night, in bold, underlined letters, I scrawled, 'I will not let Leifer define my life any longer.'

In the end, the prosecution did try to redact parts of my book relating to my marriage and Lily's birth, but the defence insisted on having access to those parts, too. Their request was granted.

All I wanted now was Leifer out of my head and out of my life. To do that, I had to get through the trial.

Director of Public Prosecutions v Malka Leifer commenced on 7 February 2023. In the first video diary I recorded during the trial process, I am lying in bed, my hair fanned out on the hotel pillow. 'There are one hundred men and women arriving in court this morning and fifteen of those will not only be judging Leifer's crime, but also judging me and my sisters,' I confided to the camera, detailing the jury selection process.

Nestled in a queen bed at the Quest Southbank, it was difficult to grasp that all those years of fighting had led to this moment. That morning, I turned over and closed my eyes, but my mind was filled with images of what I imagined was transpiring at the County Court, just 2.3 kilometres away.

By mid-morning, the prosecution called to give us an update. A jury of fifteen had been selected, drawn at random from a hat. Not one person had asked to be excused from the case, although the defence had requested the removal of one teacher. The final judging panel would consist of only twelve jurors, but they had chosen fifteen in case of any unforeseen circumstances during what was expected to be a lengthy five-week trial.

After the jury was sworn in, the opening statements were given. We could not be present during this phase, and I decided to stay offline, avoiding any media coverage. However, later that night, someone sent me an article featuring a table of all twenty-nine charges, detailing each charge's name, location, and who it had impacted. I hadn't known this would be released to the press. As I read the words discussing my body – Hadassa Erlich's breasts – they felt alien, as though they belonged to someone else. I felt both disconnected and exposed at the same time. I closed the page and retreated inside.

'I'm doing this all for you,' I whispered to the image of my younger self in my mind, the one who had endured so much in silence, too terrified to speak up. I was not her anymore.

After saying goodnight to Nicole and Elly, I popped a sleeping pill and lay down. It had been years since I had relied on medication for sleep, but as the trial drew closer, sleep became increasingly elusive. Half an hour later, when the pill had yet to calm my racing mind, I yelled out to Nicole, hearing her restlessness from across the hall, to see if she was okay. 'A bundle of nervous energy,' she yelled back at me. Nicole was first up; she would take the stand the next day.

The morning started early. I had woken at five and been unable to lie still for another minute. I managed to shower, dress, make a coffee, tidy my room and even sit down to do some painting before the film crew arrived. I had introduced Nicole and Elly to the allure of adult paint-by-numbers, explaining that the focus required to find and fill the tiny shapes was almost meditative.

The film crew messaged to say they had arrived, and within minutes, Adam, the director, accompanied by his producer, Gabrielle Weiniger, a sound technician and a videographer entered our apartment carrying an array of equipment, including cameras, tripods, stabilisers, production monitors and the big boom microphone. I took a video of the commotion to show Lily later.

Ben, Isaac, Tamar and Elly's husband Danny also arrived, along with several friends, eager to join us on our first-day walk into court to show their support. A reporter informed me that a crowd was gathering, ready to film our arrival. By 9.30 a.m., we were ready to head out, microphones threaded through our clothing and sticky-taped to our chests. As we took the elevator down, there was little space for anything but a reassuring squeeze of Nicole's hand. I sensed her nerves, but she had a brave face on.

The film crew dropped us outside the courtside cafe, 100 metres down the road, and we walked towards the court together, three sisters united in our quest for justice. The weight of the moment felt palpable. There was a thumping in my chest, and the world seemed to be moving in slow motion. Nicole, Elly and I exchanged reassuring looks; we were in this together. Danny walked close behind carrying our bags, while everyone else trailed further behind, out of the cameras' reach. It felt odd to be in front of the cameras. I had enjoyed the relative privacy of the two years since Leifer had arrived from Israel.

Once we passed through security, we took the elevator up to the first floor, to the meeting room Merryn had reserved for us. There, we were greeted by our prosecution team: Detective Danielle Newton, solicitor Ailsa McVean, her junior, Ilya Komesaroff, and Justin Lewis, the barrister representing the OPP, along with his junior, Stephanie Clancy. As the trial had begun, they were limited in how much they could interact with us at this point, so it was a quick hello before they headed to the courtroom on the fourth floor. With a flurry of 'good luck' and words of encouragement, Merryn, Ben and Nicole followed the prosecution team upstairs.

I sat down and looked around the room. There were four walls painted white, with a wooden ledge positioned at the midpoint. A varnished conference table with three chairs placed around it and a rubbish bin in the corner. The door had a sign that read 'Reserved for the prosecution', and a window looking into a cavernous space filled with many other doors. I didn't know it then, but this bland space would become our home for nine weeks, and would oscillate between feeling like a prison and a safe haven.

After everyone had left, I opened my computer and attempted to read over my statements, as well as the transcripts I had been given of my answers in the committal hearing. I would be branded a liar if my answers differed in any way. The committal had actually triggered further memories, but I pushed these away, knowing the defence wouldn't care for any changes. It was hard to concentrate.

I was reading my statements, but nothing was sinking in. I moved to the transcripts. Over the past few months, I had compiled the answers I had given during the committal and organised them into one document. To my surprise, it revealed the story the defence had been trying to piece together with their seemingly disjointed questions. At the time, their tactics had confused me, but despite their attempts to trip me up, I had responded with clarity, and the story that emerged was undeniably my own.

Finally, the day came to an end. Nicole looked completely shattered as she stepped down from the stand. She couldn't tell us much about what happened, and it was incredibly difficult not to ask. She appeared a different person to the one who had started the day. The weight of it was evident, and I worried about her, but she told me she was ready to face Ian Hill's cross-examination and the feeling of not being believed.

Early the following week, Nicole finally stepped down from the stand. There was a heaviness around her that replaced her earlier nervous energy. She looked tired, drawn and filled with self-doubt. Elly and I tried our best to reassure her, but my mind was already consumed with thoughts of the following day. Tomorrow, it would be my turn.

That night, I took two sleeping pills, but even then, I was up at 5 a.m., pacing the apartment and speaking softly to myself as I mentally retraced the sequence of my abuse. Twelve years had passed since I gave my police statements, and over time, my memory had understandably become hazy. I had read and re-read my statements, going over them with Dassi and Tamar. The little details that I once remembered vividly, such as what clothes I was wearing or which side of the couch I sat on, were now only clear when I read them again, and the memory of her abuse was triggered in my mind.

It was still only 6 a.m. My jaw was throbbing. I massaged it gently to relieve the tension, then went in search of some Nurofen. There was a lump in my throat, as if all the words I had kept inside over the years were gathered there, waiting for release. I wondered if the lump would ease once I had spoken them aloud.

Today, Justin would walk me through my statements. I was not allowed to look at them, but his questions would lead me to a specific place in time, and I would need to recount the abuse that happened there. I scrolled through my Spotify playlist for a meditation, then I put on my headphones and went in search of my inner resolve.

I began my testimony on Tuesday, 14 February. That morning, in a moment of panic, I realised I had lost the hair tie I liked to fidget with and had no others of the same style. Danny rushed out to the chemist to buy me some more. I made my way into the court accompanied by my siblings, as well as my friends Leah, Dassi and Tessa. 'Look at all this love around me,' I gently whispered to my fifteen-year-old self. I was overwhelmed by the profound sense of belonging I felt; something I had yearned for during my younger years. I knew I had the strength to face whatever lay ahead. After exchanging hugs with everyone, I followed Merryn up to the fourth floor, Tamar at my side.

There were two doors to enter the court. The security guard opened the first, and we pressed a button to unlock the second. I bowed my head to the judge as I entered and walked through the public gallery, around the bar table, towards the witness box. Inside the box-like, windowless room, the air felt heavy and still. I tried to walk lightly; my new shoes sounded so noisy on the carpeted floor. Finally, I settled into the chair the court clerk had pulled out for me, and took a sip of water from the cup he had placed on the stand. The court didn't allow water bottles; one too many had been thrown at a judge.

Once I was seated, Judge Gamble called for Leifer to be brought in. I turned away as she was ushered through the back door and seated behind the screen that was positioned between us. The camera above me gave her a view of my profile. The court clerk knocked on the jury door, and two rows of strangers filed in. I didn't know if I should look at them or keep my gaze down. I tried not to fidget as I felt their eyes upon me.

I swore to tell the truth, and then Justin began his questioning. He stuck to the details of my childhood that I had written about in my statement. He was not allowed to ask me anything that wasn't already there. Then it was time to talk about the abuse Leifer had inflicted on me. I spoke slowly, my mind like a noisy battleground, torn between the memories I was reliving and the need to articulate them to a room full of strangers, when all I wanted was to disappear.

I could feel the red creeping over my face. *The shame isn't mine, it's hers*, I tried to remind myself. Several times Judge Gamble had to ask me to speak up. Leifer's lawyers sighed loudly and smiled as I recounted my most difficult trauma. Courtroom theatrics, I know, but I reframed their reactions as a sign that I was speaking the truth, which they didn't want to hear. Her lawyers continued this behaviour all afternoon. By the end of the day, I felt shell-shocked and emotionally drained.

The following day, all I wrote in my diary was: *Living and breathing Leifer's warped world again.* I was too tired to pen any further thoughts. I also recorded a short video for my future self, just three seconds long, saying, 'Dassi, you got through this.' Isaac had sat through the day with me as my support. It was the first time he had truly heard about the abuse, and he seemed just as shaken as I was. I had finished with Justin that morning, and in the afternoon, the defence had begun their cross-examination.

The third day on the stand was incredibly intense as I faced Ian Hill for his cross-examination. The courtroom began to feel like a stage where all the painful wounds of the past were laid bare. All day, I answered Ian's questions, and I couldn't help but wonder if deep down, Leifer denied the truth of what she had done even to herself. It felt so unfair that she could still play innocent while we were left to squirm and dance to her lawyer's tune. Although I knew she had no power over me anymore, in that courtroom, answering those gut-wrenching questions, it truly felt like she did.

They brought out my diary entries, and I wanted to chuckle at my younger self and at the same time cry for her innocence. Then they began reading from the chapter in this book where I detailed my confusion and distress around Leifer's abuse. The entire courtroom was silent, absorbed in the words. Merryn later told me she wished he had continued reading more. The point he had been trying to make, that my memory was so vivid for something that happened so many years ago, fell flat. I looked directly at him and expressed my wish that the memories were not so clear, adding that that's how trauma works.

Halfway through the morning, the judge excused the jury. Ian Hill intended to ask about my father, but the judge had not yet ruled that he would allow this line of inquiry in front of the jury. The fate of that decision rested on the answers I gave at this moment. The defence asked a series of questions, followed by a few from the prosecution. Then I was given the draft of my book and asked about this paragraph:

> At some point I'm not sure when I confessed to the principal
> that I wanted to share something I was troubled about ...
> Mrs Leifer set me up for a private phone call with a rabbi's
> wife ... I was able to tell her that my father gave me hugs that
> were uncomfortable.

Both parties asked me which year the incident took place. I searched my memory desperately; I believed those calls had been made in Year Ten, but there was no clear memory to tie it to a specific time. 'I cannot provide a definite answer,' I told them.

For the rest of the trial, Ian would use this uncertainty to accuse me of lying. 'Why would Dassi go to her "abuser" for help about another abuser? And why would Leifer give her the name of her mentor without being worried that she might be exposed?' he would posit to the court. That day I was dismissed for an early lunch. Both sides needed time to argue this issue before the judge. I would be told when Judge Gamble had made his decision.

The afternoon was no easier; a decision had not yet been made, but the cross-examination continued on other matters.

On my fourth day in the witness box, I could barely climb out of bed. My body felt depleted, as if there was nothing left to give. The stress and exhaustion had caused my blood pressure to drop, leaving me dizzy and light-headed. Reluctantly, I took some midodrine, a medication to raise my blood pressure. It lasted only four hours, and I knew I would crash once it wore off. I set a reminder on my phone to take another dose at lunchtime.

It was Friday, and I prayed that it would be my last day on the stand, so I could enter the weekend without the weight of this trial hanging over me.

It seemed to me that Ian's tactic that morning was to bore everyone to death. He asked the same questions repeatedly in various ways, about details I had already confirmed I did not know. He wanted to know which classes I had attended the day of an incident, or how many and which teachers were at camp. I remembered the abuse, not the particulars of the days when it occurred, and his questions made it seem like my memory was unclear. In his closing arguments, he informed the court that Dassi Erlich had said 'I don't know' 160 times. Of course, he could spin it however he pleased; I was only allowed to answer the questions he asked.

I could feel my younger self being forced to endure the pain all over again. At the end of the day, I was asked to return on Monday. That afternoon, all the film crew captured was my slumped back as I desperately searched through my computer bag for midodrine and almost fainted in the back of their car.

An hour or so later, with the medication on board and accompanied by the film crew, I went to Freda's house, where the family had gathered for Friday night dinner. The setting sun cast a warm glow over her dining room, and I sat on the floor and cuddled her elderly Labrador. For the first time that week, I laughed, watching Freda's sons, Sam and Alex, attempt to bake the perfect bagel. The cacophony in my mind felt much quieter.

With a stomach full of pizza, I returned home to collect a few belongings, but my apartment felt like a different world. I touched the plants, the cat tower, but they seemed to belong to a life I no longer recognised. It was hard to imagine it was a life I would return to one day. The trial had begun, I told myself; that meant it would eventually have to end.

Over the weekend my emotions swung wildly. I cried, I laughed, I danced around the room from the surge of adrenaline and then collapsed and couldn't move at all. I spent some time gaming with Lily at her father's house.

I couldn't understand why the defence was allowed to try and break me, and why I was expected to remain composed in the face of such pain. What did a moment of vulnerability imply? Falsehood? The system felt deeply unjust to me, as if it punished victims for having the courage to speak up. It seemed designed to penalise those who had already suffered.

Monday marked the fifth and final day of my testimony on the stand. Judge Gamble allowed the defence to ask me about my father, and I told the jury how he had touched me inappropriately. Ian's questioning insinuated that I could not have been entirely unaware of sexual abuse, suggesting that my prior abuse somehow made me knowledgeable about such matters. I had to fight every urge to scream at him. It was utterly infuriating to have my trauma used against me in such a callous way. *Twelve years of remembering in such excruciating detail is over now*, I told myself that night. *I give myself permission to forget.* I had done my part. What they did with my truth was now up to them.

I accompanied Elly into the court on her first day on the stand and spent the day with Nicole in the bland room downstairs. But on Elly's second day of testifying, I woke up feeling absolutely dreadful, completely unable to get out of bed. The stress had finally taken its toll on my body. My mind hadn't yet registered that I was no longer on the stand. The rest of the week, as Elly bravely faced the jury, I tried my best to support her from a distance, too unwell to go to court. She too endured an awful weekend before finishing her testimony on the following Monday.

Once the three of us had finished our time on the stand, we were allowed to observe the remainder of the trial. However, the prosecution strongly advised against entering the courtroom, fearing the jury might look for our reactions to the proceedings. They said we would be provided a link to watch it online, but the defence objected. Ultimately, the judge allowed it, but due to some ridiculous demand of the defence, we were each asked to sign an affidavit saying we were watching the proceedings alone. It was a busy Tuesday morning. Merryn rushed around, up and down the floors, collecting papers and pens, preparing three handwritten affidavits for us to sign. I was panicked. Shua would face the court soon, and I was determined not to miss his testimony.

The prosecution took Shua through the statement he had provided them in 2011. They were not permitted to ask him anything else. Shua testified that I had spoken highly of Leifer and considered her a surrogate parent. He also claimed to have overheard Nicole and me discussing plans to harass Leifer, with laughter, as if it were an exciting prospect. And with this, my ex-husband became the star witness for the defence, who repeatedly emphasised his words over the next five weeks. Ian Hill never shared my explanation with the court – that the so-called 'harassment' referred to a phone number of Leifer's we had received while she was living freely in Israel, which Nicole and I had discussed calling to confront her.

The defence argued that we had fabricated the allegations and spent a decade pursuing justice out of a desire to harass someone we had once admired. They were not required to provide a legitimate reason for why anyone would do this, they could suggest as they pleased. Ultimately, it was up to the jury to decide what they believed.

The jury was also not allowed to know of Leifer's escape to Israel, her attempts to evade extradition, or any events that had occurred during her time away from Australia. With so many crucial pieces of the puzzle missing, we couldn't fathom how they could arrive at the right decision.

In that windowless, featureless white room, Elly, Nicole, Danny, Merryn and I watched the courtroom, three floors above, online, each with our earphones in, so that technically we were 'watching it alone'. Knowing in advance what would be reported in the media provided us with some semblance of control. As we listened to other witnesses give their versions of our story, and sometimes get it terribly wrong, we moved around restlessly, silently hoping that the truth would find its way to the surface. We gripped the edges of the table, the frustration sometimes escaping in expletives. At times, one of us would hurriedly rush to the toilet, keeping an AirPod in to ensure we didn't miss a moment.

During our lunch break, we discussed our plans to move back home. The Victims Assistance Program had helped fund a three-week stay in the serviced apartment for the time we were on the stand. We had not thought past that, nor anticipated how all-encompassing the rest of the trial would be. The thought of returning to an empty house terrified me. Every trauma in my life had been picked at and pulled apart, triggering old coping mechanisms and self-destructive urges at a time when I had no energy to fight them. Lily and our cat Stormi were living at her father's house, and I questioned if I could be a present mother in this headspace. Recognising the toll this was taking on us, Isaac and Ben offered to help fund an additional two weeks at the Quest hotel.

The days began to meld into one another, each following a similar routine. Every morning after getting ready we would steal a few moments for paint-by-numbers before Danny or the film crew picked us up. We would squeeze into the middle row each vying for the spot that wouldn't be filmed. The videographer would sit in the front, turning his camera back, leaving the seat directly behind him out of frame. The sound technician would crouch in the third row, head ducked down to avoid being seen on camera.

The walk into court always left us feeling exposed, as the court photographers would rush to grab their cameras at the sight of us. Later, we would check to see which dress had made the news, although eventually, we began to repeat the same outfits. Danny always offered to pick up coffee if we hadn't had time to stop by The Firm, the cafe next door to the court, and sometimes, Isaac, Tamar, Ben or our nephew M would join us in the room. David Seeman popped in one day; Ted Baillieu too. On occasion, friends came as well.

Now that we had given our evidence, the prosecution team was allowed to speak with us, and most mornings we met at 10 a.m. to hear what they could share of the day ahead. All day, we would watch the court from our meeting room, together with our support worker Merryn. Sometimes, during lunch breaks, we met with the prosecution team again. Other times, we would step outside to soak in the sun, hoping for a boost of serotonin, or we'd walk to Nick Mazzeo's office, located around the corner from the court.

Nick allowed us to use his conference room for filming, and there we would debrief in front of the cameras, sharing our reactions to what we had seen and heard.

By 4.30 p.m., either Danny or the film crew would drive us back to the Quest. Some days this was followed by more filming, which we always grumbled about. Once alone, we would unwind by painting, music, mindless TV, and ordering Uber Eats. As often as we could, we would leave the city for a few hours and spend time with our kids. Occasionally we also had sessions with our therapists. Then it was a sleeping pill, meditation, and off to bed. Get up and repeat.

On 1 March the case was suddenly adjourned, an unusual occurrence once a trial has begun. Both parties were called into a closed court. We pleaded with Ailsa to tell us what was happening, but she wasn't allowed. The whole day we worried it was a mistrial. By the next morning we had worked ourselves up into a panic, and we arrived in court full of anxiety. It turned out the judge had simply been unwell and didn't want anyone to know. We wondered if he had any appreciation of the profound impact this case was having on us.

The next major setback came when two of Elly's charges were dropped. New legislation about sexual abuse had come into law on 1 December 2006. During cross-examination, Elly had mentioned that the first time Leifer abused her was in the summer of 2006 around the time of the school play, a period that spanned two possible weeks, both before and after 1 December.

The timing was crucial. Depending on which day the abuse occurred, the name of the incident would change under the law, but not the punishment. Unable to determine the exact timing, the prosecution was forced to drop these charges.

While new legislation had been passed earlier that year to address such gaps in the law, it had not yet been tested in court. Justin told us the judge was unlikely to apply it in our highly sensitive case, as it could become an immediate point of appeal.

It was heart-wrenching to witness Elly sitting there, head in her hands, tears slowly rolling down her face as the charges were read out in court, and the jury was informed that Leifer had been acquitted of those charges. 'Acquitted' felt so painfully wrong, but it was the formal way it had to be recorded. Two charges dropped at the stroke of a politician's pen, for a trauma that Elly would have to carry for the rest of her life.

We were four weeks into the trial. The witnesses had all testified, and the case now moved to legal arguments. We decided to take a day off from court and watch the proceedings online from our apartment instead. Justin had told us that the judge had a book of standardised jury instructions and had to carefully choose the relevant ones, customising the wording to fit our case. We listened to the lawyers arguing over what the judge would instruct the jury. It sounded like a game, where our trauma was irrelevant, and each side was trying to score points in their favour. Feeling depleted, we decided to turn off the link. I found it incomprehensible that anyone would willingly subject themselves to this process if they weren't telling the truth.

Closing arguments began. We were back in the meeting room with our earphones in. As I listened, my chest was tight and my fists clenched. It was the first time I'd heard the specifics of Elly and Nicole's abuse, laid out in excruciating detail, and it was even more challenging to hear than my own. I watched the reporters through the link, their pens moving rapidly, capturing every word of my sisters' pain and suffering. It was disconcerting to see their trauma turned into a story for public consumption. But the media had another story that day. Judge Gamble had instructed a mother to leave the court, claiming her breastfeeding was a distraction. The story dominated commercial TV and made front-page headlines over the weekend.

The following Tuesday, when the trial had resumed, the judge addressed the jury regarding his actions. He proceeded to read them the transcripts of his remarks to the woman he had asked to leave. It wasn't long before another woman entered the room with her baby and began breastfeeding in protest.

Ian Hill was addressing the issue when Judge Gamble interrupted him. 'You might want to have a look behind you so you can gauge what we're dealing with,' the judge said. 'The lady concerned has just exposed her breast and is breastfeeding the baby in court as we speak.' We watched this entire incident unfold over the link with raised eyebrows, our hands over our mouths.

After a long and draining day of Ian Hill's closing arguments, which labelled Elly as unreliable and uncooperative, Nicole as a liar, and me as having false imaginations, we enjoyed a complete shift in focus and attended Isaac's wedding on a sunny Thursday evening in Melbourne.

When the date had been set, we could not imagine the intensity of the trial or how disconnected we would be from normal life. The wedding was as beautiful as it was jarring. We made a conscious decision to set aside the courtroom drama and to refrain from discussing it. The beachside restaurant was the perfect place to welcome Isaac's new wife into our family.

That night I lay in bed, unable to sleep. I had barely slept all week, even with the increased dose of sleeping pills.

The relentless stress had destroyed my body and my mind. Every allergy was triggered, and my POTS condition was as unstable as it had ever been. When I closed my eyes I felt as if I was standing on a precipice, on the verge of falling into an abyss from which I would not find my way back. It felt as if all my coping skills had crumbled away and I was my vulnerable teenage self again. My therapist and I had begun to speak about hospitalisation. After tossing and turning for six hours I eventually got up, dressed and prepared for another day at court.

The week that followed pushed me to the very brink of my endurance.

The trial was adjourned for six days due to Judge Gamble contracting Covid. The very next day, our paternal grandmother passed away. Three days later, I was by Elly's side during a prenatal scan when she learnt she had miscarried her baby. The overwhelming loss seemed a burden too heavy for any family to bear. I had no time or capacity to mourn my grandmother, or to grieve Elly's loss. I felt like I was trudging through thick, suffocating mud, and I struggled to make sense of it all.

On 21 March I was admitted to the Ramsay Clinic Albert Road, the same hospital where I had previously been admitted to the mother and baby clinic. As fate would have it, the 'mother and baby' ward was now an adult ward, and I was given the same room that had housed me twelve years earlier.

I sat opposite my therapist in the same room, by the coffee table Lily had clung to as she learnt to walk. All around were echoes of my past, but I did not see this as a step backwards, but rather as a testament to my strength. I understood I needed a safe space, and had sought help.

Between the support of the hospital and my therapist, I was finally able to get some sleep. While my sisters went home, I now slept at the hospital each night. And two days later, the jury retired to commence their deliberations.

In our pre-trial musings, Elly, Nicole and I had this whimsical idea that we would pop into other courtrooms to pass the time while waiting for the jury. How innocent we had been to believe there was distraction to be had during this emotional rollercoaster.

Back in our white-walled room, we were like caged animals, pacing to and fro in an ever-tightening web of worry. Nicole had been nominated as the person who would receive the call, and we jumped every time her phone beeped. After a morning of dashed hope, we begged her to mute every contact but Ailsa's.

When a verdict was called, the judge would immediately summon the jury into the courtroom to deliver it without delay. Missing the verdict was a real possibility – the court would wait for nobody. Even the prosecution team, who had their office down the street, decided against returning there. Instead, they found spaces within the building to work, often joining us in our room to share in the collective anxiety.

After four days of silence from the jury, the pretence of work was abandoned. More and more, Danielle, Ailsa, Justin, Stephanie and Ilya joined us in our now very crowded room, and together with Merryn, Danny, Nicole, Elly, M and myself, we always found something to laugh at to ease our intense nerves. We felt incredibly fortunate with our prosecution team.

Reports came in that upstairs, the halls of the fourth floor were lined with reporters, all navigating this wait just as we were. One morning Michelle Meyer brought us kosher pastries. Seeing our appreciation and hearing that the prosecution team also loved the kosher treats, she made it a daily tradition.

The emotional turmoil of Tuesday, 28 March was too overwhelming for my already sleep-deprived mind to handle. Having heard from the jury twice, and the judge almost taking a verdict on those charges the jury had reached a unanimous decision on, the jury had advised the judge that with some more time, they stood a realistic chance of reaching unanimous verdicts on all. We were allowed in court, but no verdict was taken, and the jury were dismissed to continue deliberations the next morning.

Back at the hospital, I sat in the shower, fully dressed, the cold tiles reminding me I was real. My mind felt broken; I was trapped in a dissociated state, detached from the world around me. Thankfully, my therapist prescribed a stronger sleeping pill. I fell asleep early and woke feeling a lot more present.

It was minute-to-minute survival for another whole week. We kept turning to the prosecution for their estimates, but our case was unprecedented for them – the longest trial, the most charges, an extraordinary number of days for jury deliberations.

On 3 April at 3.30 p.m., nine days after the jury began deliberations, Nicole's phone rang: verdicts on all charges at 3.45 p.m. We ran around in circles, unsure what to do with ourselves. I trembled uncontrollably, and my vision went hazy. I texted all my family and friends who had shared the weight of my anxiety as it spilled over and became intertwined with theirs. Everyone in my life had been sitting in this waiting game with me.

We took the lift to the fourth floor.

The public gallery was packed. Leifer had been brought up from the cells and was sitting in the dock, waiting for her judgement. We wanted to sit behind the prosecution and face the foreman, but the judge had asked that the seats behind the jury box be reserved for us. Elly, Nicole and I sat on the plastic chairs, clutching each other's hands tightly. This moment was the culmination of everything we had fought for. I couldn't even register how I felt. I kept taking deep breaths, because it didn't feel like I was breathing at all. The tension in the room was palpable.

'Not guilty,' the foreman said.

I felt like the ground had crumbled beneath my feet. *Not guilty, not guilty, not guilty, not guilty.* Four more times, like a sledgehammer to my mind.

I looked at Nicole; those were all five of her charges. Devastation washed through me. I wanted so badly to turn back time and shield her from this pain. We had failed. Malka Leifer would walk free that evening; the prosecution had prepared us that if there were no guilty verdicts, she would leave Australia that night.

But then: 'Guilty,' the foreman said.

I didn't know if I had heard correctly. I was in an emotional tailspin, trying to process what was happening. 'Guilty,' the foreman said again.

They saw! They saw the sexual abuser that she is! I shouted in my head. I didn't know how to feel. How could they see Malka Leifer as an abuser but not see the suffering she had inflicted on my sister? I was so confused.

Ten of my charges, guilty; four charges, not guilty. Elly's charges were all proven, all found guilty. I felt vindicated, angry, grateful, confused. I didn't know how to reconcile the fact that some parts of our trauma had been acknowledged while others had been dismissed. The pain I felt for my sister surpassed any other feeling. Nicole stood up and stared at Leifer; Leifer did not look at her.

We sat in our meeting room on the first floor for an hour. Nicole kept repeating that she was okay, and was holding onto the fact that Malka Leifer had been rightfully exposed as the sexual predator she was. We were all in a state of shock. The prosecution sat with us for a while and then gave us some time alone. The silence did nothing to ease our shock, and eventually we agreed it was time to face the media.

Despite the whirlwind of emotions, we walked out with smiles on our faces. Regardless of the complexity of the justice system, one thing remained certain: Malka Leifer had been rightfully convicted as a paedophile and rapist.

Malka Leifer was guilty. Malka Leifer is guilty.

'We have waited eleven years to say those words,' Nicole said outside court.

We walked up and down Lonsdale Street for an hour, with friends, family and the film crew following us, unsure of what to do next. Every moment had always led to this point; we had not imagined the other side. Eventually, we collapsed on the couches at the empty cafe near the court while we figured out the next steps. Danny booked us a hotel room, and then he and Tamar went to source some food. In our trackies, we raised our celebratory drinks as the film crew captured the moment. When they finally left, Elly, Nicole and I looked at each other, still grappling with the surreal reality of it all.

The next morning, I lay in my bed at the Albert Road Clinic and scrolled through the beautiful messages from people across the world. I ignored the media requests and trolls, letting Elly and Nicole handle the media. This moment, a lifetime in the waiting, was mine. I didn't owe the media any words; I didn't even have them yet.

The nurse brought me the *Herald Sun*. The front page screamed 'Justice at last' and then inside they had printed our words outside court: 'She's guilty – the whole world will know now'.

The huge shadow that had hung over me all my life seemed to shift slightly. In its own unfair and twisted way, justice had been served. There was no more fighting.

I felt a sense of peace settle within me. Finally, from today, I could walk away from something I had been walking towards my entire adult life.

CHAPTER 27

What now

I made myself a lifelong promise while walking away from my trauma that for every misstep – and there will be many missteps – I will get back up. That promise was something I almost forgot the evening I was discharged from hospital, a week after the guilty verdict was handed down.

Back at home after a three-month absence, I walked around the dying garden that my gorgeous neighbour Barb had helped me plant, looking for signs of life in the once-thriving sanctuary. I wandered in circles thinking about the conversation I'd had with Shua and Lily several days prior. Sitting at Esther's dining table, under the swinging pendulum of her kitchen clock, Lily had spoken of the stability she'd experienced residing solely with her father and grandmother throughout the trial, having spent her childhood shuttling between two homes. It was a stability she wanted to preserve – for now, she would not be returning home. I could not hear her that night. It would take me time to truly understand her need and to reconcile with her decision. That evening, in my monochromatic garden of yellow, grieving the loss of motherhood as I had known it, the future seemed lost and hopeless.

The evening sun cast a light too bright for my swollen and red eyes. I retreated indoors and searched urgently through my diary for an entry I had made twelve years prior, on my first night home from the psychiatric hospital in 2011, when life bore a similar hue of uncertainty. I located the note I was seeking: 'Goals for the next five years'. Underneath, my 24-year-old self listed a set of goals to serve as anchors in the new future I was forging. I chuckled at 'never drink alone, only socially'. I am not a drinker. At the time I had only tried alcohol twice, but I had been worried it would become a crutch in the world of foreign social interactions.

I studied the remaining goals: 'finalise my divorce, learn how to drive, improve my writing, maybe one day author a book, finish my police report', and realised not only had I met them, I had exceeded them. My achievements reach far beyond the lofty expectations I had set more than a decade ago. I sat back with my hands behind my head, eyes closed and a faint smile on my face, envisioning the next chapter of my life. I thought about the public fight I had undertaken, but also of the private battles that had waged within my body for as long as I could remember. I didn't want to fight anymore. Outside the court I had spoken to the media about healing, but what did that really mean? What did I need to heal?

Opening my eyes, I composed a new list of thirty goals I hoped to achieve. It would be a lot of work. This time though, I knew my strength.

A week later, I received a call from Ted Baillieu. The evening after the verdict, Victoria Police announced they had closed their investigation into those within the Adass community who had helped Malka Leifer escape Australia and evade justice. Ted had voiced his criticism of this decision, and along with former politician Philip Dalidakis, wanted to draft a letter urging the police to reconsider their position. He was seeking my approval.

With a voice coloured by shock and frustration, I told Ted the story of another of Leifer's victims, who had returned from overseas to face a civil trial against Adass School. The night before the trial was supposed to commence, community members had received a text urging them to protest outside the home of this victim – an appalling act, intended to harass and bully. This followed a week of intimidation which had started the moment the victim had disembarked from the plane. 'Ted, there is little fight in me right now,' I confessed, 'but the hope the community learnt from our journey has disappeared, and now I believe reopening the investigation is vitally important.'

Accountability was a part of healing, but it was not enough. There exists an entire network of structures in many parts of our society that allow abusers to commit their heinous acts and then be protected. Those structures need to be dismantled. Silence, isolation, leadership authority, rigid gender roles, community loyalty and obedience, limited education and fear of excommunication are embedded in the very fabric of the Adass community. The leaders of that community have to appreciate that these conditions create a fertile ground in which abuse could thrive. 'I think the letter is a good idea. Perhaps at this point, fear of consequence is the only catalyst left for change,' I told Ted.

Ted Baillieu and Philip Dalidakis were from different political parties, but united in their desire to see justice prevail. They composed a compelling three-page letter addressed to the Chief of Police on 30 April, describing the decision not to investigate those who facilitated Leifer's escape as a 'shameful breach of faith'.

... Mrs Leifer was spirited away to Israel from Australia in extraordinary circumstances in the early hours of Thursday the 6th of March 2008, they said, noting Justice Rush's civil finding which decried the 'deplorable' conduct of those who helped Leifer escape.

... If a person or persons sought to pervert the course of justice, ignored previous allegations of sexual abuse, ignored mandatory reporting obligations, prolonged the suffering of victims by 10 years plus, cost Victorian Taxpayers millions of dollars, wasted Victoria Police time, sought to sully the relationship between Israel and Australia, funded the escape of a serial sex offender and sought to cover up serious crimes, Victorians would at the very least expect a full and thorough Police Investigation. We again urge you as Chief Commissioner to ensure a full investigation of these issues is undertaken as soon as possible.

On 2 June 2023, thirty-three days after the letter was delivered, Victoria Police Chief Commissioner Shane Patton wrote to Ted Baillieu to confirm the police had resumed their investigation into the Adass Israel School board. I ticked a little checkbox on my healing spreadsheet under the title 'justice'.

Two months had passed since the conclusion of the trial and the plea hearing was drawing near. During the two-day hearing, both the prosecution and defence would present submissions on the factors that the judge should weigh up in determining Malka Leifer's sentence. I would also deliver my victim impact statement to the court – the official, sanctioned way for the profound impact of Leifer's abuse to be taken into account.

I had procrastinated the task until the eleventh hour, engrossed in completing the final chapters of this book and chasing slivers of peace wherever I could find them. At that point, I didn't want anything to do with the legal system. The notion of raking through my trauma held no appeal. My siblings and I organised a weekend away, sans partners or kids. The trial had ruled our lives like an omnipresent dictator, and we escaped to the country to liberate our family from its grip. I yearned to consign the whole Leifer ordeal to the past, but there were still some steps to take.

On the night before I was to submit my statement to the prosecution for their review, I confronted the abyss of pain head-on, and invited all my emotions to sit with me at the table. Then I peeled back the layers I had woven over the years to shield myself from the fact that Leifer's abuse had fired a metaphorical gunshot through the very fabric of my life, forcing me, since then, into a perpetual state of shifting and adjusting to mask the void she had created.

I remember the first time Malka Leifer told me she cared, I wrote. I *was sixteen years old, existing in a world absent of adult care. "I love you like a mother," she told me. There were no words I longed to hear more. She learnt of my desperation in order to exploit it. I dream sometimes of the future I could have had.*

I wrote all night. I could have poured my words into pages for months and still not exhausted the impact she'd had, but I chose to condense my statement to two pages. My goal was for the exercise to be more empowering than it was retraumatising.

I then shared my statement with the social worker at the Victim Assistance Services, and after her review and approval, I sent the pages through to Ailsa. The defence were given an opportunity to examine my statement before the hearing, as it was their right to object or cross-examine me on anything I had written. I was relieved to hear my statement was accepted in full.

I addressed the packed courtroom of family, friends and a sea of media, making a concerted effort to keep my voice steady and conceal the quiver in my limbs that threatened to overcome me. I looked at Judge Gamble several times, hoping to meet his gaze, but he did not look up. As I read the final paragraph, I turned to look at Leifer, and in a voice filled with resolve I read the closing words: 'Malka Leifer, you shattered my trust, stole my body, and altered my life's course, but you could not break my spirit. Today, I stand as a survivor. Your darkness does not define me. Instead, I choose to focus on the light within myself, the love that surrounds me, and the power of my own voice. I will continue to heal, grow and thrive. I am resilient, I am powerful, and I am so much more than the limitations you imposed on me.'

Her face remained unmoved, and seemingly indifferent.

As I sat down to listen to Elly read her statement, I felt a shift inside me. It was as if part of my heart and mind had suddenly opened up and there was light in a place where only shadows had dwelled. In the stillness of my inner world, I spoke gently to my younger self. 'This, right here, reclaiming my power, is an important part of my healing.'

I hadn't anticipated that my entire statement would end up online, as I had misunderstood the reporter's request for it.

Elly gave a brave and deeply poignant statement. I saw tears on the faces around me as she revealed that, during the trial, her baby's heart had stopped beating, resulting in a miscarriage. She couldn't help but wonder if the stress had played a role, as there seemed to be no other explanation. Her husband, Danny, gave a statement too, as a family member deeply affected by the abuse and the insidious intrusions it had on the love and trust within their marriage.

Nicole, who had consistently voiced her intent to deliver a victim impact statement at the end of our long journey, was unable to give one in the courtroom because, devastatingly, the jury had not been able to find Leifer guilty of the charges relating to her abuse. Instead, she would craft a short statement to deliver to the media outside the court during the lunch break.

I was in awe of my sister's seemingly endless reservoir of strength. In front of a cluster of microphones on the steps of the County Court in Lonsdale Street, she spoke of her driving motivation for presenting her statement. 'I speak on behalf of the countless survivors who silently endure these battles, their voices silenced by a legal system that often falls short of delivering true justice. I see you, I feel for you, and I stand in unwavering solidarity with you,' she proclaimed.

Predictably, for the remainder of the plea hearing, Leifer's legal team emphasised her challenges and advocated for a reduced sentence. Ian Hill then had the audacity to urge the judge not to put too much weight on our victim impact statements because we had failed to acknowledge the impact other abuse had on our lives – something we were forbidden to mention. He almost had Elly back on the stand for cross-examination before the judge ruled against him. At the conclusion of the final plea hearing, Judge Gamble set a sentencing date for 24 August.

That night, wrapped in a blanket on the couch, I opened my spreadsheet and thought about the goals I aspired to accomplish before that date. The end of the chapter loomed so tantalisingly near. I wrote to Michelle Meyer. 'Michelle, I have thought about the foster care initiative and if the group agrees, I am happy to take on the role of organising the event.'

In the stretch of time between the committal and the trial I had become aware of a pressing issue in the Jewish community. Within a single year I had fielded almost a dozen calls about young boys and girls from the ultra-Orthodox communities running away from home. The insular nature of these communities often left these teenagers ignorant of their vulnerabilities in the outside world.

When one such teenager found a refuge in my home, with the awareness of both child protection and her parents, I embarked on a month-long endeavour to create a culturally sensitive safety plan. Many frustrating phone calls and meetings later, I realised the support she needed did not exist.

Michelle Meyer had invited me to join a group called the Child Safety Community of Practice (COP), comprising professional and committed individuals dedicated to fostering a secure environment and ensuring the safety and wellbeing of children in the Jewish community. With this issue in mind, I joined the board and raised the possibility of training community members as foster carers. Placing a vulnerable teenager in a home outside the community often meant they were less likely to seek assistance.

Over the years, I have maintained contact with another young girl residing in an abusive household within a community that often dismisses the existence of parental abuse. Even with police involvement, she continues to endure a harrowing home life where she is devalued and mistreated. Child protection agencies adhere to stringent criteria for removing children from their homes and, within the seclusion of the Jewish community, it can be challenging to determine when abuse has reached the threshold for intervention.

Every conversation with this young girl, who embodies a strength and resilience far beyond her years, serves as a reminder of why we must do better. I once asked her why she didn't run away. 'There's nowhere safe to go, Dassi,' she told me. Even her decision to reach out to me, if discovered, could alter her life dramatically.

As I draft this final chapter, I am in discussion with the COP about raising awareness of the need for foster carers within our community. I am also collaborating with Leah Boulton and Pathways Melbourne about the increasing need for support among under-eighteens. Pathways, which currently focuses on assisting adults, has funded a community research project to explore ways to extend its support to vulnerable teenagers who are grappling with questions of faith, while still safeguarding their familial bonds. For some young individuals, questioning means potentially losing everything they have ever known.

It's 11.17 p.m. on 9 September (I'm down to the deadline for this chapter), but even at this late hour there is a fire within me and the colour of passion on my cheeks. I am excited to see what a united community can accomplish. I feel a surge of electricity emanating from my core. I am ready to channel everything I have learnt and honed into a cause that strikes such a profound chord within me. I want to become the pillar of support that was absent in my own challenging journey. This isn't merely a project; it is a symbol of my inner fortitude, and a homage to the incredible force of healing.

* * *

With these new projects underway, the weeks to sentencing passed quickly. When the day finally arrived, the walk into court brought tense muscles and a swamp of flashbacks. Our entire family, including Henry, Marilyn and several friends, filled the seats beside the ever-present media. Such was the public interest in the case, many of the reporters were live blogging. We had agreed to answer a few questions for a single news channel before entering the court, and already we had been besieged by a throng of cameras. 'I'll be very happy if I never have to face cameras again,' I told Nicole. Even in the courtroom there was a restless energy in the air. This was the zenith of a journey that had spanned years and the globe.

In the week leading up to this day the three of us had spoken countless times. We were scared that Leifer would receive a lenient sentence and walk away with time served. We were haunted by the case against Jeffrey 'Joffa' Corfe, a prominent member of a football cheer squad, who had pleaded guilty to sexually penetrating a child under the age of sixteen. Corfe had received a sentence that did not include any jail time. I was in touch with the victim, Alex Case, who had also waived anonymity and gone public with his concerns. Alex wrote that he was redirecting his anger into petitioning the government to make the system easier on victims, reform the law around sentencing and ban the use of character references for abusers.

During my own research on sentencing, I had stumbled upon two very troubling facts: first, that sexual crimes involving minors weren't referred to as rape but as sexual penetration; and second, that the maximum sentence for raping an adult was twenty-five years, while the maximum sentence for raping a child aged 12 to 16 years was ten years. I had to read that several times to fully grasp the disturbing implications.

As I walked into the crowded courtroom with the prosecution team, there was a storm of chaos in my mind. Before taking my seat, I waved to Ted Baillieu and David

Southwick in the gallery. After standing and bowing to the judge, we settled in for what turned out to be a very long time. Judge Gamble's delivery of the sentence stretched for longer than three hours and was punctuated by two breaks, in which I had to pace the halls to restore my circulation. We had grown used to our case breaking new ground at every turn. So, when our legal team informed us that it was their longest sentencing to date, we casually added this to our ever-expanding collection of unprecedented events.

Judge Gamble's words during the sentencing held tremendous significance. For purposes of recording the judgement, pseudonyms were used. I was given the name of Laura Watson and Elly was named Rachel Harris. These are some of his remarks:

The complainants were subjected to a very difficult upbringing due to the cruel and unpredictable way their mother behaved towards them,' he stated. 'Each was mistreated and witnessed the mistreatment of their siblings. Their mother neglected and abused her children regularly, both physically and emotionally. She also threatened them. The physical abuse included slaps, kicks and pinching as well as the use of objects, including straps. This caused bruising and other marks.'

… And it appears that at no stage did the complainants' father intervene to offer any form of protection or respite from his wife's erratic and emotionally damaging treatment of their children.

On any view, it was a miserable home life for the complainants, who were starved of love and affection and left in a perpetual state of fear and confusion.

There was a gentle expansion of my chest as I felt the validation weave through my childhood vulnerability.

Finally, my suffering was acknowledged by a world that for all my young life had seemed oblivious to our anguish.

The judge went on.

> To the extent that Ms Watson and Ms Harris feel a personal sense of guilt or shame for what occurred, they should not. They were completely innocent victims of the predatory behaviour of Mrs Leifer, and it is she and she alone who should feel guilty and ashamed for what occurred.
>
> ... This case is striking for just how vulnerable each of the two victims were and for the calculating way in which the offender, Mrs Leifer, took callous advantage of those vulnerabilities in order to sexually abuse them for her own sexual gratification. This is a serious aggravating feature in respect of all of the offences.

As I sat listening to the judge, waiting for the sentence to be handed down, it felt as if the world had narrowed to this singular moment of reckoning. His words echoed slightly in the silence, each syllable carrying the weight of justice long awaited. I sat taller after Judge Gamble spoke of my shame and how it was not mine. I shut my eyes briefly and pictured his words taking root in the garden of self-compassion I had been growing. A garden that one day would outgrow the shame. I drew in a deep breath and smiled to myself as I refocused on the sentencing.

The smile was wiped off my face when the judge went on to say:

> It seems most unlikely that she will ever have the opportunity to gain access to girls and young women in any similar setting again, whether in Australia, Israel or some other country. So, I consider that the opportunity for Mrs Leifer to reoffend in

this or any similar fashion is therefore negligible, if not non-existent.

I struggled to make sense of what I was hearing. I turned to look at my family, who had the same expression on their faces. The judge had completely failed to grasp the intricacies and complexities of ultra-Orthodox communities, where the chances of reoffending could be alarmingly high.

Finally, at 12.52 p.m. on 24 August, we learnt the sentence. Malka Leifer, the former principal of Adass Israel School, who had used that position to abuse me and my sisters, had been sentenced to fifteen years in jail. Judge Gamble imposed a non-parole period of eleven and a half years, but with time served of just over 5.5 years, Leifer would be eligible for parole in 2029.

I sighed with immense relief and my facial muscles relaxed. Fifteen years was significant, even if it could never match the magnitude of what Leifer did. Justice for sexual crimes was rare, and I understood just how seldom sentences like this were heard.

Nicole, Elly and I left the courtroom with smiles on our faces. 'We are showing that the voices of survivors will not and cannot be silenced, no matter the obstacles,' I told the horde of cameras outside court. For us, Malka Leifer's incarceration was a stride towards our recovery, knowing she was unable to harm anyone else. Our satisfaction was not born of revenge but of the guarantee of safety we had so long pursued.

Later, we received word that Leifer had packed her bags in anticipation of leaving the Dame Phyllis Frost Centre that day. According to community rumour, her family was very disappointed by the return on the $5 million they'd spent on legal fees. Despite all the money and power at their disposal,

Nicole, Elly and myself, along with a chorus of thousands, a diligent prosecution team, a learned judge and a jury of twelve, had put an abuser behind bars.

The campaign illuminated a different path for me. Despite the weight of my trauma, which could easily have eroded my faith in humanity, I stand in awe of the collective strength that unfolded before my eyes. It is compelling evidence of the inherent goodness that resides in every individual. For me, healing is understanding that while many people are eager to erect shields around perpetrators, there are many more individuals who are determined to tear those shields down.

One of the rewarding aspects of having a more public presence is the chance to meet and speak with people from all walks of life. These interactions, beyond satisfying my innate curiosity and broadening my understanding, have transformed strangers into friends, allies and fellow advocates, fostering a deeper sense of connection, community and shared purpose. I've had conversations so far beyond the imagination of the person I once was that I find myself pausing and quietly laughing at the extraordinary way my life has unfolded.

My list of goals centres around the absence of the chaos that consumed my life for so long. Occasionally, I slip into a meditation and glimpse a tiny shard of peace, which I am confident will one day expand into something more significant. I have this picture in my mind. In it, I am swaying on a garden swing beside Lily with a purring cat on our laps, surrounded by a tapestry of flowers in every imaginable hue.

In this picture, years in the future, those fleeting slivers of Zen are more lasting, and the inner turmoil that raged for so long has been extinguished. There is a stillness to my body that is not of dissociation but of presence. I feel a contentment with who I am and what I have achieved, still with a keen curiosity, but unfettered by the desperate circles that once framed it.

I understand that a life marked by significant trauma may always carry a hint of chaos. But the chaos is different now. I can observe it, accept it, and move through it without feeling the need to fight it.

A welcome silence resides inside me now. It's a silence I could not fathom until I experienced it and realised how loudly I had been screaming – a scream only I could hear.

I continue to breathe new life into my garden, and the small patches of green that surface hold the promise of fresh growth.

My mother told me repeatedly that I was 'nothing but a pretty face'.

She made me believe I was worthless. I was that little girl who thought being a nothing was better, because a 'nothing' doesn't feel. It has been years since her words haunted my thoughts, but if they ever return, I know how I'll respond:

I'm proud of the woman I've grown into, the one my younger self always yearned to meet. I am everything I need to be.

ACKNOWLEDGEMENTS

Writing *In Bad Faith* was a tough yet transformative journey, and I am grateful for the incredible individuals whose light, support and expertise illuminated this path from start to finish.

I extend my thanks to the entire team at Hachette for their unwavering enthusiasm and hard work. Louise Adler's belief in this book from the start, even post-Hachette, and Vanessa Radnidge's seamless takeover and kind, patient support, regardless of missed deadlines, were invaluable. Vanessa's encouragement and commitment led to the completion of this book. Ellen Whinnett, a constant guiding presence with meticulous attention to detail who steered this book through messy first drafts, showed me how to hone second drafts and worked with me to find a way through the challenges of writing my childhood. Her dedication meant this book finally reached the finish line. Thank you for working alongside me every step of the way. Special acknowledgement to Vanessa Lanaway and Chrysoula Aiello for their exceptional efforts in copy editing and polishing the manuscript. And Emily Lighezzolo, a publicist determined to ensure that this book and I have the smoothest journey through the media.

I have the deepest appreciation for Dr Deborah Rechter, both my mentor and writing coach, who devoted many mornings of her own time to enrich the depth and meaning of my work, helping shape not just my writing but my perspective on storytelling.

I owe a debt of gratitude to my therapists for helping me through the daunting process of facing my trauma to translate it onto paper.

The survivors I had the privilege of meeting on this journey, named or unnamed, stand as a testament to the significance of this book. Those who refused to stay silent and those who are constrained and remain unheard.

Acknowledgements

My heartfelt thanks to my incredible friends, who stood by me through the rollercoaster of writing this book: Dassi Herszberg, my rock, for not minding when weekends away turned into writing frenzies; Belinda Hawkins, for the tranquil refuge of her country house where my first chapter found life; Rory and Regina, for offering respite when chaos overwhelmed; Barb, for hosting sunny days in her garden with those talkative chooks; my aunts, Mandy and Susan for their early draft feedback; Leah Boulton, for letting me create in her plant-filled sanctuary beside her cuddly cat; Nathan Vale, for shifting his work to my house to sit beside me; and to my nephew M for those marathon twelve-hour writing sessions on opposite sides of my sinking couch as he studied for university.

To my extended 'adopted' family who shared countless coffee moments and always asked for updates on my writing process, thank you.

In the three years of writing, two of which were amidst Melbourne's numerous lockdowns, there were stretches I couldn't write at all. My sisters and brothers championed me from the start and gave me permission to write fragments of our shared past. They are the pillars that hold this story together. Dalia's unseen but palpable encouragement echoes in every word, just as I know it would be if she were here. Tamar helped to reconstruct the history that came before my time. Nicole and Elly fact checked the parts of our journey we shared. Isaac read every chapter eagerly and provided immediate feedback. Ben was ever ready to get whatever I needed when I was holed up at home on a writing roll.

To my beloved siblings, your constant presence, unyielding belief and encouragement breathed life into this book and fuels the fire of my resilience. From the bottom of my heart, thank you.

And finally, and most importantly, to my daughter, you are my greatest joy and deepest source of love. You give profound meaning to my journey. You are truly everything to me.

RESOURCES

If you or someone you know is in immediate danger, call **000 in Australia** or **111 in New Zealand** immediately.

The following services can put you in touch with the best service for your needs.

1800RESPECT

This national family violence and sexual assault counselling service is available 24 hours a day, 7 days a week. It's confidential and free to call. They can also help with advice about online safety if you think someone is watching your online activities.

To contact 1800RESPECT:

- call **1800 737 732** to speak with a professional counsellor
- use the services directory on the **1800RESPECT** website to find help in your area: 1800respect.org.au/services/search
- go to the **1800RESPECT** website: 1800respect.org.au

1800RESPECT has also developed free apps. **Daisy** connects you to services in your local area – including legal, housing, financial and children's services. And **Sunny** supports women with disability impacted by sexual assault and family and domestic violence, so they can understand what has happened and know their rights.

Bravehearts

Bravehearts is an Australian child protection organisation dedicated to the prevention and treatment of child sexual abuse. They support survivors and victims of child sexual abuse, and their non-offending family members, with accessible and affordable counselling, case management and advocacy.

To contact them:

- call **1800 272 831** between 8.30 a.m. and 4.30 p.m. Monday to Friday AEST
- go to the Bravehearts website: bravehearts.org.au.

Kids Helpline

Kids Helpline is a free service for young people aged 5 to 25.

To contact them:

- call **1800 551 800** at any time
- go to the Kids Helpline website: kidshelpline.com.au

Lifeline

Lifeline offers personal crisis support services if you're affected by family and domestic violence, or feeling suicidal.

- call them on **131 114** at any time.
- read more on the Lifeline website: lifeline.org.au/get-help

MensLine Australia

MensLine Australia is a phone and online support service. They provide specialist help to people affected by family and domestic violence. They also offer support to people using violence.

To contact them:

- call **1300 789 978** at any time
- go to the MensLine Australia website: mensline.org.au

National Legal Aid

National Legal Aid can help you find the legal aid commission in your state or territory. Read more about their services on the National legal aid website: nationallegalaid.org

Pathways Melbourne

pathwaysmelbourne.org

Pathways Melbourne supports and empowers people from

Orthodox and ultra-Orthodox Jewish communities who are questioning their lifestyle, practices and beliefs.

Suicide Call Back Service
Suicide Call Back Service is a nationwide service providing 24/7 phone and online counselling to people affected by suicide.

To contact them:
- call **1300 659 467** at any time
- go to the Suicide Call Back Service website: suicidecallbackservice.org.au

Women's Legal Services Australia
www.wlsa.org.au
Their mission is to promote a legal system that is safe, supportive, non-discriminatory and responsive to the needs of women.